Does Mark 16:9–20 Belong in the New Testament?

Does Mark 16:9–20 Belong in the New Testament?

David W. Hester

Foreword by David H. Warren

WIPF & STOCK · Eugene, Oregon

DOES MARK 16:9–20 BELONG IN THE NEW TESTAMENT?

Copyright © 2015 David W. Hester. All rights reserved. Except for brief quotations in critical publications or reviews, no part of this book may be reproduced in any manner without prior written permission from the publisher. Write: Permissions, Wipf and Stock Publishers, 199 W. 8th Ave., Suite 3, Eugene, OR 97401.

Wipf & Stock
An Imprint of Wipf and Stock Publishers
199 W. 8th Ave., Suite 3
Eugene, OR 97401

www.wipfandstock.com

ISBN 13: 978-1-4982-0158-2

Manufactured in the U.S.A.   03/12/2015

Images used by permission from the Center for the Study of New Testament Manuscripts (www.csntm.org).

The faculty and staff of the Turner School of Theology at Amridge University supported and encouraged me to develop this theme for my dissertation. The faculty and staff of the V. P. Black College of Biblical Studies at Faulkner University, where I teach, supported me in bringing this work to publication. The congregation where I preach—Springville Road Church of Christ—has demonstrated its love for the Truth time and time again. My late father, Benny W. Hester, believed I could go as far as I wanted in my education. He passed away before he could see me receive my doctorate. My mom, Mary Anne Hester, has been just as supportive. My wife, Brenda, is always at my side, giving love and encouragement every step of the way. Our two sons, Will and Jonathan, are in the midst of their educational journey. They have also been completely on board. It is to Brenda, Will, and Jonathan that this work is dedicated.

Contents

Foreword by David H. Warren | ix

Introduction | 1

Chapter 1
Modern Scholarship on Mark 16:9–20, 1965–2011 | 10

Chapter 2
External Evidence | 86

Chapter 3
Internal Evidence | 125

Chapter 4
A Proposal Concerning the Origin of Mark 16:9–20 | 145

Bibliography | 157

Foreword

Did Mark really intend for his gospel to end at 16:8? Or was his original ending lost, and someone else later supplied the traditional ending of 16:9–20? Could Mark have intended to write more but was somehow prevented from supplying his story with a suitable conclusion? Curiosity indeed feeds our speculations.

But forget Mark for the moment and any other man. What did God himself intend? This is the primary question that demands our attention. What most people fail to realize, including scholars, is that all of these possible scenarios could still fall under the providence of God. Even though ancient Jews did not believe that Moses prophetically wrote of his own death in the last chapter to Deuteronomy, they still regarded all thirty-four chapters as canonical and thus authoritative. According to the Babylonian Talmud (*b. Baba Bathra* 14b–15a), Joshua, the successor to Moses, wrote the last eight verses of Deuteronomy, describing Moses's death. And Joshua's sons Eleazar and Phinehas completed the book of Joshua, after Joshua's death (Josh 24:29–33). And Gad the seer and Nathan the prophet completed the two books of Samuel after Samuel's death (recorded early in 1 Sam 25:1). Even though someone besides the original authors supplied the conclusions to these canonical books, the Jews still attributed them to Moses, Joshua, and Samuel respectively.

So, does Mark 16:9–20 belong in the New Testament? This is the central question that Dr. David W. Hester attempts to answer in this volume. And he does not treat it as a theological question per se but as a historical question, albeit a historical question that surely has theological implications. And, yes, he does venture into speculation. How could he not? But he frames his answers with historical phenomena. Why does no church father in antiquity object to the addition of these verses (as you will see, no,

Foreword

not even Eusebius)? The final warning of the Bible in Revelaton 22:18–19 is repeated several times elsewhere (Deut 4:2; 12:32; Josh 1:7; Prov 30:6), showing that it is a general principle to be applied to the whole of Scripture. No one may *add to* or *subtract from* God's word. Given this strong prohibition, why does Jerome include Mark 16:9–20 in his Latin Vulgate in spite of his awareness that nearly all Greek manuscripts in his day (the late fourth century) lack it (*Epistle 120: To Hedibia* 3)? Even two centuries earlier, Irenaeus quotes from Mark 16:19 and attributes these words to "Mark" (*Against Heresies* 3.10.5). In making this quotation, he expresses no doubts or misgivings, though he is quite conscious of incurring divine condemnation should he add anything to Scripture (ibid. 5.30.1). Irenaeus clearly believed that Mark wrote Mark 16:19, and apparently he is unaware of any textual problem. He is our first indisputable witness to how Mark's gospel ended, and his copy of Mark is older than any copy that we possess today.

The Greek manuscripts, the ancient versions, statements by early church fathers, modern arguments based on vocabulary and style—here in this volume you will find all of the relevant evidence brought together and presented. Dr. Hester even includes photographs of several key Greek manuscripts so that you can actually *see* the evidence for yourself. He begins his study with a careful and complete survey of modern scholarship over the past fifty years, beginning with Kenneth Clark, whose presidential address before the Society of Biblical Literature in 1965 stirred William Farmer to write his own dissertation on *The Last Twelve Verses of Mark*.

I remember when I purchased Farmer's monograph in the summer of 1976, after my first year of Greek, and began reading his preface, where he mentioned the presidential address of Clark. The "Catholic Edition" of the New Testament portion of the Revised Standard Version (RSV) had just been released, and Clark began his address with some observations on this new edition of the old RSV. He noted that in this new "Catholic Edition," the text of Mark 16:9–20 had been restored to the main text of Mark, although a footnote warned that "some of the most ancient authorities bring the book to a close at the end of verse 8." In the original RSV, published in 1946, the text of Mark 16:9–20 was relegated to a footnote with type that was much smaller than that of the main text of Mark. This treatment of Mark 16:9–20, as if to diminish its importance, fueled one of the many complaints leveled against the old RSV by conservative Christian scholars. And many of these same voices called for a new version, and their cries

Foreword

eventually led to the publication of the New International Version (NIV) in 1973.

When the original NIV appeared, Mark 16:9–20 was printed with the same font size as the rest of Mark, although a line set it apart with the following note: "The most reliable MSS omit Mark 16:9–20." In 1978, this note was reworded for the second edition of the New Testament: "The two most reliable early manuscripts do not have Mark 16:9–20." In 1984, for the third edition, this note was reworded again: "The earliest manuscripts and some other ancient witnesses do not have Mark 16:9–20." And yet in all of these editions, the text of Mark 16:9–20 remained in the same font size as the rest of Mark's text. This situation changed, however, in 2002, when Today's New International Version (TNIV) retained the same wording for the note, but now the text of Mark 16:9–20 was printed in a noticeably smaller font size than the rest of Mark, and it was italicized. And this same practice was followed in the 2011 edition of the NIV. Of course, this note in its latest version is palpably wrong, for Irenaeus's copy of Mark apparently had Mark 16:9–20, and it would certainly count as *the earliest* known manuscript of Mark's gospel.

When the New Revised Standard Version appeared in 1989, the text of Mark 16:9–20 was printed in the same font size as the rest of Mark's gospel, though enclosed with double brackets rather than separated with a line. But what an ironic situation has developed! The newest NIV has followed the practice of the old, controversial RSV, while the new RSV has adopted the policy of the old, conservative NIV.

Perhaps Dr. Hester's volume can help reverse the tide once again for those who cherish the Bible as the divine, inspired word of God.

Dr. David H. Warren
Faulkner University

Introduction

In the spring of 1987, I was a senior Bible major in my last semester at Freed-Hardeman College (now University) in Henderson, Tennessee. One of the classes I took was Critical Introduction to the New Testament. Having already taken the companion class on the Old Testament, I looked forward with eager anticipation to delving into the questions of authorship, dating, and other issues. In the course of our study, we addressed the ending of the Gospel of Mark. The Greek courses I had previously taken served to introduce me to the problem. Now, we entered into it in more detail. When the time came for us to choose a topic for the paper we were to write, I made sure I chose the ending of Mark. Our professor guided me with patience and understanding, pointing me to the proper sources and gently giving me reminders to allow the evidence to speak. I thoroughly enjoyed the process. My conclusion at that time was that Mark 16:9–20 should be included in the text, with a footnote indicating that the two oldest manuscripts did not contain the passage—indicating doubts about its originality with Mark. However, I remember being bothered by the fact that Irenaeus's second-century testimony in favor of Markan authorship was given less weight than I thought it should. At any rate, I thought at the time that this was as far as the evidence could go.

I did not revisit the issue for over twenty years. By that time, I was now a doctoral student at the Turner School of Theology at Amridge University in Montgomery, Alabama. In the course I took on the Synoptic Gospels, I chose to write my paper on Mark 16:9–20. I expected to arrive at the same conclusion from twenty years before. In the course of my research, though, I was surprised to discover two things: first, some of the pieces of evidence that had been cited against the passage were shown by Bruce Metzger to actually favor it. Second, the amount of material that had been written in

Does Mark 16:9–20 Belong In The New Testament?

the intervening years concerning Mark 16:9–20 was huge. As a result, my interest in the passage was rekindled. This also greatly helped me to make my decision concerning my dissertation topic. The more I delved into the articles and books written on the problem, the more I was convinced this was the subject that needed to be addressed. What settled the matter for me was reading *Perspectives on the Ending of Mark: 4 Views*, by David Alan Black, Darrell Bock, Keith Elliott, Maurice Robinson, and Daniel Wallace. Published in 2008, this was the summary of a conference, previously held, which addressed the ending of Mark. To say that I was pleasantly surprised is an understatement. I was now convinced that the issue had to be revisited, and that a different perspective from the norm was ripe for presentation. Thus it was that in 2012, I finished work on the dissertation that serves as the bulk of this book. My dissertation committee, headed by Dr. Jim Smeal, was vital in focusing my research and strengthening my arguments. While Jim did not necessarily agree with my conclusion, that did not prevent him from offering helpful suggestions and encouragement throughout the process. He fully supported me all the way, as did the committee. I owe a debt of gratitude to them. They are all Christian gentlemen and scholars of the very best sort.

During the process of working on the dissertation, I at times was frustrated by certain attitudes and positions adopted by many of the scholars who wrote the articles and books I used concerning Mark 16:9–20. While I could not include my thoughts at the time in my work, I mentally filed them away for future use, if and when I was approved for publication. That time is now.

As indicated above, I was bothered by my perception that the testimony of second-century witnesses (such as Irenaeus) was given less weight than I thought they deserved. Why was this so? Were these witnesses telling the truth when they testified that Mark wrote the passage? There is absolutely no indication that they were doing otherwise. Were they mistaken? While such is within the realm of possibility, it is unlikely—given the attitude of the early church concerning the integrity of Scripture, and the biblical prohibitions against adding to the Word of God. How could such early witnesses knowingly proclaim that the passage was from Mark, if they knew that the opposite was true?

It is a presupposition on my part that the Holy Spirit fully inspired Mark, as well as all of the New Testament writers. The conservative position (or "high view") of Scripture is simple: The Holy Spirit fully inspired the

Introduction

writers of the New Testament, down to the words they chose, without overriding their individual skills and abilities. Without impugning the beliefs of any scholar, it is my strong conviction that the process of inspiration must be factored into the discussion concerning Mark 16:9–20, or for that matter, the study of any biblical book or passage.

John Mark is held forth by many to have written a masterpiece; sometimes to the point that his Gospel seems to be elevated by scholars above those written by Matthew, Luke, and John. That said—if the Holy Spirit chose the words for Mark to use, without overriding his skills and abilities—is it sensible to limit the way in which Mark wrote? To put it another way: John wrote his Gospel, as well as the epistles of John and Revelation; there is a huge difference in style between the Gospel of John and Revelation, yet both came from the same author. As will be seen, even scholars who do not hold Mark to have written 16:9–20 nevertheless admit similarities between the passage and the rest of the Gospel of Mark.[1] Is it thus a leap of reasoning to say that the same author could have written both? If the Holy Spirit chose the words, and utilized the intelligence, skills, and abilities of John Mark, such is entirely reasonable. John Mark quite obviously was a very gifted author. The Holy Spirit realized this, and utilized him to the fullest—as he did with the rest of the authors of the Gospels. Each author was chosen to write a unique Gospel for a unique audience for a unique purpose. They each told the same story from unique perspectives.

Yet, this very idea—that each author of the Gospels wrote his own eyewitness account, by the full inspiration of the Holy Spirit (which would account for similarities)—seems all too often to be lost in the discussion. Thus it is that Green-Armytage's observations ring true:

> There is a world—I do not say a world in which all scholars live but one at any rate into which all of them sometimes stray, and which some of them seem permanently to inhabit—which is not the world in which I live. In my world, if *The Times* and *The Telegraph* both tell one story in somewhat different terms, nobody concludes that one of them must have copied the other, nor that the variations in the story have some esoteric significance. But in the world of which I am speaking this would be taken for granted. There, no story is ever derived from facts but always from somebody else's version of the same story . . . In my world, almost every

---

1. Kelhoffer, *Miracle and Mission*, 49: "Numerous parts of 16:9–20 bear a striking resemblance to Mark 1:1–16:8"; Koester, *Ancient Christian Gospels*, 295: The "vocabulary and style" of the passage "are fully compatible with the Gospel of Mark."

book, except some of those produced by Government departments, is written by one author. In that world almost every book is produced by a committee and some of them by a whole series of committees.²

In commenting on the relationship between the Gospel of John and the Gospel of Mark, Carson's remarks have bearing on the discussion:

> Regardless of whether John depends on Mark, the easiest explanation as to why John 6 and Mark 6 preserve the same order of events *is that they actually occurred in that order*. It is important to remember that the Gospels were written within the lifetime of someone who knew Jesus himself. The studies on which so much form-and redaction-criticism have been based, the works on which so much effort to delineate the 'descent of the oral tradition' turn, were careful examinations of the passing on of traditions within a pre-literate society (the Maoris) over three hundred years or more. But in the Gospels we are dealing with a literate society (as the prologue of Luke attests), with books written within decades, not centuries, of the matters they describe.³

To hold one Gospel above the others does the rest a disservice, and in turn seems to overlook the process of the inspiration of the Holy Spirit. For all that has been written concerning the "Synoptic Problem," a larger point has been missed. The four accounts that have been preserved are masterpieces in their own right. Instead of focusing on "who copied whom," and "who wrote first," attention should rather be given to each Gospel as a unit to itself. Such is not the prevailing view among scholars by far, but it must be considered. If biblical scholarship is to have relevance in the lives of people, it must get "back to the Bible," as it were, and steer away from theories of relatively recent origin. Having said that, it seems that some scholars are resistant to real change.

In 1970, the landmark book *The Structure of Scientific Revolutions* appeared.⁴ While Thomas S. Kuhn originally was attempting to perceive the physical sciences, his work had major ramifications across many academic disciplines. Terms now considered normal—"paradigms," "paradigm shift"—were revolutionary when Kuhn first used them. The "paradigm" in this context is a commitment to a framework that both defines the world

---

2. Green-Armytage, *John Who Saw*, 12–13.
3. Carson, *Gospel according to John*, 49–50; emphasis original.
4. Kuhn, *Structure of Scientific Revolutions*.

Introduction

and what the scientist would expect to see. It provides a model of reality by which a thing can be determined to be "true." Scientists operate within the rules of the paradigm as they work. Yet, although paradigms are necessary, dogmatic adherence to a paradigm makes scientists very sensitive to anything discovered that does not conform to the paradigm. Thus, over time anomalous results accumulate until a paradigm change is inevitable. Such is not at first accepted, but over time takes place. Biblical studies were not immune from scrutiny. In 2000, Shedinger wrote an article asking whether "Kuhnian paradigms" had application to biblical scholarship.[5] Shedinger's thesis was that "the academic discipline of biblical studies constitutes a poor arena for the application of Kuhn's notion of paradigms."[6] He further argued that the concept of paradigms "has little place in the discipline of biblical studies."[7] Interestingly, Shedinger pointed to the discipline of Synoptic Gospel studies as one reason why. He contrasted scientific work as "normally not marked by a debate over paradigmatic fundamentals" to "precisely the characteristic of scholarly work in biblical studies, a discipline frequently characterized by debate between adherents of differing paradigms."[8] He offered the example of the predominant presupposition of the priority of Mark and the existence of Q. "But while this is the dominant paradigm, it is not the only one."[9] He pointed to debate between the two groups, a growing number of scholars who advocate the Griesbach hypothesis, and "in biblical studies, contradictory paradigms can and do coexist within the same academic community."[10]

Yet, Shedinger acknowledged some similarities between Kuhnian paradigms and biblical research; in so doing, he seemed to contradict his assertion concerning the Mark/Q understanding of the Synoptics. He observed, "The paradigm has commanded the allegiance of a significant majority of scholars and has provided the framework for an enormous amount of detailed, paradigm-based research."[11] He pointed out that those who differed with this understanding were still held to be members of the scholarly community, unlike in the scientific community, though he

---

5. Shedinger, "Kuhnian Paradigms."
6. Ibid., 454.
7. Ibid.
8. Ibid., 458.
9. Ibid.
10. Ibid.
11. Ibid., 469.

Does Mark 16:9–20 Belong In The New Testament?

interestingly added, "Those dissenting from the Mark/Q understanding of Synoptic relationships have not created a paradigm shift; they are merely engaging in healthy inter-paradigm debate."[12]

The relevance of all of this to the question of the ending of Mark can be seen in two ways. First, the prevailing view—that 16:9–20 does not belong in the Gospel of Mark—is promoted by many of those who hold to the prevailing paradigm of Synoptic studies. Shedinger perhaps unwittingly admitted more than he intended when he said that those who dissent from Mark/Q are still working within the accepted paradigm. The presuppositions of the Mark/Q approach (developed by German scholars in the eighteenth and nineteenth centuries) thus affect the approach to the problem.

The fact is, the centerpiece of this "solution" to the Synoptic Problem—the so-called Q document—is a chimera; a will-o'-the-wisp that exists only in the minds of those willing to accept it as true. Such a document has never been discovered, or has ever been shown to even exist. Second, any major challenge to the prevailing view is often met with resistance. Such will be observed in this study by the comments of Thomas, Magness, Lincoln, Danove, and Elliott—as well as the observations by Kelhoffer and Williams concerning the hostility toward dissenting voices. As will become evident, the comments by Kelhoffer and Williams along these lines are revealing. This has ramifications as to how the evidence concerning 16:9–20 is presented in both popular and scholarly works.

Norman Geisler, who served as President of the Evangelical Theological Society wrote that the twelve verses "are lacking in many of the oldest and most reliable manuscripts."[13] Ben Witherington III wrote that Eusebius and Jerome said that the verses were "absent from all Greek copies known to them."[14] These statements, as will be shown, are false. The *Archaeological Study Bible* article on Mark 16:9–20 acknowledged that the passage is included in most texts and "several" translations, but goes on to claim that it is not in a "number" of versions; concerning Clement and Origen, it said that they "show no knowledge of any ending . . . beyond verse 8"; of Eusebius and Jerome, it went on to affirm "nearly all Greek manuscripts known to them concluded with verse 8."[15] France's comments are little better. He began by stating that it was the "virtually unanimous verdict of modern

---

12. Ibid., 470n30.
13. Geisler and Howe, *Big Book of Bible Difficulties*, 377.
14. Witherington, *Gospel of Mark*, 412–13.
15. Kaiser, *Archaeological Study Bible*, 1661.

Introduction

textual scholarship" that the text of Mark ended at verse 8; in his listing of external evidence, he affirmed that Clement and Origen "do not appear to have known" the text past verse 8, and that Eusebius and Jerome stated that verses 9–20 "was not found in the majority of the Greek MSS available to them." France also referred to the versions which include the passage and have the marginal signs and comments, and claimed this indicated "its textual status is doubtful." Concerning the evidence in favor, France mentioned it in two sentences and said, "on the whole are later than those mentioned above" in favor of omission.[16] While it must be stressed that the majority of published scholars who oppose 16:9–20 do not overstate the case, it is disturbing that too many seem to have not taken the time to investigate whether some of their statements are accurate.

I have been preaching and working with Churches of Christ for over thirty-five years. My father and grandfather (both deceased) also preached over forty years and fifty years, respectively, within Churches of Christ. Our brethren by and large hold to a high view of Scripture. They are skeptical of modern philosophies that seem to them to strike against the integrity of the Bible and the sovereignty of God. I share that conviction—not because I grew up in it, or because my ancestors believed it, but because Scripture is the final authority on all things religious. That was true in the first century, and it is still true today. It will remain so until the Lord comes again. Given this conviction, I freely admit to being passionate about maintaining the integrity of Scripture, free from philosophies which have their origin in the eighteenth century. How can one accept a template which was developed by liberal scholars who rejected the miracles of the Bible? How can one accept an approach to Scripture which was adopted in total by the Jesus Seminar? Surely it is more than a coincidence that the participants in the Jesus Seminar give much space to the "Q" document, and the four-source theory of the Synoptics.[17] It is past time for those who profess to believe in the full inspiration of Scripture to call for a paradigm shift in biblical studies. We must allow Scripture to lead us, not the other way around. Our attitude must be that of the Bereans in Acts 17:11. If they "checked up" on inspired apostles, how much more should we do on uninspired scholars? One of my graduate professors was the late Rex A. Turner Sr. He raised some questions which need to be seriously considered by all of us today:

---

16. France, 685–86.
17. Funk et al., *Five Gospels*, 12–18.

Does Mark 16:9–20 Belong In The New Testament?

> The issue at stake is inspiration. Are the Old and New Testaments inspired, or are they the product of mere men? A corollary of the issue of inspiration is the question of whether or not there is an omnipotent, omniscient, omnipresent God—a creator who is perfect in holiness and righteousness? If the Scriptures are not inspired, how can a mere man, be he, by his own admission ever so intelligent and creative, as to account for the theme of the Bible—that is, God, Man, and Jesus the Son of God?[18]

Churches of Christ have long been known for their plea to restore New Testament Christianity. It is a plea that I believe to be more relevant today than ever before. Undergirding that plea is an unshakeable faith in the Word of God. The challenge is to present that plea in a way that will appeal to all people. Mark 16:15–16, part of the passage under consideration in this volume, gives the Lord's marching orders to his disciples: "Go into all the world and proclaim the gospel to the whole creation. Whoever believes and is baptized will be saved, but whoever does not believe will be condemned." With all my life, I believe those verses to be true. I believe the Lord said it.

My grandfather, S. F. Hester, did not possess a formal degree. Yet he was educated in the Scriptures. His example of faith is etched in my memory even today. In a sermon he preached on "The Gospel of Christ," he made the point that the Gospel of Christ is plain. That is, it is designed to be understood, whether one is educated or uneducated. Pa Hester said that education is valuable, but if it was essential to our understanding God's will, he would have told us so. In fact, my grandfather said, education can sometimes be a hindrance (2 Cor. 11:3). And, as he would point out, Christ chose uneducated men to declare his Gospel the first time (Acts 4:13). Now, my grandfather was not against education at all. Indeed, he encouraged all four of his sons (who would all preach) to go as far as they could with their education. Yet his point was that we must guard against the danger of elevating human understanding and reason on the same level with Scripture.

This volume is designed to take the reader on a journey. I want you to travel the same path I traveled, and to see how I ended up where I am concerning Mark 16:9–20. We will begin by surveying the history of research from 1965–2011. It is almost a survey of my lifetime. I was born in February 1965; in December of that same year, Kenneth W. Clark made his annual presidential address to the Society of Biblical Literature. That

---

18. Turner, *Systematic Theology*, 42–47.

Introduction

address would start some to reexamine the issue of the ending of Mark. In the course of surveying the literature, attention will be given to scholarly journals and books, as well as critical introductions and commentaries. Next, the evidence will be examined. External evidence and internal evidence will be treated separately and seriously. It is my observation that all too often the external evidence is given short shrift. An attempt will be made to correct that. The internal evidence will be examined as well. Then, a proposal will be offered as to both the origin of Mark 16:9–20 and its status. I realize that my conclusion will not be accepted by everyone. I also realize that some criticism will come. That is all to be expected. I do want everyone to understand that the conclusion I offer is one which satisfies me, and is one which I know beyond any reasonable doubt does not strike against the inspiration of Scripture or the integrity of the Word of God. I only ask that the conclusion offered here be given a fair and complete hearing.

My colleagues at the V. P. Black College of Biblical Studies at Faulkner University have been fully supportive of this endeavor. I owe them, especially Dean G. Scott Gleaves, a debt of gratitude. I am honored to be a part of the great work of training preachers and biblical scholars. Dr. David H. Warren, one of my colleagues, actually served as my first dissertation committee chairman. He has offered vital help and support. I have incorporated many suggested corrections and changes he has offered. He also graciously agreed to write the Preface. I am honored to call David a friend and brother in Christ.

All of what I have said up to this point is to make the reader aware of where I am coming from in this book. Our modern society is in desperate need of ancient Truth. To be able to reach those who need it, we need to cast aside human pride and philosophies, and embrace wholeheartedly Scripture in its fullness. This includes Mark 16:9–20.

David W. Hester
October 30, 2014

CHAPTER 1

Modern Scholarship on Mark 16:9–20, 1965–2011

From the late 1800s to the late 1950s, the scholarly consensus eventually solidified against inclusion of Mark 16:9–20. In 1965, that began to change.

The SBL Presidential Address of Kenneth W. Clark

On December 30, 1965, the Society of Biblical Literature held its annual meeting at Vanderbilt University. Kenneth W. Clark delivered the presidential address on that occasion.[1] While not arguing for the acceptance of Mark 16:9–20 as genuine, Clark said: "On the other hand, the restoration of the traditional ending of Mark is a wholesome challenge to our habitual assumption that the original Mark is preserved no further than 16:8 . . . Witnesses both for and against the CE restoration as genuine are early and impressive, and we should consider the question still open and perhaps 'insoluble at present.'"[2]

---

1. The address was subsequently published as Clark, "Theological Relevance of Textual Variation in Current Criticism of the Greek New Testament," *Journal of Biblical Literature* 85 (1966) 1–16. In his address, Clark was reviewing the new "Catholic Edition" of the Revised Standard Version; hence his abbreviation "CE." Mark 16:9–20 had been restored back to the text of Mark, unlike the 1946 RSV.

2. Ibid., 9–10.

Perhaps overlooked were his earlier remarks concerning bias, which could have elicited a strong reaction from his audience: "It is also a false assurance, offered by many, that textual criticism can have no effect upon Christian doctrine. This insistent comfort implies that the text, in any form, deals only with the periphery of doctrine. It also implies a fear that emendation of the text might have evil, but never good, theological consequences. And yet it is impossible for any scholar to provide assurance to any Christian that textual studies will not affect his beliefs, even for the better."[3]

Clark's remarks were controversial; William Farmer made mention of them in the Preface to his book, *The Last Twelve Verses of Mark*, yet Clark would be mentioned by only one other scholar.[4] Over the next fifteen years, numerous books and articles were written concerning the passage that took the study into new directions. Most still denied that verses 9–20 should be included in the Gospel of Mark, save one.

1964–72: Metzger, Meye, Farmer, Linnemann, Schweizer, Schmithals, Trompf, Elliott, Van der Horst

Bruce M. Metzger had penned an overview of the textual issues of the New Testament in 1964.[5] Concluding that the passage was not from the hand of Mark, Metzger asked, "But did Mark intend to conclude his Gospel with the melancholy statement that the women were afraid?"[6] In arguing against such a position, Metzger (perhaps) unwittingly anticipated scholars who would follow after him. He made three significant points in this regard: first, such a conclusion is not an appropriate ending; second, to terminate a Greek sentence with the word γάρ is rare; third, Metzger said that it is possible that in verse 8 Mark meant to write "they were afraid of"—thus indicating that something else is needed to finish the sentence.[7] This was

---

3. Ibid., 5.

4. This is both surprising and puzzling, given Clark's stature and the content of his address. Nevertheless, a search of articles and books from the period immediately following his address (1965–70) yields no direct reply, nor any reference to it. After the work of William Farmer, Clark would not be mentioned again in either articles or books until 2000.

5. Metzger, *Text of the New Testament*, 322–26. Metzger would subsequently reprint the same discussion, with some changes, in 1968 and 2005.

6. Ibid., 325.

7. Ibid., 326.

Does Mark 16:9–20 Belong In The New Testament?

the first, but by no means the last, time that Metzger would address textual issues concerning the passage.

Robert P. Meye advocated the view that the Gospel ended prior to 16:9–20.[8] At the outset, he clearly stated his position: "This essay is written with the conviction that the history of Marcan and Gospel studies has provided us with ample evidence to compel the conclusion that Mark 16:8 was indeed the original and intended ending of the Gospel."[9] Meye then acknowledged two central problems with this position: first, "it is thought improbable that a Gospel would conclude without a narrative of the resurrection appearance(s) of Christ." The second "has to do with the apparent abruptness of an ending at 16:8."[10] In response, Meye said first that "Mark 16:1–8 clearly articulates the resurrection of Christ."[11] He also said that the response of fear of the women at the tomb pointed to "a sign that the women were at the scene of the ultimate mystery."[12] In addressing the second problem, Meye pointed to the beginning of Mark's Gospel for a proposed solution. "Markan clues are of crucial significance in the search for a solution to the Markan ending."[13] He suggested first that the abruptness of the first verse presages the abruptness of the ending. Meye also stressed that the style of Mark demanded the abrupt ending; thus, "Mark 16:8 is not abrupt as an ending when viewed in the light of the Markan beginning, or the Markan narrative in general."[14] He then stressed the use of prophecy: "In other words, what happens in Mark 16:1–8 must be understood as the fulfillment of the word of the beloved Son of God himself... The evangelist is clearly concerned to stress that all that is happening is a fulfillment of Jesus' own word... Seen in these terms the ending is forceful and complete: Jesus is risen! He goes before his disciples into Galilee! And that in fulfillment of his own word!"[15] Meye's work served as a prelude to others who would eventually follow his lead. At this point, however, his position was in the minority. Also, others would take this avenue of study into different directions.

8. Meye, "Mark 16:8."
9. Ibid., 33.
10. Ibid., 34.
11. Ibid., 35.
12. Ibid., 36.
13. Ibid.
14. Ibid., 39.
15. Ibid., 42.

Modern Scholarship on Mark 16:9–20, 1965–2011

William R. Farmer was motivated by Clark's address to write a monograph defending the authenticity of the passage.[16] Farmer divided the work into two parts, addressing the external evidence (pp. 3–75) and the internal evidence (pp. 79–103). His conclusion concerning the external evidence was that "it does not produce the evidential grounds for a definitive solution to the problem."[17] That being said, he did argue that the removal of the passage from Mark was an intentional omission—due to some Alexandrian scribes excising it because of their qualms with picking up snakes and drinking poison.[18] In part 2, Farmer addressed the internal evidence—from which he drew the conclusion that the vocabulary of the passage argues in favor of its authenticity.[19] Farmer examined the vocabulary of the passage in comparison with the rest of the Gospel by examining eighty words and phrases used in the passage.

Farmer's work came under immediate criticism, most notably from Gordon Fee.[20] After stating that Farmer's "argument is brilliantly conceived and carefully worked out," Fee added, "There are major weaknesses in both parts of the book that tend to weaken the case for Markan authorship."[21] Fee pointed out the lack of emphasis by Farmer concerning the similarities of the vocabulary and style of the passage with Gospel parallels—although Farmer did periodically compare words and phrases to the other three Gospels but perhaps not to the extent that Fee desired. Farmer's stated purpose for part 2 of his work was to compare the relationship of the passage to the rest of Mark.[22] At any rate, Fee declared, "This is an important study . . . But

---

16. Farmer, *Last Twelve Verses of Mark*, ix. Though Farmer's work was published in 1974, according to James Kelhoffer Farmer actually completed it in 1969.

17. Ibid., 74. Farmer did say that the "question can only be settled by a study of the internal evidence" (72).

18. Ibid., 67–72. Previous scholars had raised possibilities of its omission, but not to the extent of Farmer.

19. Ibid., 103.

20. Gordon D. Fee, review of *Last Twelve Verses of Mark*. Many other reviews subsequently appeared, including C. K. Barrett, *Durham University Journal* n.s. 36 (1974) 104–6; Beasley-Murray, *Review and Expositor* 72 (1975) 375; Birdsall, *Journal of Theological Studies* 26 (1975) 151–60; Elliott, *Theology* 78 (1975) 103–5; Fowler, *Dialog* 16 (1977) 148–49; and Wikgren, *Catholic Biblical Quarterly* 37 (1975) 249–50. Also see Hodges, *Bibliotheca Sacra* 133 (1976) 178.

21. Fee, *Last Twelve Verses*, 462.

22. Farmer, *Last Twelve Verses*, 83.

whether Farmer's thrust toward authenticity will convince any except those who were predisposed to be convinced remains to be seen."[23]

Eta Linnemann offered an interesting hypothesis concerning the composition of the passage.[24] After making the claim that there is a natural break between verses 14 and 15, she divided the passage into two parts—16:9–14 and 16:15–20. Her contention was that the two parts were independent; that the Gospel originally ended at verse 8, followed by elements of Matthew 28:16–17 and Mark 16:15–20. Though Farmer's work was written in 1969, he addressed Linnemann's work in his Preface to his own book. After stating that Linnemann's two-part hypothesis had "some support" from the evidence, Farmer added, "not so as to preclude 16:9–14 from being a part of the original text of Mark." Farmer's assessment of Matthew 28:16–17 being part of the original text of Mark was that it "would seem to be unnecessarily complex, though by no means impossible."[25] Linnemann's work was echoed by Walter Schmithals[26] and Gary Trompf,[27] who both argued for a division of the passage along similar lines. Though the work of Linnemann, Schmithals, and Trompf took the study into interesting areas, they never gained widespread acceptance.[28] Kurt Aland, in particular, quickly moved to refute Linnemann's hypothesis.[29] Nevertheless, the impetus had been given to others to delve deeper into the passage and surrounding issues.

Eduard Schweizer briefly addressed the question of the ending of Mark in 1970.[30] Schweizer affirmed, "Unquestionably this passage is a later addition, which has been supplied because the sudden ending in vs. 8 required such a conclusion."[31] He wrote, "Above all, this is an example of a harmony of all the Easter accounts which has probably been created for purposes of

---

23. Fee, review of *Last Twelve Verses*, 463.

24. Linnemann, "Der (wiedergefundene) Markusschluss"; as cited in Kelhoffer, *Miracle and Mission*, 35.

25. Farmer, *Last Twelve Verses*, ix–x.

26. Schmithals, "Der Markusschlub"; as cited in Kelhoffer, *Miracle and Mission*, 35.

27. Trompf, "First Resurrection Appearance," 308–30.

28. Typical of the reaction to these proposals is Phillips, "Mark 16 in Recent New Testament Studies," 53–56. Schmithals argued that 16:9–20 belonged originally to a source used by Mark; thus, Schmithals dated the passage earlier than the Gospel itself. Farmer mentioned Schmithals's work in his own preface, x.

29. Aland, "Die widedergefundene Markusschlub?"; as cited in Kelhoffer, *Miracle and Mission*, 35.

30. Schweizer, *Good News according to Mark*, 374–75.

31. Ibid., 374.

instruction. According to a very uncertain tradition this conclusion was originated by the Presbyter Ariston (AD 100)."[32] Schweizer later added, "We cannot be sure whether or not something else originally preceded this conclusion."[33] Schweizer said that the passage "is valuable because it affirms that the real objective of Jesus' resurrection is found in the proclamation of the Gospel in the world."[34]

Writing in 1971, J. K. Elliott offered his perspective.[35] After listing the manuscript evidence for all ending options, Elliott briefly addressed Linnemann's article. Calling her work "too facile," he went on to add, "If Linnemann had tried to argue against the full evidence it would have proved impossible to maintain that part of the longer ending belonged to the original Gospel."[36] Elliott then proceeded to examine the distinctive linguistic and stylistic features of 16:9–20. Specifically, thirty-two words and phrases were listed by Elliott, all of which he said at the least do not appear elsewhere in Mark—including some, he claimed, that do not appear in the other three Gospels, and in some cases nowhere else in the New Testament.[37] Elliott's work was crucial in "setting the table" for analysis of 16:9–20 based upon internal evidence. His work would eventually factor into further study.

Commenting on the Greek text of the passage in 1971, Bruce M. Metzger stated concerning NT Greek Manuscript 2386: "Although the last page of Mark closes with ἐφοβοῦντο γάρ, the next leaf of the manuscript is missing, and following 16.8 is the sign indicating the close of an ecclesiastical lection, a clear implication that the manuscript originally continued with additional material from Mark."[38] Metzger had thus affected the evidence that supported omission, taking away one piece that had up until his time been cited frequently. He would come back to the issue again in due course.

---

32. Ibid.
33. Ibid., 374–75.
34. Ibid., 378.
35. J. Elliott, "Text and Language."
36. Ibid., 257.
37. Ibid., 257–62.
38. Metzger, *Textual Commentary*, 122n1. Given this statement, one is left to wonder why Metzger did not acknowledge the space at the end of Mark in Vaticanus. Perhaps a future version of the work by a different author will correct the omission.

Does Mark 16:9–20 Belong In The New Testament?

In 1972 a groundbreaking article appeared by P. W. van der Horst, who favorably argued that a Koine Greek book could end with γάρ.[39] He utilized a parallel in the thirty-second treatise of Plotinus (*Ennead* 5.5) and attempted to show that Plotinus's pupil and editor, Porphyry, had been guided in his division of the work by Plotinus's own markings—thus having no problem ending with γάρ. If a sentence or paragraph could end this way, van der Horst argued, then why could not an entire book? Concurrent with the rise of narrative criticism in the years that followed, van der Horst's work eventually proved influential. He had taken Meye's work a step further. Initially, however, many scholars were not quick to accept his conclusion.

The same year that van der Horst published his article, Metzger announced a discovery he made which seemed to impact the evidence concerning the passage: "The present writer, having examined the ending of Mark in sixty-five Ethiopic manuscripts, discovered that none, contrary to the statements made by previous investigators, close the Gospel at xvi.8, but that most (forty-seven manuscripts) present the so-called shorter ending directly after vs.8, followed immediately by the longer ending (verses 9–20)."[40] This affected the evidence for omission in that it clarified one of the sources often cited against the validity of the passage.[41] By this time, scholarship was already moving into even more interesting directions.

1974–1976: Hug, Gideon, Anderson

Joseph Hug offered a major contribution in the study of the passage with his 1974 dissertation, published in 1978.[42] His was the first major study of the passage in the twentieth century distinct to itself. While he did not accept its authenticity to the rest of the Gospel, he accepted its canonicity. He concluded that the passage was appended at some point in the late first century to the early second century.[43] In chapter 3 of his work, he examined the vocabulary of the passage by comparing it to extracanonical Christian

---

39. Van der Horst, "Can a Book End with a ΓΑΡ?"

40. Metzger, "Ending of the Gospel according to Mark," 167.

41. E.g., Elliott (256) cited three Ethiopic manuscripts as ending at v. 8.

42. Hug, *La finale de l'évangelie de Marc*; as cited in Kelhoffer, *Miracle and Mission*, 35–39.

43. Ibid., 177–215.

writings, instead of the rest of the New Testament.[44] Hug argued in chapter 4 that the author of the passage did not write with knowledge of the other three Gospels,[45] a thesis which was accepted by the majority of those who reviewed his dissertation.[46] Generally speaking, Hug's work was valuable in that his focus was on the passage as a distinct work.

In 1975, Virtus Gideon began an examination of the history of scholarship on the passage with this comment: "The average contemporary student is no longer satisfied with the traditional explanations concerning the reliability of Mark 16:9–20. He usually permits little room for critical studies, seemingly feeling that the New Testament is not to be subjected to modern critical studies. He searches for 'pat' answers to 'pet' questions. Therefore, world renowned New Testament scholars have been forced by positions of their colleagues who advocate the veracity of these verses to reinvestigate a question formerly believed conclusively settled."[47] Gideon thus entered into a consideration of most of the writing on the subject from 1871 on. He mentioned Farmer's work, as well as Linnemann and Metzger, but curiously omitted several others.[48] In the end, Gideon concluded that the passage should be included in the Greek text, but not as a part of the Gospel itself. He said further, "Critical studies teach us that Christian doctrines should not be founded primarily upon this passage which lacks the best manuscript evidence."[49] Gideon's piece was an interesting glimpse at most of the work that had been done up to that point. However, it broke no new ground—nor did it follow up on the efforts of others.

---

44. Ibid., 39–162.

45. Ibid., 163–76.

46. Pesch, review of *La finale de l'évangile de Marc*, 368, was characteristic of the reviewers; he himself had argued in support of this position in his commentary on Mark, *Das Markusevangelium*, 2:544–56; as cited in Kelhoffer, *Miracle and Mission*, 37.

47. Gideon, "Longer Ending of Mark."

48. Gideon was another in the long line of scholars who did not mention Clark's address. It could be contended that he alluded to it in the paragraph just cited, but that is unlikely. More significantly, he did not cite van der Horst, even though he dealt with the question of how Mark ends and spent a great amount of space examining the question of whether a koine Greek book could end with final γάρ. Also missing from his piece was Schmithals and Trompf, which is equally curious—given the fact that the title of Gideon's work concerns recent study on the passage, and Schmithals and Trompf both wrote in 1972.

49. Gideon, "Longer Ending of Mark," 12; it is possible that he made this statement in light of v. 16 and its teaching on baptism.

Does Mark 16:9–20 Belong In The New Testament?

Hugh Anderson addressed 16:9-20 in his commentary, published in 1976.[50] Anderson wrote of the verses, "In vocabulary, style, and content they are unquestionably non-Marcan, and have a distinct flavor of the second century."[51] His conclusion was that "it was initially an independent report and was latterly attached to Mark's Gospel by some person or group who felt that the Gospel was incomplete without an appearance-story or stories, and wanted to align it with the other Gospels."[52] He further stated that "the passage reads like a manual of instruction, designed to answer questions about the Easter event and its theological meaning, and consists mainly of Easter traditions drawn from the later Gospels and Acts. From this we may judge that it comes from the earlier part of the second century."[53]

After referring to the Freer Logion and the short ending, Anderson concluded of all of them: "These Endings can hardly be regarded as canonical. Yet they do have their own intrinsic significance. They show us how the Church continued to think of Easter as central and decisive, as the hinge of history and belief and above all of its missionary proclamation and service. The Longer Ending represents one of the earliest attempts we know to construct a harmony of Easter events out of the varied data of the Gospels and Acts."[54] He wrote, "The manifold truth of Easter has never been dependent on men's ability to agree to a uniform *mode* of Jesus' rising again or to reconstruct precisely what happened."[55]

1980–85: Krauss, Petersen, Boomershine, Thomas, Childs

Veronika Krauss took the study of the passage into another direction with her dissertation, published in 1980.[56] Approaching the passage from the standpoint of biblical theology, Krauss divided her work into three parts. Part 1 addressed the authenticity of the passage (pp. 14–26); part 2, exegetical issues (pp. 27–228); part 3, biblical-theological issues (pp. 229–265). Based on the uniformity of the style of the passage, Krauss maintained

50. Anderson, *Gospel of Mark*, 358–62.
51. Ibid., 358.
52. Ibid.
53. Ibid.
54. Ibid., 361.
55. Ibid.
56. Krauss, "Verkundet das Evangelium der ganzen Schopfung!"; as cited in Kelhoffer, *Miracle and Mission*, 39–42.

16:9–20 was the work of a single author.[57] Krauss spent a significant amount of space in part 2 identifying the literary genre of 16:9–20.[58] She contended that an exact determination of the genre of the whole passage was not possible.[59] Krauss suggested that it was simply the concluding passage of the Gospel.[60] As to dating, Krauss placed the passage after the time of Acts and the Fourth Gospel but before Irenaeus—in the first third of the second century.[61] Part 3 of Krauss's work focused on a theological interpretation of the passage, wherein she concluded that the passage was consistent with the basic message of the New Testament.[62] Krauss's work is valuable in that she considered the passage as an entity to itself.

Also writing in 1980, Norman R. Petersen addressed the abrupt ending of the Gospel.[63] He began with the assumption that 16:8 marked the end of Mark. Petersen then proposed a literary approach to interpretation—namely, reader-response. He posited that the abrupt ending presented a major problem for the early readers, who expected closure.[64] Pointing back to Mark 13 where Jesus made predictions of what would happen after his death, Petersen suggested there was a matter of "eschatological urgency"[65] in solving the supposed riddle of the abrupt ending. Considering a literal interpretation, Petersen rejected it due to the clear implications thereof that Jesus' mission would be a failure and the disciples would be shown as liars. Thus Petersen wrote, "Our narrator does not mean what he says in Mark 16:8."[66] He suggested an ironic reading of the end of Mark. "The irony of 16:8, combined with the implicit directions provided by the plotting of expectations and satisfactions, constitutes an artful substitute for the obvious."[67] Rather than seeing 16:8 as an abrupt ending, Petersen saw it as an "ironic bridge" to what follows. It assumed the reader is aware of the

---

57. Ibid., 141–45, 153–57.
58. Ibid., 159–97.
59. Ibid., 158–59.
60. Ibid., 185.
61. Ibid., 228.
62. Ibid., 268.
63. Petersen, "When Is the End Not the End?"
64. Ibid., 152, 154.
65. Ibid., 159.
66. Ibid., 162.
67. Ibid., 163.

events following the end of Mark's Gospel. Petersen's article also served as a "bridge" to those who would follow after him.

Two articles appeared in 1981 from Thomas Boomershine concerning the possibility of whether Mark's Gospel could end with γάρ. The first, cowritten with Gilbert L. Bartholomew, argued that Mark essentially originated some of the techniques of narrative criticism that would be studied in detail some fifteen hundred years later.[68] Boomershine and Bartholomew rejected the argument concerning no parallels in ancient literature similar to the ending of Mark. It was highly unlikely, according to this argument, that Mark would pioneer such a technique. The authors also considered the notion that the original ending was either lost or damaged.[69] While conceding the fact that no parallels exist in ancient literature, the authors developed their arguments based upon internal evidence from Mark's Gospel. First, the use of narrative comments within the Gospel—specifically, the use of γάρ—had the same form and function as 16:8.[70] In particular, attention was given to the story of Jesus walking on the water (6:45–52) and the plot of the authorities (14:1–2).[71] The second argument was based on the "inside view"—that is, "the narrator describes the perceptions, thoughts, or feelings of a character."[72] Three passages in Mark were cited by the authors as parallel to 16:8, in that they all ended this way: the walking on the water (6:45–52), the second passion prophecy (9:30–32), and the conflict about paying taxes to Caesar (12:13–17).[73] Thus, it was argued, Mark was consistent. The third argument was that Mark ended the Gospel with a brief sentence—as was the case in many other instances within the book.[74] In this regard, Boomershine and Bartholomew departed from the standard Greek texts (Nestle-Aland and UBS) and argued that the phrase ἐφοβοῦντο γάρ ("for they were afraid") should be taken as an independent sentence, and not as a new clause in a compound sentence. They also made the point that the Gospel was likely intended to be read

---

68. Boomershine and Bartholomew, "Narrative Technique of Mark 16:8."
69. Ibid., 213–14.
70. Ibid., 214, 216.
71. Ibid., 216–17.
72. Ibid., 218.
73. Ibid., 218–19.
74. Ibid., 219–22.

orally, and that the use of γάρ at the end indicates a full oral stop prior to it.[75] That is to say, the public reader would make clear that γάρ was the end.

In his second article, Boomershine was more explicit in his use of narrative criticism.[76] He argued that 16:8 was "the climactic reversal in the motif of the messianic secret and that it emphasizes, in Mark's characteristic style, the same theme as the endings of the other Gospels."[77] In arguing his case, Boomershine responded to two other interpretations of 16:8. The first, made by R. H. Lightfoot, was that the verse should be taken as "holy awe" on the part of the women.[78] In spite of acknowledging the use of similar language in a similar way in the Gospel, Boomershine rejected this view: "While their fear is understandable and to a degree sympathetic, the dominant tone of the ending is negative."[79]

The second view was that of John Dominic Crossan, who suggested that Mark developed his Gospel as a polemic against early Christian theological opponents.[80] In assessing this position, Boomershine examined how the women were presented earlier in the Gospel. To account for Crossan's view, one must hold that the women are presented in a negative way throughout the Gospel. Yet in every instance, the women were presented as sympathetic characters as was the case in chapter 16. As Boomershine contended, "A valid interpretation of the ending, therefore, must account for the predominantly sympathetic characterization of the women."[81] Boomershine's position was as follows: "The impact of the ending, therefore, is to appeal for repentance from silence in response to the commission to announce Jesus' messiahship after his resurrection."[82] He had pointed out the development of the "messianic secret" earlier[83] and concluded, "The intended meaning of the ending is, therefore, the total effect of the ending."[84] This interpretation was given in light of how the Gospel would be read to subsequent audiences. In essence, this relied heavily upon narrative criti-

75. Ibid., 221–22.
76. Boomershine, "Mark 16:8."
77. Ibid., 225.
78. Ibid., 227–30.
79. Ibid., 230.
80. Ibid., 230–33.
81. Ibid., 233.
82. Ibid., 238.
83. Ibid., 233–38.
84. Ibid., 237.

cism as well as reader-response criticism. Boomershine's work advanced the approach to the ending. Although he did not accept the validity of Mark 16:9–20, he nevertheless prompted further study into different directions, the effect of which would eventually become apparent.

John Christopher Thomas made his own contribution to the discussion concerning Mark 16:9–20 in 1983.[85] He began by surveying the external and internal evidence available concerning the text, both for and against inclusion.[86] He turned to the question of whether the Gospel ended with final γάρ,[87] as well as the possibility that the ending may have been lost.[88] Thomas then focused upon the proposition that verse 8 was the place where the book was intended to end.[89] Based on the fact that Thomas did not criticize this view, it seems that he favored it. Thus he cited Petersen's and Tannehill's arguments as the likely solution, while rejecting Crossan in turn.[90] Thomas concluded that verses 9–20 were secondary and therefore not canonical.[91] He also suggested that the passage constituted a fifth witness to the resurrection recorded in the Gospels (assuming non-Markan origin), as well as making this assertion: "Farmer's work will probably inspire more research among those who for theological reasons *feel compelled to cling* to 16:9–20."[92]

Brevard Childs issued his landmark work on the New Testament in 1987. Putting forth his views on canon theology he devoted a short section to the long ending of Mark, and thus added a new twist to the discussion.[93] Having already stated his belief that the book ended at verse 8 and was thus intended to be read for the church, Childs indicated his conviction that verses 9–20 were added later.[94] Yet Childs stated,

85. Thomas, "Reconsideration of the Ending of Mark."

86. Ibid., 407–12. Thomas paid particular attention to the arguments of Farmer, as well as Linnemann.

87. Ibid., 413–14. Here the arguments of van der Horst and Trompf were addressed. It seemed that Thomas favored van der Horst's suggestion that the book ended with γάρ. He in turn rejected Trompf's proposal.

88. Ibid., 414–15.

89. Ibid., 415–18.

90. Ibid., 417–18.

91. Ibid., 418.

92. Ibid., 418–419; emphasis added. As will be seen, subsequent authors would use even stronger language in downplaying the notion of the passage being canonical.

93. Childs, *New Testament as Canon*, 94–95.

94. Ibid., 92–94.

> The significance of the expanded ending has usually been disregarded by modern critical scholarship, but it is wide-ranging in effect. Mark's Gospel received its canonical shape by the addition of an ending which clearly does not stem from the original author. Yet the addition is not simply a pious gloss attached to one late textual tradition, but rather an early expansion which helped to form the dominant textual tradition . . . This evidence supports the conclusion that the expanded ending to Mark entered the text during the process of forming a fourfold Gospel collection . . . For Mark to function within the fourfold collection his Gospel has been brought into conformity with the other three.[95]

This proposition encouraged another area of study for modern scholarship. If this were true, then the writer of verses 9–20 relied upon Matthew, Luke, and perhaps John. In due course another scholar would pick up on this possibility.

1986–89: Mirecki, Mann, Magness, Metzger, Myers, Stock, Lincoln

Paul Mirecki's 1986 dissertation, sponsored by Helmut Koester, relied upon form-criticism, as opposed to previous efforts which had stressed textual criticism.[96] Chapter 1 of his work reviewed a limited number of articles that addressed the passage.[97] Chapter 2 utilized form critical methodology in analyzing the passage itself.[98] He began the chapter by proposing that the passage displays evidence throughout of triple parallelism.[99] From this Mirecki set forth to prove that it was written by not one, but by two authors.[100] Mirecki thus attempted to explain the apparent variations in the passage from the rest of the book. The remainder of the chapter examined verses 16–19 and its particular forms.[101] Chapter 3 focused upon redaction criticism of the entire passage, assuming his earlier assertions to be true.[102]

---

95. Ibid., 94–95. As will be seen, subsequent authors took issue with Childs's assertions.

96. Mirecki, "Mark 16:9–20."

97. Ibid., 1–25. Mirecki reviewed Farmer, Hug, Pesch, Linnemann, and Schmithals.

98. Ibid., 26–106.

99. Ibid., 28–29.

100. Ibid., 30–35.

101. Ibid., 35–106.

102. Ibid., 107–42.

Does Mark 16:9–20 Belong In The New Testament?

Mirecki enunciated his rationale in an appendix. Verses 9–20 of Mark, in Mirecki's view, followed 15:47—instead of verse 8.[103] This explained his attempt at reconstructing the passage, as well as his proposition that two authors penned it. Mirecki then ended his work with certain suggestions: "It is hoped that this recognition of the nature of the text as a well-written literary composition will function as a starting point for a total reevaluation of the text in terms of its own textual history, its narrative story, its relation to similar texts, and especially its puzzling relation to the Gospel of Mark."[104] While one may disagree with Mirecki's conclusions, it seems undeniable that he opened the door for additional ventures. His basic assumption that the passage should be studied on its own merit stood in contrast to those that examined it only in connection the rest of the Gospel.

C. S. Mann addressed the question of the ending of Mark at length in his commentary, published in 1986.[105] Instead of focusing on 16:9–20, he rather dealt with the reasons for why the Gospel could end at verse 8. Specifically, he mentioned the theory that the early church actually failed to communicate the message of the resurrection. In response, Mann wrote, "The juxtaposition of Jerusalem-Gentile in this literature is far older than the unwary reader may imagine and has an ancestry in the nineteenth-century Tübingen School's notion of a 'Peter-Paul' conflict (The reader will also detect the inevitable hand of Hegel—'thesis-antithesis'—on which so much history tends to be written.)."[106] Mann concluded that "Mark's manuscript was deliberately ended at 16:8."[107] He listed five reasons for this:

1. The community for which Mark wrote, on his return to Palestine from Rome, was terror-stricken and tempted to flee.

2. Perhaps some had already fled, but the call of the messenger at the tomb was to go back to the time of loyalties, a time of discipleship characteristic of the Galilee of the ministry.

3. The silence of the community's witness is inappropriate, even in a time of peril, for *he has been raised*.

4. The women witnesses had been followers and companions of Jesus in ministry, passion, and at the tomb. The members of Mark's community

---

103. Ibid., 143–45.
104. Ibid., 150–51.
105. Mann, *Mark*, 659–70.
106. Ibid., 661.
107. Ibid., 663.

are also called to be followers and witnesses, even in time of trial and distress. *"He is going on before you . . ."*

5. Mark's Gospel was, in our view, specifically designed to elicit the response: "But surely there were resurrection appearances?" The message of Mark is that there were indeed resurrection appearances, but first the community must share with the trembling women all the feelings of fear, know those fears to be in the final analysis groundless, and only then can they hear the voice the women heard—*just as he told you.*[108]

At the end of his notes on 16:1-8, Mann briefly alluded to the abrupt ending at verse 8 and said that the author of verses 9-20 was anonymous. He concluded, "Mark did indeed end his Gospel at verse 8, with the harsh *for they were afraid* (It is grammatically far more harsh in the Greek). He wrote, as we have maintained, for a community overtaken by fear, a community which needed the reassurance that even those who were the first to hear of the vindication of Jesus in the Resurrection had been terrified."[109]

Also writing in 1986, J. Lee Magness explored the ending of Mark in great detail.[110] Chapter 1 of his work presented an overview of the problem, in which Magness briefly mentioned verses 9-20 and concluded, "Overwhelming evidence demands that we reject verses 9-20 and look elsewhere for the original ending."[111] He then examined the suggestions made by previous scholars concerning the possibility that a biblical writer would end a book with γάρ. Rejecting those suggestions, he offered a different hypothesis: "Mark affirms and communicates a resurrection and post-resurrection reunion without narrating them."[112]

Chapter 2 of Magness's work set forth the proposal of "absent endings" in literature in general, and then acknowledged a possible objection: "But the leap from twentieth-century literary theory to first-century gospel is an abrupt one. Only if these principles are clearly present in the ancient literary context of which Mark was a part can we confidently claim that our assessment of Mark's suspended ending is anything other than a

---

108. Ibid.
109. Ibid., 670.
110. Magness, *Sense and Absence.*
111. Ibid., 6.
112. Ibid., 14.

modern imposition on an ancient text."[113] In chapter 3, Magness proposed that several ancient works showed evidence of suspended endings. Of particular interest to Magness were ancient epics,[114] ancient tragedy,[115] ancient biography,[116] and ancient romance.[117] In chapters 4 and 5, Magness examined the biblical evidence for suspended endings, both in the Old and New Testament. In chapter 4, Magness examined both shorter narratives and longer narratives in the Old Testament.[118] He proposed, "Suggestive foreshadowing, structural patterning, and the synecdochal function of the ending have emerged as key interpretive factors."[119] In chapter 5, Magness followed the same structure.[120] In similar fashion he suggested that suggestive foreshadowing and structural patterning was evident in the New Testament.[121] In this way, Magness set up his theory as it pertained to Mark. In chapter 6, Magness applied his theory to the whole Gospel of Mark.[122] After examining the overall structure of the book, he focused upon the miracle stories, the transfiguration narrative, and the passion narrative. He suggested that the concepts of fear and silence were placed in a positive light, that implication of outside proclamation was clear and reader participation was evident, and that foreshadowing of the angelic mandate in 16:7 was also present.[123] In chapter 7, Magness gave his analysis of the ending of Mark in light of his previous suggestions.[124] He suggested that the abrupt ending at

---

113. Ibid., 24.

114. Ibid., 28–36. Magness focused on the *Iliad*, the *Odyssey*, and Virgil's *Aeneid*.

115. Ibid., 36–40. The works of Sophocles and Euripides.

116. Ibid., 40–42. Xenophon's *Cyropaedia* and Philostratus' *Life of Apollonius*.

117. Ibid., 42–47. Magness mentioned the works of Chariton, Xenophon, Helidorus, Longus, and Achilles Tatias.

118. Ibid., 49–63. Magness examined Judg 11:29–40, the marriage stories of Gen 24 and 29:1–30 as well as Exod 2:15–21, the miracle stories of Exod 15:22–25a, 17:1–6, and 2 Kgs 4:1–7 under "shorter narratives." The books of Exodus, Ruth, 2 Kings, Song of Songs, and 2 Chronicles, as well as Genesis and Jonah, were also studied under "longer narratives."

119. Ibid., 62–63.

120. Ibid., 70–85. In particular, Magness looked at the miracle stories of Matthew, the encounter stories within the Gospels, the pronouncement stories, and the parables under "shorter narratives." The books of Matthew, John, and Acts were placed under "longer narratives."

121. Ibid., 85.

122. Ibid., 87–105.

123. Ibid., 105.

124. Ibid., 107–25.

verse 8 was "coherent closure."[125] Magness acknowledged Petersen's work, and further suggested that 16:1–8 affirmed the resurrection of Jesus and assumed the obedience of the women and the other disciples, as well as affecting subsequent readers in positive ways.[126] Magness's work would spark further interest in the ending of Mark, but a familiar name weighed in once again with yet another twist.

Bruce Metzger mentioned 16:9–20 within his work concerning the canon of the New Testament.[127] In the midst of discussing questions concerning the canon, he asserted in this regard "the question of the canonicity of a document apparently did not arise in connection with discussion of such variant readings."[128] After briefly mentioning the external evidence against inclusion of the passage, Metzger wrote: "Eusebius and Jerome, well aware of such variation in the witnesses, discussed which form of the text was to be preferred. It is noteworthy, however, that neither Father suggested that one form was canonical and the other was not. Furthermore, the perception that the canon was basically closed did not lead to a slavish fixing of the text of the canonical books. Thus, the category of 'canonical' appears to have been broad enough to include all variant readings."[129] Metzger went further in his analysis of the question of canonicity: "There seems to be good reason, therefore, to conclude that, though external and internal evidence is conclusive against the authenticity of the last twelve verses as coming from the same pen as the rest of the Gospel, the passage ought to be accepted as part of the canonical text of Mark."[130] Thus, Metzger gave weight to the passage being included in the text of the canonical Gospel. This would give impetus for others to follow and take his conclusion even further in the years that followed.

Ched Myers offered a political interpretation of the ending, as well as the Gospel, in 1988.[131] Myers addressed the objection that a book could not end with γάρ: "Such speculation can now be considered obsolete, along with the grammatico-literary objection that a book could not end in a γάρ

---

125. Ibid., 107.
126. Ibid., 117–25.
127. Metzger, *Canon of the New Testament*.
128. Ibid., 269.
129. Ibid.
130. Ibid., 270.
131. Myers, *Binding the Strong Man*, 399–404.

clause."[132] Myers quoted from Petersen's work favorably, but added, "I believe Mark is doing more than inviting the reader to finish the last stroke of the painting; the openness/ambiguity of 16:8 cannot be resolved 'aesthetically,' but only by practice."[133] He explained: "We do not entirely understand what 'resurrection' means, but if we have understood the story, we should be 'holding fast' to what we *do* know: that Jesus still goes before us, summoning us to the way of the cross. And that is the hardest ending of all: not tragedy, not victory, but an unending challenge to follow anew. Because that means we must respond."[134]

In addressing 16:9–20, Myers listed it along with the short ending and said, "I do not deem them worthy of exegesis. It is important, however, to reflect upon them as the first of a long theological tradition, which continues today, to betray the Gospel by 'rewriting' it."[135] He further labeled 16:9–20 as pseudopigrapha because of its "bald presumption to 'rescue' Mark from his own deepest narrative and ideological commitments."[136] Myers went on to say that the passage, along with the short ending, "represent the work of those who cannot see the meaning of 16:8 as an invitation to which to respond, but only as a scandal that must properly be resolved."[137] Myers termed these endings "imperial rewritings" of Mark, based upon power. "Life in the imperial sphere depends upon triumphal narrative: the eleventh-hour Hollywood rescues, the arrival of the cavalry, the 'happily ever after.' Such endings allow us to avoid confronting ourselves, our mistakes, our frailty. Why else would the story of the Vietnam war need a heavily cosmetic face-lift before appearing in high-school history texts?"[138] Myers went on to say concerning the resurrection, "Mark, at least, offers no 'proof;' did Jesus in fact appear to the disciples? We are not told. For Mark, the resurrection is not an answer, but the final question. There is only one genuine 'witness' to the risen Jesus: to follow in discipleship. Only in this way will the truth of the resurrection be preserved."[139]

---

132. Ibid., 399.
133. Ibid., 400–401.
134. Ibid., 401.
135. Ibid.
136. Ibid.
137. Ibid., 402.
138. Ibid.
139. Ibid., 404.

Modern Scholarship on Mark 16:9–20, 1965–2011

Writing in 1989, Augustine Stock dealt in a summary fashion with the endings of Mark.[140] Of 16:9–20 he said, "The passage does not appear to have been compiled originally for the purpose of rounding off Mark. Composed originally as a catechetical summary of post-resurrection events, the long ending had, apparently, an independent existence, then came to be copied at the end of Mark's Gospel some time after the appearance of the shorter ending. The short ending is the older of the two and it *was* deliberately composed to round off Mark's abrupt ending at 16:8."[141] Dating both endings in the second century, Stock proposed that the existence of the short ending in Codex Bobbiensis indicated the origin of it at that point, because of indications that Bobbiensis was copied from a second-century papyrus. "The LE was in existence at the latest by the middle of the second century, and until the thirteenth century the SE stands before the LE. This primacy points to an early origin; a date near the middle of the second century is probable."[142] In commenting on the passage Stock wrote, "The LE has been characterized as a summary mission instruction which relates the epoch of the early Christian mission from Easter on."[143]

Andrew Lincoln, also writing in 1989, followed up on the work of Boomershine, Petersen, and Magness concerning the ending of Mark and γάρ.[144] He argued that the ending was much more complicated for both ancient and modern readers—leaving more questions than one would normally expect. Given that, however, what Lincoln said concerning 16:9–20 echoed Thomas's assertion: "This reading of the ending will work with the text that ends at 16:8 and will proceed on the assumption that it is no longer necessary to argue in any great detail either that 16:8 is the original ending or that an author could have intended to end a work with the clause ἐφοβοῦντο γάρ."[145] That this was the generally accepted position at the time was evident even among conservatives.[146] Yet, the ground had been prepared for others to eventually come along and challenge this view.

140. Stock, *Method and Message of Mark*, 432–39.
141. Ibid., 432–33.
142. Ibid., 434.
143. Ibid., 436.
144. Lincoln, "Promise and Failure."
145. Ibid., 284.
146. This was apparent to the author in the spring of 1986, during a visit to Harding Graduate School with the Bible majors of Freed-Hardeman University. The seminar was on the Gospel of Mark. One of the questions addressed considered the ending. It was suggested that perhaps verse 8 was indeed the end, and Mark's genius extended to the

Does Mark 16:9–20 Belong In The New Testament?

1991–94: Hooker, Gundry, Cox, Danove, Williams

Morna D. Hooker summarily addressed 16:9–20 in her commentary published in 1991.[147] She wrote, "Everything after v.8 is written in a different style and has quite clearly been added later."[148] She added, "It is probable that this was added to Mark some considerable time after the Gospel was written, probably in the second century. The great problem, to which we must return, is whether Mark intended to end at v.8, or whether his Gospel is incomplete—either because he was unable to finish it, or because the original ending was lost."[149] She suggested on the one hand that Mark may have suffered martyrdom, or on the other hand that the final page of the codex was worn away. "In this case, however, it is puzzling that the missing portion was not copied out and replaced. Though the problem is the abrupt ending, it is remarkable, nevertheless, that an accidental break should have occurred at a point where a case can at least be made for arguing that Mark intended to stop."[150] In commenting on 16:9–20 Hooker wrote, "These verses were certainly not written by Mark: in style and vocabulary they are quite different from the rest of the Gospel."[151] In a brief paragraph Hooker reviewed the major pieces of external evidence both for and against the passage, and concluded that "the verses were probably written at the beginning of the second century."[152] She said that the passage "shows no reliance on vv. 1–8. It consists of three brief accounts of appearances of the risen Lord."[153] In an additional note, Hooker addressed the problem of the abruptness of ending the Gospel at verse 8. She ended by advocating the approach of "reader-response" criticism: "It provides us with an interpretation of the text to which author and reader together can contribute—an interpretation which corresponds with the experience of many readers of the Gospel, whether or not it was in the mind of the evangelist."[154]

---

very style of the book. In a subsequent critical introduction class, the position taken by the teacher concerning the passage was that it likely was not Markan, but should be included with an explanatory footnote.

147. Hooker, *Gospel according to St. Mark*, 382–94.
148. Ibid., 382.
149. Ibid., 382–83.
150. Ibid., 383.
151. Ibid., 388.
152. Ibid., 389.
153. Ibid.
154. Ibid., 394.

Modern Scholarship on Mark 16:9–20, 1965–2011

Robert H. Gundry addressed at length the question of the ending of Mark in his commentary, published in 1993.[155] Gundry began by acknowledging the possibility of a lost ending for Mark, but rejecting the canonicity of 16:9–20: "We should not think of that ending as canonical any more than we think of the myriad other inauthentic writings in the Textus Receptus as canonical."[156] That said, Gundry proposed that verse 8 started a new pericope, the rest of which is now lost. Listing twelve reasons in favor of such a proposal, Gundry rejected the idea that γάρ could stand at the end of a book.[157] In his notes, Gundry responded to various scholars and their theories concerning why the Gospel could have ended at verse 8.[158] He also speculated as to why Mark did not reproduce the lost ending, and why others did not.[159] In a final paragraph, Gundry speculated as to the form of a lost ending by suggesting reliance of the author upon Matthew 28 and Luke 24.[160]

Steven Lynn Cox's dissertation was also published in 1993.[161] Cox's work went back to the second century and reviewed all scholarship up until the mid-1980s, an ambitious goal to say the least. In chapter 3, Cox reviewed Farmer's work and found it wanting, especially in the area of Farmer's use of patristic evidence and internal evidence.[162] Cox ended the chapter by affirming the canonicity of 16:9–20.[163] In chapter 4, he focused on whether ἐφοβοῦντο γάρ was indeed Mark's conclusion to the Gospel. After reviewing several possibilities—an unintentional ending, a lost ending, Mark never concluded his Gospel, the ending was deliberately suppressed—Cox affirmed, "There is no textual or patristic evidence which would suggest that the ending of Mark was lost, incomplete, or suppressed. These proposals to the ending of Mark were based purely on conjecture."[164] In a lengthy section

155. Gundry, *Mark*, 1009–21.
156. Ibid., 1009.
157. Ibid., 1009–12.
158. Ibid., 1012–21.
159. Ibid., 1021.
160. Ibid.
161. Cox, *History and Critique*. The book was divided into six chapters: Introduction; Pre-Critical Positions on the Ending of Mark; Scholars Who Support the Long Ending of Mark; Theories on the Endings of Mark Other Than the Short and Longer Ending; The Short Ending; Conclusion.
162. Ibid., 85–89.
163. Ibid., 94–95.
164. Ibid., 107–8.

Does Mark 16:9–20 Belong In The New Testament?

in the same chapter, Cox examined the reconstructed ending theories of Linnemann, Trompf, and Schmithals.[165] Cox's conclusion was virtually the same as mentioned above: namely, they were "based on conjecture."[166] He ended the chapter with a look at two other optional endings—the "Freer Logion" and the shorter ending. Cox agreed with scholars who rejected the authenticity of both.[167] In chapter 5, Cox put forth his own proposal concerning the ending. Using the Ibycus Scholarly Computer (ISC) database, Cox "found that one thousand and five sentences end with γάρ followed by a period and roughly 500 sentences end with γάρ followed by a question mark."[168] His conclusion was that if that is the case with a sentence, then it stands to follow that a paragraph, chapter, or work could end with γάρ as well. Cox then quoted from Homer, Isocrates, and Plotinus—all who ended a paragraph with γάρ[169]—but then undermined his proposal by writing: "The ISC did not list any ancient works that end with γάρ except Mark 16:8 followed by 16:9–20 in the textual marks."[170] In this, Cox emphasized what many scholars had stressed; namely, that no ancient work ends with γάρ—and that Mark would have been the first to do so. Other scholars would eventually come back to this same point. Cox's conclusion in chapter 6 put forth proposals for future research, following a summary of his work. An appendix listed the patristic writers who either quoted from or alluded to 16:9–20, which was helpful—though exact references were not given for each one.[171] Taken as a whole, Cox provided a summary of almost all of the studies up to that point concerning 16:9–20.[172]

The same year that Cox's work appeared, Paul L. Danove published his own work.[173] His thesis was clearly stated at the beginning: "The thesis of this book is that the evangelist intended to end the Gospel at 16:8, that the narrative has been constructed to demand a literal interpretation of the ending (the message was not delivered), and that the literal interpretation

---

165. Ibid., 110–32.
166. Ibid., 131.
167. Ibid., 133–45.
168. Ibid., 152.
169. Ibid., 155–56.
170. Ibid., 157.
171. Ibid., 217–22.
172. He did not reference Mirecki's work, and only mentioned Hug's study in a footnote.
173. Danove, *End of Mark's Story*.

engenders a carefully crafted crisis of interpretation which does not admit to narrative resolution but establishes textual grounds for resolving the narrative outside the story world and in the life of the reader."[174]

Danove divided his work into two parts: part 1 generated the methods of analysis (comprising chapters 1–4) and part 2 applied the method to the Gospel of Mark (comprising chapters 5–8). Chapter 1 established a definition of plot based on the writings of Aristotle and contemporary authors.[175] Chapter 2 proposed a structuralist approach to plot analysis using construction grammar, based upon the work of Charles J. Fillmore.[176] Danove demonstrated how this could be applied by using Mark 6:14–29.[177] In chapter 3, Danove proposed a phenomenological model of narrative communication in which the implied reader is crucially involved in the process.[178] Chapter 4 attempted to integrate the structuralist method of plot analysis with the phenomenological model of the implied reader by utilizing linguistic frames; specifically, the narrative frame.[179] Danove then applied this technique to Mark 6:17–29 as an example.[180]

In chapter 5, Danove briefly examined the text of Mark in connection with the ending. While he gave an overview of some of the external evidence, he unfortunately was dismissive of patristic evidence.[181] For Danove, the textual evidence was not enough: narrative technique was the deciding factor in dismissing 16:9–20 as a valid ending and making 16:8 the end of the Gospel.[182] Danove further asserted, "External criteria also establish that a conclusion in γάρ is at least acceptable according to the canons of contemporary literary practice,"[183] thus tipping his hand as to his approach. Chapter

---

174. Ibid., 1.

175. Ibid., 8–11.

176. Ibid., 30–54. Danove relied upon Fillmore's work extensively in this chapter, referencing both an unpublished manuscript and a published work.

177. Ibid., 49–54.

178. Ibid., 55–75.

179. Ibid., 78–87.

180. Ibid., 110–15.

181. Ibid., 120n5. Danove categorized it as "redundant." Concerning the possibility that such evidence might pinpoint a date for any particular ending, he offered this response: "This, however, is not a necessary conclusion but only a possible one, since knowledge of these endings does not imply any given context for them."

182. Ibid., 126–30.

183. Ibid., 130.

6 analyzed the plot structure of Mark, utilizing narrative technique.[184] Based upon this structure, Danove analyzed the implied reader of Mark in chapter 7. He assumed that the implied reader was proficient in Koine Greek and the Septuagint, could recognize structural types and could recognize reliable narration.[185] Chapter 8 brought all of Danove's proposals together concerning the ending of Mark. He argued that 16:8 provided a "textually grounded, readerly guided response."[186] Danove argued that verse 8 provided a challenge to the reader to proclaim the message, serves as a "tender trap" rhetorically speaking in that it provides an opportunity for greater faith, and constituted ironic narrative communication.[187] While Danove's work was based on patently modern methods of plot and communication analysis, many of the points he raised were intriguing. However, his all too brief treatment of the textual (and especially the patristic) evidence was problematic. From a scholar of Danove's stature, it was disappointing to see a lack of emphasis upon the evidence concerning authenticity.

1995-99: Hester, Helton, Terry, Williams

In 1995, J. David Hester (no relation to the author) built upon the work of Danove in his own analysis of the ending of Mark.[188] Hester focused upon "the role of the women and the young man as part of a specific narrative strategy" in the ending of the Gospel.[189] He utilized Danove's theory in developing his idea: "It is my function here to show how these characters participate, through the lack of fulfillment of specific narrative indicators, in 'trapping' the implied reader, and thereby forcing actual readers into making a series of decisions regarding its completion."[190] Hester presented the women of 16:1–8 as crucial in developing the unfolding plot of the

---

184. Ibid., 132–66.

185. Ibid., 169–78. Danove also assumed that the reader was a Christian who maintained a "high" Christology, 187–91.

186. Ibid., 205–21.

187. Ibid., 221–28.

188. Hester, "Dramatic Inconclusion." Danove helped Hester in the composition of the article. In his first footnote, Hester said, "My thanks to Dr. Paul Danove, Villanova University, Philadelphia, PA, for his encouragement and discussions (some of which I have attempted to refer to here) concerning the following interpretation." Hester also referred to Danove's 1991 dissertation concerning irony and plot.

189. Ibid., 63.

190. Ibid.

end of Mark's Gospel. "They are, in other words, protagonists, therefore entrusted by the reader with the success of the story."[191] From there, Hester seemed to diverge into a semi-feminist interpretation.[192] Hester then focused upon the young man of 16:5–7.[193] After stressing the importance of the young man to the conclusion, Hester presented seven possibilities as to his identity.[194] He then added his own suggestion: that the young man was more of a literary device, including all of the possibilities, plus acting as some sort of angelic messenger.[195] In this, he would have served as a figure to tie everything together—until the abrupt ending of 16:8, which to Hester served as an ironic conclusion, requiring "actual readers, disappointed by the role they are expected to play (implied reader) to enter the story and act upon it."[196] To Hester, the meaning of the abrupt ending was clear: "It is the actual reader who either fails or completes the story."[197]

In 1996, J. Stanley Helton attempted to examine the connection between the long ending of Mark and churches of Christ.[198] He attempted to demonstrate this through the example of J. W. McGarvey, who had initially advocated Markan authorship of Mark 16:9–20, but then backed away from that position later in his life after more textual evidence had surfaced. Those items of evidence were the discovery of the Vaticanus (B) manuscript, the Sinaiticus (ℵ) manuscript, the absence of the text in several Armenian manuscripts, and several other pieces of evidence against Markan authorship—which, Helton surmised, McGarvey would have known about by reading Westcott-Hort's appendix volume to *The New Testament in the*

---

191. Ibid., 64.

192. Ibid., 65–69. Hester contrasted the actions of the women with the disciples, and cast the women as having authority that seemed to be on par with the twelve. Hester also quoted approvingly from Elizabeth Schüssler Fiorenza.

193. Ibid., 71–80.

194. Ibid., 78–79. They were: (1) Symbolic representation of early church baptismal rites and theology; (2) A Joseph figure whose story is based upon a combination of Old Testament texts; (3) Christological typology; (4) The young man fleeing from the scene (in 14:51–52 and connected with 16:5–7) is an anticipation in the story of Jesus' eventual "escape" from the authorities (through resurrection); (5) The figure represents a Christian martyr transformed from symbolic death to heavenly reward; (6) Connection between the two figures in 14.57 and 16.5, who are two distinct, though related, figures symbolizing two of the Maccabean martyrs; (7) The figure was a baptism initiate.

195. Ibid., 79.

196. Ibid., 84.

197. Ibid., 85.

198. Helton, "Churches of Christ."

Does Mark 16:9–20 Belong In The New Testament?

Original Greek.[199] Helton thus attempted to correct the historical record by introducing McGarvey's revised position on Mark 16:9–20, as opposed to the popular view that McGarvey never changed in his advocacy of Markan authorship.[200] While Helton seemed to get sidetracked in his work,[201] he brought out useful information concerning McGarvey. Helton drew the article to a close by suggesting that McGarvey's revised position "anticipated by a hundred years Bruce M. Metzger's alternative,"[202] that is, that Mark 16:9–20 should be regarded as canonical. After quoting Metzger, Helton then entered into a brief discussion of the literary status of the ending of the Gospel by mentioning the theories of van der Horst, Boomershine and Bartholomew, and Petersen.[203] He seemed to agree with the view that the Gospel ended at 16:8.[204] Helton suggested that McGarvey's position if he were living in modern times would be that the ending to the Gospel was lost. Helton admitted that such a position on the passage would be "hypothetical, based on presuppositions about how Mark had to end his literary production."[205] The article provided a valuable correction to McGarvey, and thus added to the information to be considered.

Bruce Terry made a contribution to the discussion concerning Mark 16:9–20 in 1996, issuing an unedited article originally written in *Firm Foundation*.[206] He stated his purpose from the outset: "Textual critics usually object to Mark's authorship of these verses on the basis of supposed differences of style between them and the rest of the Gospel of Mark. However, an in-depth study of the stylistic features in question reveals that almost all of them can be found elsewhere in Mark."[207] Terry began the study by first examining five objections concerning the juncture of verses eight and

---

199. Ibid., 36–40.

200. Ibid., 40–50.

201. He critiqued several living preachers—Thomas Warren, Rubel Shelly, Neil Lightfoot, William Woodson, and Jack P. Lewis—but emphasized those deceased preachers who exemplified, according to Helton, "the debating tradition of the twentieth-century Churches of Christ" (40).

202. Ibid., 50.

203. Ibid., 51–52.

204. Ibid., 52.

205. Ibid., 51.

206. Terry, "Style of the Long Ending"; originally published as "Another Look at the Ending of Mark," in *Firm Foundation* 93 (Sept. 14, 1976).

207. Ibid. Terry categorized those features "under four headings: juncture, vocabulary, phraseology, and miscellaneous."

nine. The first two—the subject of verse 8 is the women, whereas Jesus is the presumed subject of verse 9; the other women of verse 1–8 are forgotten in verses 9–20—were quickly addressed. "Although this section does begin with these stylistic features, they are also found together five times elsewhere in Mark."[208] This set the tone for the remainder of the article. The objection that Mary Magdalene was introduced as a new character was addressed by Terry. After classifying it as a flashback, he pointed out that similar flashbacks were used at least four times elsewhere in Mark. To the objection that the use of ἀνάστας δέ ("Now rising") and the position of πρῶτον ("first") in verse 9 are ill-suited in a continuation of verses 1–8, even though they would be appropriate at the beginning of a comprehensive narrative, Terry observed that verse 9 started a new section, and was not a continuation of verses 1–8. Terry then addressed the objection that verse 8 ended with γάρ. Citing nine Markan passages, Terry stated that there were three and four word clauses in those passages that contained γάρ. "Thus Mark did know how to use γάρ in short sentences."[209]

Moving to the vocabulary of Mark 16:9–20, Terry addressed the claim that there were sixteen words not used elsewhere in Mark.[210] To this, he replied that eight of the sixteen had their word root elsewhere in the Gospel. Most strikingly, though, was what he found when he examined Mark 15:40–16:4:

> One finds not just sixteen such words, but twenty to twenty-two, depending on textual variants. This shows that the author knew quite well how to use in a brief passage many new words which he had not previously used . . . Thirteen of these sixteen words found only here in Mark are used only once. But this is not as unusual as might be thought. In the 661 undisputed verses in Mark, there are 555 words that are used only once (WUOO) in this book; however; the distribution of words used only once is not uniform in Mark. For example, the first twelve verses of chapter 1 contain 16 words used only once in Mark, and the first twelve verses of chapter 14 contain 20, even though both of these chapters have ratios that are less than 1 such word per verse.[211]

---

208. Ibid.

209. Ibid.

210. Terry only focused here on single words, while Elliott's work included both words and phrases.

211. Ibid.

Does Mark 16:9–20 Belong In The New Testament?

Terry further analyzed the ratio of words used only once to verses, and found that Mark 16:9–20 had a ratio which was well within the ratio for both chapters and sections within the Gospel. Similarly, Terry dealt with the objection that three of the sixteen words in question were used more than once. He found in an analysis of words used only once in a twelve-verse span "that there are 77 such words in the undisputed verses of Mark plus 5 proper nouns." Terry addressed the objection that two of Mark's favorite words (εὐθέως or εὐθύς, "immediately"; πάλιν, "again") were not found in Mark 16:9–20. To this, Terry replied, "this is to overlook the fact that not only do the last twelve verses of Mark not contain these words, the last fifty-three verses do not contain them." Examining 650 sets of twelve consecutive verses in Mark, over 35 percent did not contain the three words. "It is hardly an objection to say that the last twelve verses are in the same category with more than one-third of the sets of twelve consecutive verses in the rest of the book."[212]

Terry addressed objections based on phraseology in a similar fashion. He demonstrated that Mark "knew how to use a large number of new phrases in a single section," and then proceeded to show that variations of many of the phrases were found elsewhere in the Gospel. As to various miscellaneous objections, Terry demonstrated from comparing other passages in the Gospel that Mark certainly had the competence to pen such a passage as Mark 16:9–20.[213] In his conclusion, Terry appealed to the concept of "peak" to explain the use of so many rare stylistic forms in one place:

> Peak is an area of grammatical turbulence. Little used features become prominent in peak sections and often used features are abandoned. Background devices become foregrounded and vice versa. In languages around the world, peak has been shown to occur in sections of climax and denouement, and sometimes inciting incident, in narratives told by good storytellers. If the crucifixion is the climax, the resurrection is the denouement. One would expect this to be a peak area in which the use of expected stylistic features is abandoned in favor of less frequently used ones. This is exactly what is found in the increased use of words used only once in Mark in the last five chapters. Rather than revealing that Mark is not the author of these last twelve verses, this different cumulative style may show that he was a good storyteller.[214]

212. Ibid.
213. Ibid.
214. Ibid.

Modern Scholarship on Mark 16:9–20, 1965–2011

Given the fact that internal evidence had been appealed to frequently by many scholars against Markan authorship of 16:9–20, Terry's work constituted a challenge to the position advocated by the majority. It would not go unnoticed.

In 1999, Joel F. Williams produced an overview of different literary approaches to the end of Mark and proposed his own solution.[215] After briefly examining the external and internal evidence, Williams rejected Mark 16:9–20 as being Markan and asserted that 16:8 was where the Gospel originally ended.[216] From there, Williams examined the various literary approaches that had been taken—in particular, those of Magness, Boomershine, Lincoln, Pesch, Peterson, and Hester. His own conclusion was an attempt at a compromise of views: "Mark ends his Gospel by juxtaposing a promise for restoration in 16:7 with an example of failure in 16:8 . . . Christian experience according to Mark involves an interplay between divine promise and human failure, and so he appropriately ends his narrative with both an encouragement and a warning."[217] The contrast between Williams and Terry demonstrated the contrast in views concerning Mark 16:9–20 as the twenty-first century dawned. Williams exemplified the view of those who accepted the received wisdom of the majority of scholars concerning the passage, that it was not Markan. A cursory overview of the evidence, it seemed, was all that was needed to demonstrate this. Petersen and Terry, on the other hand, represented a small number of scholars, like Clark in 1965, who did not consider the matter to be closed. Their numbers would increase.

2000–2003: Kelhoffer, Iverson, France, Thomas and Alexander, Croy

James A. Kelhoffer contributed his own ambitious study concerning Mark 16:9–20 in 2000.[218] A revision of his dissertation submitted to the University of Chicago, Kelhoffer explained that it "seeks to offer a comprehensive explanation for the origin and distinctive features of Mark 16:9–20."[219] In particular, Kelhoffer was "interested for some time in second-century

215. J. Williams, "Literary Approaches."
216. Ibid., 22–24.
217. Ibid., 33–34.
218. Kelhoffer, *Miracle and Mission*.
219. Ibid., ix.

Does Mark 16:9–20 Belong In The New Testament?

Gospel traditions and in the early Christian mission," and thought that a study into Mark 16:9–20 would assist in those areas.[220] Chapter 1 gave a thorough history into the scholarship surrounding Mark 16:9–20, from Andreas Birch (1801) to Steven Cox (1993).[221] In describing the consensus of scholars prior to 1969, Kelhoffer wrote:

> The vast majority of critical scholars were united in their estimation of the Longer Ending until about thirty years ago. No part of the LE reflects the ending Mark the evangelist intended for his Gospel. In addition, the passage itself consists of a later author's conflation of texts that were probably borrowed from one or more of the NT Gospels. Like their nineteenth-century counterparts, most recent scholars, having reached this conclusion concerning the non-Markan authorship of Mark 16:9–20, have been content to abandon its investigation. Since Mark did not write the LE, it is either a "false" (and embarrassing) interpolation or not worthy of serious attention by NT scholars.[222]

This observation was not only surprising but also quite revealing in calling to attention the general attitude of scholars against a reexamination of the authenticity of Mark 16:9–20—hearkening back to Clark. Kelhoffer continued: "A move towards the serious re-evaluation of this consensus began perhaps with the 1965 Society of Biblical Literature presidential address of Kenneth Clark, who stated that the question of the genuineness of these verses was 'still open' and perhaps 'insoluble at present.'" Although Clark himself did not explicitly argue in favor of this position, his comments were an inspiration to William R. Farmer, who responded with a monograph "in response to" Clark's address.[223] Kelhoffer subsequently critiqued Farmer's work, as well as those of Hug, Krauss, Mirecki, and Cox.[224] His propositions concerning Mark 16:9–20, as developed in the book, were wide-ranging. Chapters 2 and 3 addressed whether the author of Mark 16:9–20 had access to a copy of one or more of the NT Gospels. Chapter 4 put forth the view that Mark 16:9–20 is not a fragment of another lost work, but was written to finish Mark. Chapter 5 compared the miracles section of Mark 16:9–20 with those described in the second and third centuries. Chapters 6 and 7

---

220. Ibid.
221. Ibid., 1–47.
222. Ibid., 32.
223. Ibid., 32–33.
224. Ibid., 33–46.

focused upon the description in 16:8 of picking up snakes and drinking poison and compared them to similar descriptions in ancient literature. Kelhoffer's seemingly ambitious scope was not ill-advised.

As for Kelhoffer's position concerning the date of Mark 16:9–20, he connected it with the unity of the passage itself. Arguing against the compositional theory of Hug, Kelhoffer made the case that the passage was written by a single author, not redacted.[225] Concerning the style and language of Mark 16:9–20 and how it compares to the rest of the Gospel, Kelhoffer wrote: "Numerous parts of 16:9–20 bear a striking resemblance to Mark 1:1–16:8 . . . Such perceptiveness to the subtleties of the style of 1:1–16:8 bespeaks an author who had read Mark very closely . . . the LE's numerous Markan words and phrases reflect an effort to imitate the style of the work which this author augmented."[226] Kelhoffer, while still rejecting Markan authorship of Mark 16:9–20,[227] thus stated that the passage had many similarities to Mark 1:1–16:8 due to the author's attempt to finish the work. He explained this by saying, "These allusions also point to the intentional imitation of all four of the NT Gospels."[228] He then mentioned parallels with Acts. In chapter 3, Kelhoffer addressed the connection of Mark 16:9–20 with the four Gospels. He devoted special attention to answering the contention of Hug, who said that 16:9–20 used common written sources to those of the four Gospels.[229] After examining selected passages in 16:9–20 and comparing them to the four Gospels, Kelhoffer claimed, "the author of the LE wrote with knowledge of copies of these writings."[230] This in turn affected Kelhoffer concerning the date of composition of the passage itself. "The fact that the author of Mark 16:9–20 wrote in conscious dependence on one or more MSS of the NT Gospels suggests a *terminus post quem* for the LE's composition after these four Gospels had been collected and compared with one another, which probably would not have occurred earlier than 110–120."[231] After rejecting the notion that 16:9–20

---

225. Ibid., 51–65. Thus, Kelhoffer also by extension answered similar claims made by Linnemann, Schmithals, and Trompf.

226. Ibid., 49, 73, 121.

227. Ibid., 121. "Taking up the earlier metaphor from an American baseball game, there are enough "strikes" against the LE to "strike out" the case for its authenticity many times over."

228. Ibid.

229. Ibid., 130–37.

230. Ibid., 150.

231. Ibid.

Does Mark 16:9–20 Belong In The New Testament?

was a forgery, Kelhoffer put forth the idea that the passage was a second-century witness to "the existence of a four-Gospel canon.[232] He also took to task the claim of Helmut Koester, who claimed that prior to AD 200, the four Gospels were not regarded as Holy Scripture; Kelhoffer judged this claim to be "inaccurate."[233]

Chapter 4 constituted a lengthy in-depth study of the unity of 16:9–20, by examining various parts of the passages and comparing them with other literary forms.[234] Kelhoffer specifically built off of the work of Mirecki, while critiquing his central claim that the passage bore evidence of an earlier narrative.[235] Kelhoffer affirmed that 16:9–20 should be considered as a single unit.[236] Consequently, when considered along with the evidence from second-century Christian authors, Kelhoffer dated Mark 16:9–20 to ca. AD 120–140.[237] Kelhoffer also claimed that the author of Mark 16:9–20 wrote it for the specific purposes of continuing the story from 16:8 and finishing it.[238] In chapter 5, Kelhoffer set forth to compare the statements concerning miracles in Mark 16:17–20 with similar statements from the rest of the New Testament, as well as second- and third-century works.[239] He found a discontinuity with the relevant New Testament passages, save for John 14:12–14 and 1 Corinthians 12:9–10.[240] As for the apocryphal works and apologists of the second and third centuries, Kelhoffer concluded that 16:9–20 was closely related to them.[241] Accordingly, Kelhoffer placed 16:9–20 in a second-century context.[242]

Similarly, chapters 5 and 6 compared the signs of picking up snakes and drinking deadly poison with similar statements in antiquity.[243] Although exact parallels concerning picking up snakes do not exist in Jewish or Christian writings, numerous Greco-Roman writings depicted similar

---

232. Ibid., 155.
233. Ibid.
234. Ibid., 157–244.
235. Ibid., 189–238.
236. Ibid., 169.
237. Ibid., 175.
238. Ibid., 243.
239. Ibid., 245–339.
240. Ibid., 281.
241. Ibid., 280, 337.
242. Ibid., 338–39.
243. Ibid., 340–472.

images.²⁴⁴ In Kelhoffer's treatment of poison, he again examined ancient literature which seemed to parallel what was written in 16:18. He found numerous references, and drew this conclusion: "Two individuals whose experiences match the expectation of Mark 16:18b are Homer's Odysseus and especially the patriarch Joseph, and are therefore the most likely candidates for the heroes whose immunity to poison may have inspired the LE's fourth sign."²⁴⁵ An Epilogue summarized Kelhoffer's conclusions;²⁴⁶ in it, he raised speculations concerning the author of Mark 16:9–20. Kelhoffer contended that the author "stood at a critical transitional period in the history of early Christian literature."²⁴⁷ Paradoxically, Kelhoffer wrote that second-century Christians would not have necessarily accepted him.²⁴⁸ Regardless of whether or not one considers Kelhoffer's conclusions valid, his study serves as a significant piece in its treatment of all of the various issues involved with the passage.

Following up on his own work, Kelhoffer published an article about Eusebius of Caesarea that was originally intended to be a part of his dissertation.²⁴⁹ In particular, Kelhoffer's focus was upon Eusebius's response to a question of Marinus concerning an apparent discrepancy between Matthew 28:1 and Mark 16:2, 9. In his two responses, Eusebius "offers a window to a point in time when 'nearly all the copies' of Mark ended at Mark 16:8."²⁵⁰ Kelhoffer wished to examine in detail what copies of Mark were known to this author, "the practice of 'textual criticism' in the early and medieval church and the significance of these claims for contemporary scholarship on the Markan endings."²⁵¹ Kelhoffer noted at the outset that "roughly 99 percent" of the copies of Mark include 16:9–20 at the end.²⁵² He then briefly discussed the authorship of *Gospel Problems and Solutions To Marinus*, stating that it had been unquestioningly accepted as being from Eusebius "on the basis of rather little evidence," and thus "needs to be

---

244. Ibid., 407–11.
245. Ibid., 470.
246. Ibid., 473–480.
247. Ibid., 479.
248. Ibid., 480.
249. Kelhoffer, "Witness of Eusebius' *ad Marinum*." In a footnote, Kelhoffer explained the process of how the article came to be composed separate from his dissertation.
250. Ibid., 79.
251. Ibid.
252. Ibid.

tested" in future studies.[253] Kelhoffer also stated that part of Eusebius's work has not survived, though how much "must remain an open question."[254]

After offering his own translation,[255] Kelhoffer addressed the answers given by the author to the question of Marinus. The first reply indicated that there was a question as to the genuineness of Mark 16:9-20. The second reply was that there was no contradiction between Matthew's account and Mark's account. The author used a word from 16:9 to show that the two accounts referred to two different events (Matthew concerning the timing of the resurrection, Mark with the appearance to Mary).[256] Kelhoffer also referred to a related question in part 2.1, in which the author concluded that there was no contradiction between Matthew and John concerning post-resurrection narratives.[257] Kelhoffer proposed to examine the claims and assumptions of the answers given, which he subsequently did.[258] Kelhoffer focused upon the seemingly contradictory responses given by the author. The response to Marinus's first question—16:9-20 is not part of Mark—seems to stand in contrast to the response to the second question (as well as the third), that the answers may be complementary. Interestingly, Kelhoffer seemed to be sympathetic with the possibility that the first answer came from the pen of Origen, and that the second answer came from Eusebius himself, who corrected Origen.[259] After suggesting that the identity of the author was not certain, Kelhoffer said "the writer's primary purpose is *to defend the integrity of scripture*," not to examine text-critical questions in detail.[260] In examining the text-critical implications, Kelhoffer stressed the harmonizing response of the author to the second question.[261] Kelhoffer then went on to state:

253. Ibid., 81.
254. Ibid., 82-83.
255. Ibid., 83-89.
256. Ibid., 90-91.
257. Ibid., 91.
258. Ibid., 91-96.
259. Ibid., 92-93. This was the cautious conclusion of Westcott and Hort, based on the use of the optative mood by the author for the first answer—suggesting reservation.
260. Ibid., 93-94; emphasis original. "Had this particular question about Matt 28 and Mark 16 never been a concern, it is likely that the precious information contained in the answer concerning the content of MSS of Mark would not have been preserved here."
261. Ibid., 94.

Such a harmonizing approach to the manifold character of sacred scripture has obvious implications for the eventual prevalence of Mark 16:9–20 in nearly all manuscripts of Mark. In contrast to the unusually judicious attitude toward textual evidence in answer one, the blatantly uncritical perspective of answer two reveals something important about the argument for retaining the Longer Ending as a reliable, and presumably original, part of Mark's Gospel. The criterion assumed here is that, *if a passage like the Longer Ending can be shown to agree with other received texts, its authenticity should not be questioned.*[262]

While repeating his conviction that 16:9–20 was composed in the second century, Kelhoffer acknowledged that the passage had similarities to the other Gospels. This, he asserted, would explain the unquestioned acceptance of the passage.

Kelhoffer then entered into a lengthy discussion of analogous claims concerning Eusebius's work in early and medieval Christian writings.[263] In the course of this, Kelhoffer suggested that the author had available both Sinaiticus and Vaticanus, among others.[264] Interestingly, he also suggested that "this author's claim to knowledge of a more 'accurate' textual tradition for the end of Mark may constitute something of a rhetorical device."[265] The writings of various authors were then examined at length.[266] Kelhoffer demonstrated that the difficulties concerning the end of Mark "continued to be recognized through the early and medieval periods.[267] Evidence both for and against inclusion were passed along. Kelhoffer's conclusion was that the problems in the text of Mark were "likely both credible and, to a certain extent, verifiable" by the fourth century or earlier.[268] The testimonies of subsequent authors attested to that tradition and were opposed by some. Kelhoffer suggested that the textual tradition known to early authors needs to be examined carefully.[269] Kelhoffer then offered his position, based upon

---

262. Ibid., 95; emphasis original.

263. Ibid., 97–109.

264. Kelhoffer acknowledged the missing pages in Sinaiticus, 1420 and 2386.

265. Ibid., 98.

266. Ibid., 99–109. They were: Jerome, Hesychius of Jerusalem, Severus of Antioch, Victor of Antioch, Minuscules 20 and 215, Theophylactus of Ochrida, Euthymius Zigabenus, Minuscule 199, and Eusebius of Caesarea.

267. Ibid., 108.

268. Ibid., 110.

269. Ibid., 111.

Does Mark 16:9–20 Belong In The New Testament?

the opinions offered by ancient and medieval authors he examined: "An awareness of the text-critical problem concerning Mark 16:9–20 does not necessarily lead to a decision to refrain from making use of this passage."[270] He also called for careful study and use of patristic witnesses in connection with Mark 16:9–20.[271] The questions raised by Kelhoffer concerning Eusebius and Mark 16:9–20 were significant. The implications for future studies would likewise be important. His work set the stage for much of what would follow.

Kelly Iverson examined the possibilities of the ending of Mark in a 2001 study.[272] After he briefly reviewed the evidence, Iverson rejected the authenticity of Mark 16:9–20. He subsequently proposed that verse 8 was the end of Mark's Gospel, and reviewed the arguments of van der Horst, Magness, Boomershine and Bartholomew, Lincoln, Hester, Williams, Peterson, and Danove. In the end, he embraced the view of Lincoln and Williams, with a slight adjustment. Iverson wrote, "It may very well be that Mark has intertwined promise, failure, and the messianic secret into the ending."[273] Thus while Iverson's work was a decent summary of one particular perspective concerning the ending of Mark, the same could not be said concerning its treatment of the issue of authenticity. At best, it was a cursory review of the evidence—which unfortunately did not take into consideration Kelhoffer's (2000) work.

R. T. France addressed the authenticity of Mark 16:9–20 in a concise treatment in his commentary, published in 2002.[274] France first responded to modern interpretations of an abrupt ending at verse 8. After examining the claims made by such authors as Magness, Peterson, Van der Horst, and Danove, he affirmed: "My own inclination is to side with the increasingly unfashionable minority who find an intentional ending at 16:8 an unacceptably 'modern' option."[275] After refusing to speculate as to what happened to the ending, France proposed what the ending might have looked like by focusing on the double indication by Mark that Jesus would meet with the disciples in Galilee (14:28; 16:7), and the ending of the Gospel of Matthew—which according to France suggests Mark "intended something

270. Ibid.
271. Ibid.
272. Iverson, *Irony in the End*.
273. Ibid.
274. France, *Gospel of Mark*, 671–74; 685–88.
275. Ibid., 673.

similar as the conclusion of his work."[276] In an appended note, France intended to "set out as simply and clearly as possible"[277] the evidence for the ending of Mark. After setting forth the external evidence, France addressed the content of 16:9–20. He first compared selected verses from the passage to parallels in Matthew, Luke, and John, and then stated "in vv. 17–18 some of the 'signs' which are related in Acts are summarized, and v. 20 is virtually a summary of the whole book of Acts in a nutshell."[278] France acknowledged that the reference to drinking poison and picking up snakes is "the only element which is not easily accounted for."[279] France then highlighted the difference in style of 16:9–20, and the awkward transition from verse 8. He wrote, "For these reasons, the almost unanimous conclusion of modern scholarship is that both the Shorter and Longer Endings, in their different ways, represent well-meaning attempts, probably sometime in the second century, to fill the perceived gap left by the 'unfinished' ending at 16:8."[280]

John Christopher Thomas again wrote concerning Mark 16:9–20 in 2003. Along with Kimberly Ervin Alexander, he looked at the passage in light of Pentecostal hermeneutics concerning miraculous gifts.[281] Thomas and Alexander examined various literature from Pentecostalism.[282] As a result, "it began to become clear that the place of Mk 16.9–20 was unrivaled within the early Pentecostal literature in position and significance!"[283] In addition, they reviewed Pentecostal response to the textual problems connected with Mark 16:9–20.[284] Their conclusion was that "these early Pentecostals were neither unaware of the textual problems associated with Mk 16:9–20 nor unprepared to respond to these problems."[285] The authors then reviewed both the external and internal evidence concerning Mark 16:9–20.[286] After briefly asserting that the passage contains "a large number

---

276. Ibid., 674.
277. Ibid., 685.
278. Ibid., 687.
279. Ibid.
280. Ibid.
281. Thomas, and Alexander, "And the Signs Are Following."
282. Ibid., 149–57.
283. Ibid., 149.
284. Ibid., 157–59.
285. Ibid., 157.
286. Ibid., 161–65. Thomas and Alexander unfortunately listed three Ethiopic manuscripts as omitting the passage, even though Metzger had already conclusively shown

of words ... that occur nowhere else in Mark, in some cases the whole of the New Testament,"[287] the authors appeared to recognize that there were those who would point out the opposite: "However, given the remarkable differences between 16:9–20 and the rest of the Gospel, it is more probable to assume that any Markan peculiarities found in 16.9-20 are either the result of the compiler's attempt to imitate Markan style or, as is more likely, coincidental."[288] The authors then considered the origins of Mark 16:9–20.[289] In particular, they agreed with Kelhoffer concerning date, though they placed the passage about AD 115–130.[290] As for canonicity, they compared the passage with other disputed passages and concluded that Mark 16:9–20 had much stronger evidence for acceptance.[291] A section examined the passage itself to see how it fit in with the rest of the New Testament—in particular, Acts.[292] The authors concluded with a few remarks concerning the place of the passage in Pentecostal theology.[293] Thus, while affirming that the passage was not written by Mark, they asserted its place in the canon.

N. Clayton Croy changed the nature of the debate with his book, published in 2003.[294] In it, he addressed the matter of the ending. However, his approach was novel. He proposed that not just the ending was possibly damaged, but also the beginning of the Gospel, "through some mishap ... not too many years after its composition."[295] Croy examined scholarly opinion concerning how Mark ended the Gospel.[296] After agreeing that Mark 16:9–20 was a secondary addition, he then showed how positions concerning the ending shifted.[297] In chapter 2, Croy suggested a reason for the shift in consensus: "I propose that the cause of the shift was the advent of 'New Criticism' in the guild of biblical studies and other developments

---

that the three manuscripts in question do contain it (161).

287. Ibid., 162.
288. Ibid., 163.
289. Ibid., 163–65.
290. Ibid., 164.
291. Ibid., 165–67.
292. Ibid., 167–70.
293. Ibid., 170.
294. Croy, *Mutilation of Mark's Gospel*.
295. Ibid., 12.
296. Ibid., 18–32.
297. Ibid., 22–30.

Modern Scholarship on Mark 16:9–20, 1965–2011

in academia and society in general during those decades. A corollary to this proposal is that the shift was not caused *primarily* by the introduction of new evidence . . . much more important was . . . 'the development of new methodologies.'"[298] Croy listed five factors behind this cause: the influence of New Criticism, the rise of the author/decline of the reader, the assumptions of modernity (the newer is better, recent is superior), the sociology of knowledge ("group think"), and the *Zeitgeist* of the twentieth century (pessimism, alienation, disorder). Indeed, when considering all of the literary approaches to the ending of Mark, one is inclined to agree with Croy: "I must confess to being very skeptical about all of this. When literary critic Frank Kermode compares Mark's riddling narratives to those of Frank Kafka, I prefer to think that biblical scholarship should perhaps wake up and *smell* the Kafka. Mark is a Gospel, a proclamation of good news; not a brooding, inexplicable, existentialist riddle."[299] In chapter 4, Croy attempted to present all of the arguments for the mutilation of Mark's Gospel.[300] In particular, he addressed the question of γάρ: "So, can a book end with γάρ? Van der Horst says that we cannot deny this possibility, and he is right . . . But to point out the obvious, all things that are *possible* are not equally *probable* . . . It is still quite awkward for a *narrative* to end as the Gospel of Mark does."[301]

Croy also argued for a truncated Gospel from grammar, theology, tradition, logical coherence, narrative expectations, literary convention, and textual additions—including Mark 16:9–20.[302] In chapter 6, he addressed all of the various literary explanations concerning the ending—including those of Petersen, Boomershine and Bartholomew, Magness, Lincoln, Danove, and Hester.[303] After rejecting all of the literary theories, he suggested three possibilities: Mark was an incompetent storyteller, Mark was a protomodernist, or Mark was the victim of accidental damage.[304] Croy agreed with the last possibility, due to the disruption evident in the textual tradition which might have come from physical damage to the manuscript. He went one step further in chapter 7, asserting that the front of the Gos-

298. Ibid., 34.
299. Ibid., 42.
300. Ibid., 45–71.
301. Ibid., 49.
302. Ibid., 50–66.
303. Ibid., 72–112.
304. Ibid., 106.

pel was also damaged.³⁰⁵ "Something originally preceded Mark 1:2 but has been lost."³⁰⁶ Croy suggested in chapter 8 that the Gospel was published in codex form and was mutilated between AD 65 and 85.³⁰⁷ Croy was realistic: "For the present, it would be a step in the right direction if more persons began to regard the debate as 'far from settled.'"³⁰⁸

2004: McDill, Kelhoffer, Burkett

Writing in 2004, Matthew McDill argued for the inclusion of Mark 16:9–20 in the Gospel.³⁰⁹ His approach was twofold: explore the evidence to see whether the passage belonged in Mark; and, if so, he wished to examine the structural features of the passage.³¹⁰ After an overview of the external evidence, McDill seemed to be conclusive: "One might acknowledge that a substantial case can be made for the LE's originality based on external evidence."³¹¹ He hedged this, though, by stating that "the external evidence is not as decisive as some make it out to be"³¹² because much of the opposition is based upon internal evidence. Thus, McDill considered two of the main internal arguments—vocabulary and style, and the connection between verse 8 and verses 9–20.³¹³ This he did by relying primarily upon Terry's study. McDill's conclusion was straightforward: "There is currently a great deal of literature that attempts to prove that such an ending [at verse 8] is grammatically acceptable and has literary significance that fits into Mark's style. The purpose of this review of internal evidence is to establish the possibility of arguing that the LE fits into Mark's style and that its connection to v. 8 is not insurmountably awkward. Again, one might at least begin his study of the matter with the understanding that the current consensus of scholarship may not be as conclusive as it appears."³¹⁴ In his proposed solutions, McDill offered two possibilities: first, if Mark's

---

305. Ibid., 113–36.
306. Ibid., 124.
307. Ibid., 137–63.
308. Ibid., 164.
309. McDill, "Textual and Structural Analysis."
310. Ibid., 27.
311. Ibid., 31.
312. Ibid.
313. Ibid., 31–33.
314. Ibid., 33.

Modern Scholarship on Mark 16:9-20, 1965-2011

Gospel were a record of Peter's preaching, then Mark may have added Mark 16:9–20 at a later time. Second, if the Gospel originated in Rome, then that would explain the geographical dominance of Mark 16:9–20 in the textual evidence; and, the omission of the passage may have been due to a scribe either accidentally or intentionally omitting it.[315]

McDill's treatment of the canonicity of Mark 16:9–20 was quite interesting.[316] He asked, "Should the Bible scholar interpret the square brackets around the LE in the UBS 4th edition to mean 'this really does not belong in the text?'"[317] While accepting the canonicity of the passage, he raised some intriguing questions: "Although many scholars have not forthrightly objected to the LE's canonicity, many are doing so in practice. Without saying so, it appears that many scholars are concluding that if the LE was not in the original MS or if it was not written by Mark, then the LE does not belong in the canon. As was pointed out earlier, for example, there are many works that do not deal with the LE exegetically or theologically. How many preachers continually avoid preaching Mark 16:9–20 due to the textual questions surrounding it?"[318]

In the course of fleshing out the question of canonicity, McDill called attention to some key implications. "If scholars continue to neglect this passage in their exegetical, linguistic, and theological inquiries, then biblical studies in Mark will be hindered. Such scholarly work will also not be at the disposal of preachers who do attempt to preach this text . . . If Mark 16:9–20 is canonical, and it continues to be treated as non-canonical by biblical scholars, theologians and preachers, then the church will be robbed of one of its important commission passages."[319] McDill then turned his attention to the structure of Mark 16:9–20.[320] He contended, as did Terry, that the passage is a discourse unit, based on its language—including content, parallelism, and thematic unity. His analysis of the structure of Mark 16:9–20 was intriguing, raising other questions which could be pursued in subsequent studies. His work was thus added to the number of those who advocated the authenticity of the passage.

---

315. Ibid., 33–34.
316. Ibid., 35–37.
317. Ibid., 35.
318. Ibid., 36.
319. Ibid., 37.
320. Ibid., 38–42.

Does Mark 16:9–20 Belong In The New Testament?

James Kelhoffer revisited Mark 16:9–20 in the midst of an article concerning the use of the term "Gospel" in the second century.[321] In particular, he argued against the view of Koester that the term "Gospel" did not refer to an authoritative writing—or a collection of Gospels—prior to Justin Martyr. Kelhoffer affirmed again his own dating of 16:9–20 (AD 120–150), and affirmed that the four Gospels "were available in one place for the passage composed by the author of the Longer Ending."[322] Kelhoffer went on to show that Koester's assumptions concerning the Gospels prior to AD 200 were inaccurate—in part based upon Mark 16:9–20.[323] Since the four Gospels were incorporated into the passage, according to Kelhoffer, Koester's contentions about supposed differences between second-century and fourth- and fifth-century usage of a Gospel were without foundation.[324]

Delbert Burkett presented his view of the ending of Mark near the end of the first of a proposed three-volume study of the sources of the canonical Gospels.[325] In chapter 1, Burkett began his study with an "Introduction to the Problem"; he summarized the main current solutions to the Synoptic Problem. His basic view was that "the simpler theories do not work."[326] Chapters 2 and 3 focused on "Markan Redaction Absent from Matthew and Luke" and "Matthean Redaction Absent from Mark and Luke." In these chapters, he focused on "benign omissions," that is, words, phrases, and themes that are found frequently in Mark or Matthew respectively but not in the other two Synoptics, and for which there are no discernible grammatical or ideological reasons for their omission. From these, he concluded that Mark did not serve as a source for either Matthew or Luke (denying any theory of Markan priority) and that Matthew did not serve as a source for either Mark or Luke (denying any theory of Matthean priority). He also stressed the "minor agreements" between Matthew and Luke against Mark. In chapters 4 and 5, Burkett set out to find "Sources Common to Mark and Matthew" and the "Sources Common to Mark and Luke" by comparing the order of pericopes in those Gospels. Burkett proposed that Mark and Matthew had common sources, as did Mark and Luke. Burkett noted the similarly ordered pericopes in each set of compared Gospels as a particular

---

321. Kelhoffer, "How Soon a Book."
322. Ibid., 10.
323. Ibid., 12–13.
324. Ibid., 12.
325. Burkett, *Rethinking the Gospel Sources*, 252–63.
326. Ibid., 5.

Modern Scholarship on Mark 16:9–20, 1965–2011

sequence and then, at each point the order diverges, noting this as a different sequence. Thus he concluded that there were three distinct sources shared by those Gospels.

In chapter 6, "Conflation in Mark," Burkett concluded that Mark conflated his sources that were shared by Matthew and Luke. Chapter 7 presented Burkett's proposal, "Toward a New Theory." It proposed that a basic Proto-Mark including a common Synoptic core went through two independent revisions, producing Proto-Mark A and Proto-Mark B. Proto-Mark A served as a source for Matthew, and Proto-Mark B served as a source for Luke. Canonical Mark was written using Proto-Mark A and B as well as other shared sources. Chapters 8–11 discussed the scope and possible historical setting of Proto-Mark, Proto-Mark A, Proto-Mark B, and the kerygmatic source. It was chapter 12, "The Making of Mark," that presented Burkett's view of the ending of Mark—at the end of other selected portions of the Gospel. Burkett critiqued the traditional approach of scholars against 16:9-20 (he also quoted Clark's 1965 comments on the passage),[327] and specifically examined some of the internal evidence cited against it. Viewing the problem through the lens of his new approach, Burkett offered direct criticism of a supposed "Markan style," as articulated by the UBS committee: "The problem with this argument is that those who use it never make explicit their presuppositions about what constitutes 'Markan' and 'non-Markan' style. Implicitly they presuppose that Mark's style is coterminous with the style of Mark 1:1–16:8."[328]

Burkett argued that since Mark had compiled his Gospel by relying upon outside sources, then 16:9–20 did not differ markedly from the rest of the Gospel. He then set out to propose how the shorter ending came to be (the ending of proto-Mark), that Proto-Mark A was followed by Matthew—ending with a Galilean resurrection narrative, that Proto-Mark B was followed by Luke and ended with a Jerusalem resurrection narrative, and that Mark ended with 16:9–20—conflated from Proto-Mark A and Proto-Mark B. Burkett then posited possible reasons for the "confusion in the manuscript tradition," speculating that a scribe omitted 16:9–20 for various possible reasons which led to the omission in א and B; that in a separate line of tradition, 16:9–20 was not omitted; that some scribes knew both traditions and reattached 16:9–20, some with asterisks, obeli, and others without; that a scribe had a copy of Proto-Mark, and took the short

---

327. Ibid., 253.
328. Ibid., 254.

Does Mark 16:9–20 Belong In The New Testament?

ending and reworked it at the end of 16:8—which is preserved in the Old Italian manuscript k; and that scribes who knew both the short and long endings of Mark included them both in that order.[329] Thus, another scholar was willing to present a different view concerning not only the ending of Mark, but also the composition of the Gospel itself. Burkett unhesitatingly affirmed his belief in the authenticity of 16:9–20: "Given our theory, both the stylistic features of the longer ending and the editorial procedure used in it suggest that it came from the same person who edited 1:1–16:8, i.e., the evangelist Mark."[330]

2006–2007: Iverson, Bridges, Stein, Spencer, Snapp

Kelly Iverson built upon Croy's work with his own article, published in 2006.[331] After briefly mentioning past research on final γάρ, he stated his thesis: "If accurate, Croy's research could have an impact on the continued debate over Mark's ending. The purpose of this study is to investigate Croy's assertion, specifically, the kinds of literature in which γάρ is followed by a period. It is hoped that the study will provide a balanced assessment of Croy's research and contribute to the ongoing debate over Mark's ending."[332] The scope of Iverson's work was enormous (third century BC to second century AD), but was aided by the CD-ROM version of *Thesaurus Linguae Graecae*.[333] Of all the texts containing final γάρ, two were found to be identical to Mark 16:8.[334] Polybius[335] (third century BC) and Dio Cassius[336] (second century AD) gave examples of what Iverson called "a legitimate example of a final γάρ construction in the body of a narrative work."[337] About Dio Cassius's work, Iverson claimed that it was

---

329. Ibid., 262–63.
330. Ibid., 256.
331. Iverson, "Further Word on Final Γαρ."
332. Ibid., 81.
333. Ibid.
334. Iverson found 272 instances of final γάρ; 16 of those "hits" resembled the Gospels, 12 occurred in dialogue, and one was 16:8. The two to which Iverson refers were found in historical texts. Ibid., 81–86.
335. *Historiae* 2.60.1.1.
336. *Historiae Romana* 63.19.2.3 (SI81.5).
337. Iverson, "Further Word," 86–87.

"an excellent parallel to the construction in Mark,"[338] and said the two references were "understated" by Croy.[339] In his evaluation of Croy's work, Iverson asked: "But does the relative infrequency of final γάρ in the narrative genres as compared to the philosophical and other technical genres argue against Mark's abrupt ending? Croy responds in the affirmative; I am not so sure. To argue for a hypothetical longer ending based on the scarcity of this particular construction is difficult, given the current parameters of the discussion."[340] Iverson thus judged Croy's assessment as "inadequate" and "tentative."[341] To obtain the entire body of extant literature, Iverson obtained figures from *TLG s Canon of Greek Authors and Works*—namely, 17,729,880 words.[342] After examining all of the data, Iverson stated: "The fact is *concluding γάρ statements are extremely, extremely rare at all times and in all genres*."[343] He then began to draw his conclusion: "In and of themselves, the data suggest nothing. They can be marshaled to argue for a hypothetical lost ending or the abrupt ending ... The point of this article is not to argue for a particular theory but to demonstrate that the usage of final γάρ is inconclusive and can be utilized with equal force to support the case for a mutilated text or the intentional, abrupt ending."[344] Iverson then offered some suggestions for future researchers: "What the research does affirm is that scholars should use caution in utilizing final γάρ as a basis for postulating a theory of Mark's ending. Barring significant discoveries of new literature, statistical probability and literary parallels provide little direction in this ongoing debate. The use of final γάρ from the third century BCE to the second century CE indicates that both theories are possible, but it does not render one theory more probable."[345] Iverson's work called for a drawing back from hard, fast positions concerning final γάρ and Mark 16:8. Thus it seemed that the scholarly mood was shifting, as subsequent works would demonstrate.

---

338. Ibid., 87.
339. Ibid.
340. Ibid., 87.
341. Ibid., 88.
342. Ibid.
343. Ibid., 93; emphasis original.
344. Ibid.
345. Ibid., 94.

Does Mark 16:9–20 Belong In The New Testament?

Carl B. Bridges wrote concerning Mark 16:9–20 in 2006.[346] His objectives were threefold: "(1) Document the unremarkable claim that the writer of Mark 16:9–20 shows knowledge of the other three Gospels; (2) Speculate that whoever wrote the Longer Ending did so to finish the Gospel for collection with the other three; and (3) Argue that present-day preachers may use the LE with few reservations about its canonical status."[347] After briefly reviewing the external evidence, Bridges assumed "that the author of 1:1–16:8 did not also write the LE."[348] Bridges also suggested that the author of Mark 16:9–20 drew upon the four Gospels.[349] Bridges then set the *terminus ante quem* for the composition of 16:9–20 at AD 165, the death of Justin Martyr, though Bridges stated that "the LE appeared sometime before the last quarter of the second century; how much earlier, we do not know."[350] It was at this point that Bridges proposed an interesting theory. After establishing the date of collection of the Gospels before AD 180, when Irenaeus discussed the four Gospels in *Against Heresies*, he stated:

> If the LE and the four-Gospel codex both appeared sometime in the second century, the temporal proximity of the two events proves little. It is much like placing an accused murderer and his victim in the same state but not in the same house on the night of the crime. However, the conjunction in time does leave open the possibility that the two events might have some further connection. Specifically, whoever composed the LE may have done so to prepare the Gospel of Mark for inclusion in the new collection of four Gospels into one codex. As long as the Gospels circulated independently, the Gospel of Mark with its abrupt ending—whether through Mark's design or the loss of the final page or two—might have been left as is. But as soon as Mark became part of a collection of Gospels, each of the others with its own account of Jesus' post-resurrection appearances, the collectors may have felt the need to supply a similar ending for Mark.[351]

Thus, while Bridges held that another hand penned Mark 16:9–20, he maintained that the passage was ancient and possibly was added not

---

346. Bridges, "Canonical Status."
347. Ibid., 231.
348. Ibid., 234.
349. Ibid., 236.
350. Ibid., 237.
351. Ibid., 238–39.

long after Mark had been completed.[352] Building upon this point, Bridges discussed the canonicity of the passage.[353] He listed three standards to determine canonicity: "its conformity to the 'rule of faith,' its connection to an apostle, and its widespread use in the churches."[354] Bridges then stated:

> The LE fits these standards well enough. It conforms to the historic faith in that it draws from the canonical Gospels and Acts for its material. It enjoyed widespread—though not universal—use in the churches as the manuscript tradition suggests. Its apostolic connection is admittedly weak, not to say nonexistent, but the standard of apostolicity has been used very flexibly, allowing the church to affirm the canonical status of works that seemed to deserve it. Most importantly, if the LE was composed specifically to finish this Gospel for collection with the other three, we could consider the "complete" Gospel of Mark the canonical version.[355]

Bridges added, "to assign canonical status to the LE would not give aid and comfort to snake handlers or other King-James-only groups,"[356] perhaps giving an insight as to the reluctance of some to accept inclusion of the passage. He concluded, "About all this modest proposal would do would be to give the church a collection of four complete Gospels to be used without hesitation."[357]

Writing in 2007, Robert H. Stein wrote an article in which he contended that Mark 16:8 was not the intended ending to the Gospel.[358] Stein began by briefly reviewing the evidence for the various endings of Mark. Apparently Stein agreed with Hengel[359] and Kelhoffer and dated 16:9–20 "to the first decades of the second century."[360] However, he stated "there is no doubt that 16:9–20 was not written by the Evangelist."[361] Stein then put

352. In a footnote, Bridges said: "The reader will notice how many times I have used words like 'speculate,' 'may,' 'might,' and so on. What we need is a dozen or so newly discovered second-century Gospel manuscripts to shed some light on these issues" (239). Indeed.
353. Ibid., 239–42.
354. Ibid., 241.
355. Ibid.
356. Ibid., 242.
357. Ibid.
358. Stein, "Ending Of Mark."
359. Hengel, *Studies in the Gospel of Mark*, 167–69.
360. Stein, "Ending of Mark," 82.
361. Ibid., 84.

forth the arguments for the Gospel ending at verse 9, including a lengthy list of quotations from authors attempting to give reasons for an intentionally abrupt ending.[362] Stein then commented, "Here it should simply be noted that the intended readers/hearers envisioned by these suggestions are for the most part very unlike the actual readers that Mark had in mind. They appear to be more like highly educated twentieth and twenty-first-century existentialists than like first-century Christians, the great majority of whom could not read or write."[363] He then examined reasons why 16:8 is not the intended ending and that the ending is missing, "whether by accident or it was intentionally mutilated or something happened to Mark and he never finished his Gospel (whether death, persecution, or some other reason).[364] This is what Stein advocated; he took issue with those who suggested that it is difficult to hear Mark: "But is not this the point? Does not the great dissatisfaction with 16:8 as Mark's intended ending found among the scribes indicate that 16:8 was seen as a totally inappropriate ending?"[365] He continued:

> Are "less sophisticated readers" more reliable or less reliable guides for interpreting Mark's Gospel than modern-day literary critics, who are deeply entrenched in Kafka-like existentialism and a reader-response hermeneutic? Are not Mark's intended readers, who treated Mark 16:1–8 as an "historical narrative," more reliable interpreters of Mark than modern-day "reader-response" critics who apply the rules of fictional narrative to Mark's text? I would suggest that Mark's 1st-century, unsophisticated Christian readers, familiar with the Gospel traditions concerning Jesus' resurrection and his appearances to his disciples, would not only find 16:8 a difficult ending for Mark but an impossible one. And since Mark wrote with such an audience in mind, this argues that 16:8 is not his intended ending.[366]

Stein argued that the promise of Jesus to meet the disciples in Galilee weighed heavily against verse 8 being the intended conclusion to Mark.[367]

---

362. Ibid., 86–88.
363. Ibid., 88.
364. Ibid., 89.
365. Ibid., 91.
366. Ibid., 92.
367. Ibid., 93–95.

As to the reason why the Gospel was not finished, Stein did not offer an opinion on any of the possibilities.[368]

Also writing in 2007, Aída Besançon Spencer offered yet another modern interpretation of the abrupt ending.[369] After very briefly touching upon the external evidence, she offered her thesis: "If we examine the movement of the book itself, we will discover that 16:8 is a most appropriate way for the Gospel to end. Why? Because Peter's denial drives the Gospel of Mark. That is why it has to end the way it does."[370] She then attempted to show from the Gospel of Mark how it emphasizes the unbelief and the hard hearts of those who feared—even including the disciples.[371] She then compared this perceived emphasis with the other three Gospels, and claimed that Mark stressed the lack of understanding more than Matthew, Luke and John.[372] Spencer concluded by claiming that the women at the tomb stood as "a synecdoche of the whole Gospel. The women model the dual inclinations of amazement and fear. The reader, too, is asked, by implication: will you be another hardened heart, incapacitated by fear, or will you repent, be forgiven, and proclaim Jesus, the crucified Messiah, God's Son, resurrected from the dead?"[373]

James E. Snapp offered another perspective on Mark 16:9–20 in 2007.[374] After examining the external evidence at length,[375] he drew two preliminary conclusions: (1) An appeal to the two oldest manuscripts of Mark 16 rather than to the oldest evidence is insufficient; it is essentially an appeal to climate. (2) The Long Ending of Mark received widespread acceptance as part of the Gospels in the second and third and fourth centuries.[376] Snapp addressed the internal evidence briefly, mainly relying upon Terry's work: "The most formidable internal-evidence-based objections against the Long Ending do not consist of evidence that Mark could not have written it; they consist of evidence that Mark could not have written the Long Ending

---

368. Ibid., 98.
369. Spencer, "Denial of the Good News."
370. Ibid., 270.
371. Ibid., 273–77.
372. Ibid., 277–80.
373. Ibid., 281.
374. Snapp, "External Footprints and Internal Fingerprints."
375. Ibid., 1–10.
376. Ibid., 10.

as the ending of the Gospel of Mark."[377] Snapp then listed four pieces of internal evidence cited against Mark 16:9–20: "(1) The sudden shift between 16:8 and 16:9. (2) The use of ἐκεῖνος as an absolute in the Long Ending. (3) The positive focus on signs, in contrast to Mark 8:11–12. (4) The focus on events which, in Luke, are located in and around Jerusalem rather than in Galilee."[378] His conclusions concerning the internal evidence were definitive: "None of these textual fingerprints eliminate Mark as the author. Cumulatively, however, they indicate that the Long Ending was not composed by Mark in order to complete the Gospel of Mark. The first and fourth pieces of evidence also indicate that the Long Ending was not composed by anyone to complete the Gospel of Mark. They suggest that the material we now know as Mark 16:9–20 existed as a freestanding document before being attached to the main portion of the text of the Gospel of Mark."[379]

Snapp addressed the view, advocated by Kelhoffer and others that the author of Mark 16:9–20 purposefully borrowed from the four Gospels in order to end Mark "in a way that would imitate the writing style of Mark and the writers of the other canonical Gospels."[380] Snapp stated:

> That theory requires a special sort of author. The author would be bold enough to add his own literary creation to the Gospel of Mark, but timid enough not to adjust the jarring shift between 16:8 and 16:9. He would be thoroughly acquainted with the Gospel of Luke, and yet write that the disciples rejected the two travelers' report (in 16:13), which is not suggested by Luke, and he would present Jesus' subsequent appearance to the disciples as if it occurred some time after the two traveler's report, which also is not suggested by Luke. He would be so cautious that he consulted the Gospels and Acts sixty times, but also so bold that he inserted unparalleled material about serpent-handling (which Mk. 16:18 does not suggest to be accidental) and poison-drinking. Though dependent upon Matthew, Luke, and John, he would differ from all three by relating that main group of disciples rejected Mary Magdalene's announcement that Jesus was alive and had been seen by her. And this author, though he realized that the Gospel of Mark ended with an explicit forecast of an appearance in Galilee, would decide not to use John 21, and would choose instead to summarize events

377. Ibid., 11.
378. Ibid.
379. Ibid.
380. Ibid.

which anyone acquainted with the Gospel of Luke would locate in and around Jerusalem rather Galilee.[381]

Snapp was not impressed with this, as evidenced by his response: "Such an author is, I believe, complicated beyond the point of plausibility. The theory of a mad mimic ought to be rejected in favor of a much simpler and more credible explanation of the textual fingerprints in the Long Ending."[382] Snapp remarked that Mark 16:9–20 existed separately from the rest of the Gospel as a freestanding document originating in Rome.[383] Snapp then gave his scenario as to how the various endings of the Gospel were disseminated in all of the different textual streams:

> The transmission-history, to the extent that it can be traced by extant evidence, corresponds to what one would expect to result from the scenario described above: the Long Ending was accepted as part of the Gospel of Mark in Gaul, Rome, Asia Minor, and Syria. In Egypt, the Abrupt Ending was disseminated in Gospels-books, and affected the earliest level of the Sahidic version, one branch of the Old Latin version, and the ancestry of the Sinaitic Syriac. The Short ("Intermediate") Ending was composed in Egypt, possibly in the late second or early third century by a copyist who did not appreciate that John 21 was a continuation of the thread of Mark's narrative. In the late third century, when copies with the Long Ending circulated in Egypt (non-Byzantine copies, with "And in their hands" in 16:18), copyists who were puzzled by disagreeing exemplars combined the two endings, placing the Short Ending first so that it would round off an otherwise abruptly-ending pericope. Such copies formed the text-base of the Ethiopic and Bohairic versions, and influenced the Sahidic version also. Copies with the Abrupt Ending were taken from Egypt to Caesarea (by Origen, among others) and it was these cherished copies, or their descendants, that Eusebius described as the "accurate copies" in his comments to Marinus. Eusebius' comments were perpetuated by Jerome, and were capsulized in marginalia in f 1 and related copies. Armenian translators in the fifth century, influenced by either an exemplar prepared by Eusebius (one of the fifty codices), or by his comments and Canons, did not include Mark 16:9–20 in the Armenian version. The translators who produced the Old Georgian version followed the Armenian version. Meanwhile,

381. Ibid.
382. Ibid.
383. Ibid., 12.

copies with the Long Ending as part of the Gospel of Mark circulated everywhere else the Gospels were known.[384]

He thus concluded: "Wherever copies or copyists or translators were more firmly linked to the initial Roman dissemination of the Gospel of Mark than to an Egyptian Gospels-text, the Long Ending was accepted as part of the Gospel of Mark. Those who want their copies of the Gospel of Mark to contain the ending that was in the Gospel of Mark when it was initially released for church-use should do likewise."[385] Whether one agrees with Snapp's scenario, at the least he further called into question the prevailing view concerning the authenticity of Mark 16:9–20. As it was, there had already been a head-to-head meeting concerning all of the positions relative to Mark 16:9–20, and the results would be published in short order.

2008: Black, Bock, Elliott, Robinson, Wallace, De Jong

David Alan Black in 2008 edited a volume of papers presented at a conference entitled "The Last Twelve Verses of Mark: Original or Not," held in 2007 at Southeastern Baptist Theological Seminary in Wake Forest, North Carolina.[386] In his preface, Black expressed his "hope that this volume will help a new generation of students to sift through the evidence—through the claims and counterclaims—and to establish a responsible historical basis for the answer to the question: Are the last twelve verses of Mark original or not?"[387] That this question would be asked spoke to how far the discussion had come since the mid-1960s.

Chapter 1, written by Daniel Wallace, advocated the position that Mark ended at 16:8.[388] He began by noting presuppositions that one may have in entering such a discussion.[389] Specifically, Wallace mentioned one's view on source criticism, textual criticism, and presuppositions about bibliology,

---

384. Ibid., 16.

385. Ibid., 17.

386. Black, *Perspectives on the Ending of Mark*. In addition to editing the book, Black also presented a paper at the conference. Wallace, Robinson, Elliott and Black (in that order in the book as well as the conference) presented their respective positions, while Bock concluded by responding to all of the presentations. Both Terry and Snapp were present for the conference.

387. Ibid., xii.

388. Wallace, "Mark 16:8."

389. Ibid., 1–10.

particularly the doctrine of preservation.³⁹⁰ At this point Wallace characterized an unpublished 1988 essay by Wilbur Pickering as advocating the doctrine of preservation. Wallace thus went on to criticize the doctrine by recounting his own philosophical journey away from preservation to that of a "reasoned eclectic."³⁹¹ Wallace then examined the external evidence.³⁹² Concerning Mark 16:9–20, he affirmed that "95 percent of all Greek MSS" contained it.³⁹³ He also added, "the raw data can be quite deceiving . . . I used to be impressed by the sheer volume of MSS on one side of a textual problem."³⁹⁴ Curiously, Wallace only devoted two brief paragraphs and one footnote to the actual evidence in favor of 16:9–20.³⁹⁵ The bulk of that particular section addressed the argument of Farmer, that Alexandrian scribes omitted the passage.³⁹⁶ When he addressed the external evidence in favor of ending Mark at 16:8, Wallace remarked, "This discussion won't take much space because there aren't many of these documents."³⁹⁷ However, he devoted all of the section to a detailed examination of every piece of evidence in favor of exclusion.³⁹⁸ To his credit, Wallace acknowledged that Clement and Origen, though both silent concerning Mark 16:9–20, cannot be reliably used against the passage.³⁹⁹ The remainder of the section highlighted the testimony of Eusebius and Jerome, the Intermediate Ending of Mark, notations in some manuscripts, and the various "endings" of the Gospel

---

390. Ibid., 3, 5. "Preservation" here refers to the belief that God had preserved the Scriptures so that there must always be manuscript testimony to the original text.

391. Ibid., 6–9.

392. Ibid., 10–29. "Longer Ending," 10–14, and "Short Ending," 14–29. Thus there was a certain irony in the amount of space given to each possibility.

393. Ibid., 10. As has been seen from Kelhoffer (2001), that number is 99 percent.

394. Ibid.

395. Ibid., 10–11.

396. Ibid., 11–14. This is disappointing, to be sure; however, it may be because all those who participated in the conference knew ahead of time that Wallace advocated ending the Gospel at 16:8. At any rate, a more thorough engaging of the evidence in favor of inclusion would have been useful.

397. Ibid., 14.

398. Ibid., 14–29. Interestingly, Wallace referred in a footnote (p. 19) to Codex 2386 and 1420 as both lacking a leaf that would have contained 16:9–20. Additionally, Wallace acknowledged in another footnote (p. 20) what Metzger had found: three Ethiopic manuscripts that contained 16:9–20.

399. Wallace said they "may be" witnesses for ending at 16:8, but concludes, "There is simply no way to verify whether Clement or Origen knew of the LE. All we can say is there is no evidence that they did" (ibid., 20–21).

as evidence that it did not contain Mark 16:9–20.[400] Wallace addressed the internal evidence briefly, "because J. K. Elliott's essay in this volume focuses on internal evidence."[401] In one paragraph, Wallace listed the key points raised (vocabulary, syntax, style, and context).[402] Wallace offered this criticism: "What marks most of these studies is an unprincipled approach that picks bits of willy-nilly, but never argues on sound linguistic principles as to whether Mark could have written this section."[403] Nevertheless, Wallace referred approvingly to Kelhoffer and Williams, who both concluded that Mark did not write Mark 16:9–20.[404] Wallace then rested his case upon three points: the cumulative argument of all the linguistic peculiarities of the passage; his contention that "a few Markanisms" within Mark 16:9–20 are not enough to prove its authenticity; and, the Intermediate Ending and Freer Logion have several Markan features that are not found in Mark 16:9–20, yet they are not authentic—thus supposedly showing that similar features could occur in Mark 16:9–20 "without implying anything about authenticity."[405]

Wallace concluded his essay by offering the theory for Mark ending at 16:8. He made three points in support, by responding to three main objections. First, regarding the objection that an open-ended book is a modern convention, Wallace relied upon the work of Magness and argued for Mark fitting into the literary conventions of his own day. He also put forth the view that Luke consciously emulated Mark's style in his ending of the book of Acts.[406] Second, in replying to the argument that the final leaf of the Gospel was either lost or destroyed, Wallace contended that Mark was written on a scroll, instead of a codex; if so, it would have been very difficult for a leaf to have been damaged or lost. Finally, Wallace replied to the argument that no book could have ended with γάρ by relying upon the works of both van der Horst and Iverson, who argued the opposite.[407] Wallace ended his presentation by claiming that the ending of Mark at 16:8 was dramatic, and

400. Ibid., 21–29.
401. Ibid., 29–33.
402. Ibid., 29.
403. Ibid., 30.
404. Ibid. Wallace referred to Kelhoffer (2000) and Williams (2007).
405. Ibid., 32–33.
406. Ibid., 34–35.
407. Ibid., 36–37.

that Mark had "created a new literary genre called *gospel*,"[408] if his Gospel were written first.

Chapter 2, written by Maurice A. Robinson, consisted of a lengthy defense of Mark 16:9–20.[409] He began by listing the manuscript evidence for the short ending, the long ending, and the Freer Logion.[410] Robinson stated, "In reality, twenty-first-century scholars continue to deal with issues raised during the nineteenth century."[411] Robinson then listed the patristic evidence in favor of inclusion of Mark 16:9–20.[412] He contrasted at the outset two groups of witnesses—the "speculations of the fourth and later centuries" of Eusebius, Jerome, and Victor of Antioch, and the second-century testimonies of Justin Martyr and Irenaeus. Robinson commented, "Under almost any other circumstances, these citations should outweigh patristic speculations of some two centuries later."[413] Robinson stated his conviction that Justin Martyr weaved Mark 16:20 into his *Apology*, noting that the three-word combination in question only appears in that particular verse in Mark.[414]

Robinson referred to Irenaeus's unquestioned use of the ending of Mark 16:9–20 in *Against Hersies*—"declaring the LE to be a component part of the Second Gospel in a period long predating that of ℵ, B, Eusebius, and Jerome."[415] Robinson attempted to further make his case by paralleling the possible intentional shortening of the ending of Mark with the 1919 poem of Marianne Moore, "Poetry," which appeared in several versions over a 50 year period—complete with a "long form," a "short form," and an "intermediate form"—along with "variant readings," each created by Moore. Robinson asserted, "In Moore's case we know the entire transmissional history; with Mark we have 'only hints followed by guesses.'"[416] Robinson further paralleled the commentators upon Moore with those of the Markan ending.[417] "Of course, had the earlier long version of Moore's poem *not* initially

---

408. Ibid., 27–28.
409. Robinson, "Long Ending of Mark," 40–79.
410. Ibid., 41–46.
411. Ibid., 44.
412. Ibid., 46–50.
413. Ibid., 46.
414. Ibid., 46–47.
415. Ibid., 48.
416. Ibid., 48–49.
417. Ibid., 49–50.

existed, the later versions would have been more difficult to interpret. A similar consideration could apply to the various Markan endings."[418]

Robinson suggested that both Vaticanus and Codex Sinaiticus possibly may have deliberately omitted Mark 16:9–20, based upon the blank space at the end of Vaticanus and a "cancel-sheet replacement" that occurs in the same location in Sinaiticus.[419] Robinson suggested several reasons for its excision; Eusebius's response to questions raised about chronology, location, and events in Mark 16:9–20 being in contradiction to the other Gospels was one such reason, as were the miracles listed in Mark 16:9–20.[420] Robinson proposed that the Intermediate Ending was created to round off a lection:

> In light of the joint inclusion of both the Intermediate and Long Ending in various Greek MSS, it is possible that the Intermediate Ending was *not* created solely to provide a conclusion to the *known* LE. The present writer suggests a plausible option, involving liturgical and lectionary concern. From early times, the Greek Orthodox Church has read the LE for Matins on the Feast of the Ascension. As the Sunday readings were developed for the Synaxarion, Mark 15:43–16:8 was assigned to the liturgy reading for the Third Sunday after Easter. Continuous-text manuscripts were used for liturgical purposes long before the creation of separate lectionary manuscripts, and in some localized quarters (Egypt in particular) the abrupt negative tone concluding that lection may have struck harshly upon those hearing such an ending publicly read, particularly when the lection involved the announcement of the Resurrection itself. The doubtful nature of such a liturgical conclusion may have provoked in some circles a pious adjustment in the form of the Intermediate Ending. Such would allow an already lengthy lection to conclude on a positive and evangelistic note without overextending the text unnecessarily. The Intermediate Ending thus would provide an appropriate conclusion to 16:8 without assuming an actual absence of the LE itself in any particular MS.[421]

---

418. Ibid., 50.
419. Ibid., 51–52.
420. Ibid., 52–55.
421. Ibid., 58–59.

At this point, Robinson engaged in a lengthy discussion of the internal evidence concerning Mark 16:9–20.[422] He included a chart of words not paralleled within Mark, compared to the other three Gospels. With only one exception, Robinson found "the supposed non-Markan words of the LE are rare even within the remaining three Gospels."[423] Robinson also addressed certain words considered to be non-Markan: "Obviously, cognate usage involving parallel root forms remains an authorial component and demonstrates that many of the supposedly 'non-Markan' terms found in the LE do fall within a reasonable expectation regarding Markan usage. Far too many problems arise from excessive claims regarding vocabulary and style involving a limited portion of text."[424]

Robinson then demonstrated parallels between Mark 16:9–20 and the remainder of Mark in style, vocabulary, theme, and composition, drawing upon Terry's work and his own explorations.[425] In each case, Robinson found that 16:9–20 complements and harmonizes with Mark. Robinson also raised the possibility that an "Elijah" theme runs through Mark, and Mark 16:9–20 would be needed to finish the Gospel since "a true ending of Mark (whether the LE or some speculative "lost" ending) would require Christ's ascension in order to complete the 'Elijah motif' within that Gospel."[426] Thus, Robinson claimed that internal evidence was not as overwhelming against Mark 16:9–20 as it had been presented previously. After a fifteen-point summary of his essay, Robinson declared "the continued canonical acceptance and promulgation of the LE as the *only* fitting conclusion to Mark's Gospel."[427]

In chapter 4, J. K. Elliott discussed issues concerning the text of the ending of Mark and internal evidence against Mark 16:9–20.[428] In beginning

---

422. Ibid., 59–74.

423. Ibid., 61.

424. Ibid., 62. In a footnote, Robinson goes even further: "Elliott ("Text and Language," 262n20) suggests that the various tallies of 'non-Markan' terms within the LE are 'low' and represent an 'undercount.' In contrast, the present writer suggests that *overcounts* in this matter are more frequent, and in most writers these exist primarily to embellish an *a priori* view of LE non-authenticity based primarily on its absence from MSS ℵ and B."

425. Ibid., 64–74.

426. Ibid., 67–68.

427. Ibid., 78.

428. Elliott, "Last Twelve Verses."

Does Mark 16:9–20 Belong In The New Testament?

the section on external evidence,[429] Elliott acknowledged the vulnerability of ancient manuscripts to damage; it was "an eventuality we may have to accept."[430] He also admitted that only two early Greek MSS and one medieval MS end at 16:8.[431] Yet, concerning ℵ and B, Elliott made some concessions. After pointing out the blank space in B at the end of Mark and stating that the space was not big enough to include Mark 16:9–20, he stated in a footnote that "the issue is not clear-cut."[432] Concerning ℵ, Elliott pointed out the replacement leaf at the end of Mark, as well as the fact that "the last six columns of Mark are stretched out, although the opening four columns by D (a scribe of this manuscript—dh) in this replacement are not stretched out."[433] After pointing out that this scribe was also likely connected with B, Elliott said, "Some have argued that this means we are concerned effectively with only one MS witness to the text of Mark ending at 16:8 rather than with two independent early Greek manuscripts."[434] He also stated, "Thus the Greek external evidence is not crystal clear in its witness as far as ℵ and B are concerned."[435] This was significant, coming as it did from a Greek scholar who defended the short ending of Mark. However, he quickly added the manuscripts which included the intermediate and longer endings as additional witnesses against Mark 16:9–20. He also listed the versions which ended at 16:8, as well as the witness of Eusebius and Jerome.[436] Elliott then entered into a discussion of the internal evidence.[437] Though he deferred to his 1971 study, he nevertheless listed fourteen words and phrases from Mark 16:9–20 he either termed as "non-Markan," or "only here in Mark."[438] After noting in a parenthetical aside how many of the features occur more than once, he added this blunt statement: "It is self-deceiving

---

429. Ibid., 81–87.

430. Ibid., 81.

431. Ibid., 82.

432. Ibid., 84. Elliott said that one of his students had demonstrated the possibility of inserting the text into the space. Elliott then wrote, "Several years ago there was much discussion about this topic in the papers circulated by the Majority Text Society."

433. Ibid., 85.

434. Ibid., 86.

435. Ibid.

436. Ibid., 86–87.

437. Ibid., 88–99.

438. Ibid., 88–89.

to pretend that the linguistic questions are still 'open.'"[439] Elliott offered his view that Mark did not end with 16:8. His conclusion was that no ancient author would have ended any work "with a postpositional particle."[440] He offered that a continuation of verse 8 existed, but that the final page of Mark was lost.[441] When he addressed the contents of Mark 16:9-20, Elliott was even more direct. He called the passage "an inferior piece of writing, plodding and grey."[442] He continued: "I am unwilling to credit Mark with the incorporation of this allegedly previously composed ending into his new Gospel . . . I am disinclined to believe that it was Mark, the innovative composer and creative theologian, who took over, unrevised, a paragraph such as vv. 9-20, especially as it may well have disagreed with his own theological stance."[443] Elliott further explained his position that the original ending was lost, and that Mark 16:9-20 had been "concocted" to fulfill the ending. He also in turn rejected the theories that Mark somehow had invented a new sophisticated style.[444] In his summation, Elliott referred approvingly to Kelhoffer's (2000) work—that Mark 16:9-20 was a second-century writing—and then added, "we must make it clear that it was inappropriately cobbled on as a conclusion that can scarcely be said to develop or belong to vv. 1-8."[445] Elliott affirmed the canonicity of Mark 16:9-20 while denying Markan authorship.[446] He then entered into a polemic against "inerrancy, as narrowly defined by some." Calling it "indefensible," he equated the "inerrancy" he spoke against as the position that there were absolutely no errors in the original text of the New Testament.[447] He then stated: "The Bible

439. Ibid., 89. From a scholar like Elliott, this kind of assertion is disappointing, to say the least. Based on the wording of the statement, it seems that he was replying to the 1965 address by Clark. As it was, he referred to his earlier work and made no reference to any dissenting voices.

440. Ibid.

441. Ibid.

442. Ibid., 91.

443. Ibid., 91-92. In a footnote, Elliott explained: "For instance, the teaching that believers will be granted miraculous powers and that signs will prove the truth of the preaching is against Mark 8:11-13." This overlooks that Jesus was speaking to the Pharisees who were not interested in proof; it also overlooks all of the miracles (signs) that Jesus had already performed and would perform.

444. Ibid., 93-95. In this, Elliott relied upon Croy's work; again, though, Elliott disappointingly used a harsh word—"concocted"—to describe the writing of 16:9-20.

445. Ibid., 98. Once again, Elliott's choice of words is unfortunate.

446. Ibid., 99-102.

447. Ibid., 99. Elliott equally was critical of both the defenders of the Textus Receptus

Does Mark 16:9–20 Belong In The New Testament?

may well be a collection of inspired writings or an inspired collection of writings (i.e., writings not intended by their authors to be so, but deemed to be so by later Christians) but whether those definitions can help to decide on the rough and tumble of textual variation is improbable. The sooner that the language of inerrancy is dropped in the context of textual criticism the better it will be for scholarship."[448] Elliott then affirmed the canonicity of Mark 16:9–20, based upon the long practice of inclusion of ancient texts into Scripture which were disputed.

Chapter 4, written by David Alan Black, presented his position that Mark 16:9–20 was composed by Mark as a later addition to his Gospel.[449] Black summarized his views on the external and internal evidence—stating from the outset his belief that Mark 16:9–20 was genuine and from the hand of Mark.[450] The bulk of the chapter was Black's presentation of his position concerning the development of the Gospels.[451] He divided the phases of development of the Gospels into four sections.[452] According to this view Matthew was the first Gospel written, in order to both answer the charges of the Jews against Jesus and also to serve as a handbook of teaching for the early church.[453] The second phase was when the Gospel of Luke was composed, as an aid for Paul to be able to integrate Jewish Christians with Gentile converts.[454] Since Luke's Gospel could not be published until after

---

and the Majority Text; yet, he seemed to go a step further: "To argue that a particular strand of the MS tradition, typically the text represented by the Textus Receptus, or the Majority text, uniquely preserves, through 'providential care,' those inspired words in their entirety ignores the scientific results of textual criticism as practiced in the past century or more, and such preconceived conclusions alienate academic discussion that depends on open and free inquiry."

448. Ibid., 100–101.

449. Black, "Mark 16:9–20 as Markan Supplement," chap. 4 of *Perspectives on the Ending of Mark*.

450. Ibid., 103–6. Black characterized the external evidence as crucial, and the internal evidence against 16:9–20 as "overstated." While he referred approvingly to Terry's work, it was disappointing that Black did not present his own findings concerning these areas.

451. Ibid., 106–21. Black himself said that this was a variation of the "Two Gospel Hypothesis" of Bernard Orchard and William Farmer; Black preferred the term "Fourfold Gospel Hypothesis," coined by Farmer and taken from both Irenaeus (*Against Heresies* 3.2.8) and Vatican II's *Dei Verbum*.

452. The Jerusalem Phase, AD 30–42 (Acts 1–12); the Gentile Mission Phase, AD 42–62 (Acts 13–28); the Roman Phase, AD 62–67; and the Johannine Supplement.

453. Black, "Mark 16:9–20," 110–12.

454. Ibid., 112–16.

the crisis concerning circumcision had abated, Paul sought Peter's help in giving public assurance that Luke was in harmony with the apostles. Peter thus delivered a series of five lectures concerning the life of Jesus, possibly with the scrolls of Matthew and Luke at hand. This constituted the third phase. Mark arranged for individuals in the audience to write down Peter's words as he uttered them. When Peter was finished, his remembrances were warmly accepted—though he himself did not wish for them to be published in his own name. Luke's Gospel was thus able to be published. Black further speculated that Mark 16:9–20 was added by Mark following the death of Peter in an edition of the text which would include the death and resurrection of Jesus. Since the edition of Mark without those verses had already been in circulation, this would explain the divided textual tradition.[455] The fourth phase was the Johannine supplement. John published his Gospel to supplement the information given in the Synoptic Gospels. He gave information not published in the other three, and sought to strengthen the faith of Christians. A couple of byproducts would be a refutation of Gnosticism, and a "quiet polemic" against Judaism.[456] Black summarized his presentation in his conclusion, and called for all followers of Christ to adopt the evangelistic theme of Mark. He specifically referred to Mark 16:15—"Go into all the world and preach the Gospel to every creature"—and implored churches to take the Great Commission seriously.[457]

Chapter 5 presented Darrell Bock's response to the participants.[458] He began by listing three points upon which all agreed: the variants for both the short and long ending of Mark are very old; what is taught in Mark 16:9–20 is taught mostly elsewhere in the New Testament; and, everyone desires to work with hard evidence—though Bock added that internal evidence should also be included as tangible evidence.[459] Bock then mentioned presuppositions. He referred to Pickering's 1988 paper, and characterized it as "unnuanced, oppositional thinking" that "does not advance discussion." Echoing Elliott, he added that it had a danger of "creating a brittle

---

455. Ibid., 116–20. In this, Black also referred to Farmer's work concerning the divided textual tradition.

456. Ibid., 120–21.

457. Black referred to Mark 16:15 twice. He said, "I have been known to go so far as to quote the Markan version of the Great Commission in public" (104). In a footnote, he said that he found only four references to the verse on an Internet database. One wonders if he thought to search any sites connected with churches of Christ.

458. Bock, "Ending of Mark."

459. Ibid., 124–25.

fundamentalism."[460] Concerning external evidence, Bock gave a synopsis of both the manuscripts and patristics.[461] He included the Intermediate Ending as evidence against Mark 16:9–20, and highlighted the testimony of Eusebius and Jerome.[462] He also listed the Byzantine lectionaries as lacking the ending.[463] Thus, Bock claimed that the external evidence was evenly divided between the short and longer endings, and that internal evidence was crucial. He added that such evidence is subjective, requiring judgment; yet, he said, "we should not think that external evidence is free of judgment that involves connecting the dots."[464]

Bock addressed Elliott's conclusion favorably, that the original ending has been lost; however, he said that it was the "second most likely solution."[465] Yet, he rejected it in the end, due to it being unlikely that no copies had circulated prior. With Robinson's essay, Bock found it "not convincing," and "not quite to the point." Bock said that "length is not an issue here" concerning a cutoff at verse 8 for liturgical reasons, and "the combination of lexical terms, grammar, and style . . . is the point."[466] The explanation Bock gave relied heavily upon Magness, as well as van der Horst and Iverson. Thus, Bock held the position that Mark intended to end at verse 8. The response of the reader would be crucial in interpretation.[467] In a postscript, Bock addressed Black's essay.[468] Bock called into question his assertion that Matthew was the first Gospel written, due to the testimony of Eusebius.[469] Bock also disagreed with Black's theory of composition be-

---

460. Ibid., 126.

461. Ibid., 128–31.

462. Ibid. In a footnote, Bock cast doubt upon Justin Martyr's citation, claiming that the word πανταχοῦ "is more common in Luke than in Mark." Yet, Bock's claim is incorrect, inasmuch as πανταχοῦ occurs once in the Nestle-Aland text in Mark, at Mark 1:28, and once in Luke, at 9:6.

463. Ibid., 129. However, the fact is that all of the Byzantine lectionaries actually *include* the ending. He also cited Elliott, "the earliest Byzantine lectionaries lack the longer ending," yet, Elliott was actually referring to a Jerusalem lectionary.

464. Ibid., 131.

465. Ibid., 132.

466. Ibid., 132–33.

467. Ibid., 134–37.

468. Ibid., 138–40.

469. Ibid., 138. Concerning *Eccl. hist.* 3.39.16; 5.10.3; 6.25.4, Bock took issue with Black's contention that Eusebius referred to Matthew writing in Hebrew style, not language. "The normal way to translate the terms in question is as Hebrew language."

cause of a lack of hard evidence and the apparent time it took to develop the canon. In the end Bock said that regardless of the position one took, "it should not significantly alter our faith."[470]

Also in 2008, Matthijs J. de Jong wrote a defense of verse 8 being the end of Mark.[471] He began by mincing no words concerning his position: "Text-critically there is no doubt that the authentic text of Mark ends at 16:8. Furthermore, the claim that the last words of 16:8, ἐφοβοῦντο γάρ, cannot be the original ending of a book, has been decisively refuted ... There are no solid arguments for suggesting the authentic gospel of Mark had a different ending from 16:8."[472] De Jong examined the women at the tomb,[473] and concluded: "The author did not aim to produce a consistent literary character but merely used the women as a vehicle for his message. He did not care that they remained silent; on the contrary, he used their silence for his explanation."[474] His thesis for verse 8 and the empty tomb was a departure from what had been written before: "Those who witnessed it remained silent about it."[475] He then attempted to explain the promises of the meeting in Galilee being unfulfilled if the Gospel ended at verse 8. A connection was attempted with the resurrection appearances of 1 Corinthians 15.[476] De Jong then rejected the idea that the empty tomb implied an assumption; rather, he said it implied resurrection.[477]

2010: Williams, Robinson, Pearse

Travis B. Williams in 2010 published his own proposed methodological procedure concerning 16:9–20.[478] Williams began his essay describing the hardened position of those who denied the authenticity of the passage:

---

470. Ibid., 141.

471. Jong, "Mark 16:8."

472. Ibid., 123. The triumphalist rhetoric aside, his claim had no basis. As has been seen, there were many in recent years who had given quite convincing arguments to the contrary.

473. Ibid., 125–31.

474. Ibid., 130.

475. Ibid., 131.

476. Ibid., 133–36.

477. Ibid., 138–46.

478. Williams, "Bringing Method to the Madness."

Does Mark 16:9–20 Belong In The New Testament?

> Are the last 12 verses of Mark 16 authentic? Could vv. 9–20 have originally been composed by the hand of the evangelist? When questions like these are posed within the world of biblical scholarship, ordinarily they are met with a resounding "No!" For the most part, the inauthenticity of the longer ending of Mark's Gospel has become almost an accepted axiom. In fact, this position is so widely held that one would assume that the evidence against its legitimacy is overwhelming. To some, even raising the possibility of the passage's authenticity might seem gratuitous, especially in light of the modern consensus to the contrary.[479]

This was enlightening, in light of what Kelhoffer had pointed out (from whom Williams then quoted directly on this aspect), and what had already appeared in print—from some who hardly disguised their frustration with having to address the questions. Williams went on to criticize the methods previously used by critics of the passage:

> From a text-critical perspective, style has been one of the major reasons why scholars have rejected the authenticity of the longer ending. Yet the problem with much of the previous argumentation is that it has been based on methodological assumptions that have yielded a somewhat less-than-convincing result. Numerous exegetes have been content with building their cases on a surface-level assessment of Markan style that consists either of the recitation of comments from past examiners or of a limited number of statistical observations. Thus, the strength of their conclusions often greatly exceeds the evidence from which the deductions are extracted.[480]

Williams even went so far as to accuse the critics of being "stuck in the ruts of the past."[481] To be sure, he was equally critical of those defending the authenticity of the passage. Saying they often would "downplay" textual issues associated with the passage, Williams accused them of being willing to "overlook or even deny the combined force of the stylistic evidence."[482] He thus proposed a "reassessment" using a "basic methodological procedure by which to evaluate the syntactical style of Mark 16:9–20 in relation to the rest of Mark's Gospel."[483] In addressing how style would be measured,

---

479. Ibid., 397.
480. Ibid., 398.
481. Ibid.
482. Ibid.
483. Ibid., 399.

Williams appealed to statistics. He also added a very interesting caveat: "The single occurrence of an unusual grammatical phenomenon does not signify dissimilarity, for there are instances of grammatical peculiarity in every author."[484] He emphasized that the accumulation of such single occurrences would signify dissimilarity. Williams also examined the syntax of the passage in relationship to the rest of the Gospel. It was at this point that Williams took a turn from those who had gone before. In discussing syntax, he again took the opportunity to criticize past critics of the passage:

> A tacit assumption among many who have dealt with the subject is that the mere existence of a grammatical construction within Mark's Gospel equates to a Markan stylistic feature or that the absence of a construction makes it un-Markan. Yet, as we shall see, such an ideology is demonstrably false. While it is true that one aspect of style is what sets an author apart from other authors, the fact that a particular construction does not appear in what remains of the author's work does not mean that he/she could not have been responsible for it. Certainly, we would admit that Mark could have composed various other grammatical formations, especially considering the limited amount of material that we actually possess and the restricted number of topics that are being addressed.[485]

Williams proposed a different approach: a different style is one that is not consistent with the way in which Mark consistently communicates it elsewhere.[486] He proposed to do this by a series of questions: Is the construction found elsewhere in Mark? Does the construction fit with Markan style? Is it an obvious stylistic feature? Does Mark use a different construction to convey the same idea? Is it part of Mark's regular style?[487] He added that he would focus on "strong indications" of an un-Markan style.[488]

After listing sixteen words that appear nowhere else in Mark, Williams focused on three words "that raise problems for the authenticity" of the passage: the divergent use of πορεύομαι, the choice of the word ἕτερος, as opposed to his use elsewhere in the Gospel of ἄλλος, and the use of θεάομαι. He then mentioned two "glaring absences:" the word εὐθύς, and the word

---

484. Ibid., 402.
485. Ibid., 403.
486. Ibid.
487. Ibid., 404.
488. Ibid. "Plus instances that have been wrongly labeled un-Markan."

πάλιν. Additionally, Williams referred to two "key absences" related to grammar: the omission of the historical present, and the way in which the story line is continued—using the word καί instead of δέ. Williams then said: "What really gives the interpreter reason for pause is that none of the major Markan peculiarities—whether lexical or syntactical—are present in the passage. This is the rub; this is what turns a lot of seemingly insignificant lexical and syntactical discrepancies into a major problem. It is this *accumulation* that weighs heaviest against authenticity."[489]

Williams then examined each disputed expression as used in its verse; he found that four of them could have been used by Mark, but that "the vast majority of instances pointed toward stylistic divergence."[490] In particular, "of the 24 stylistic expressions we examined, 8 revealed a strong, un-Markan style, and 8 more provided moderately strong proof in this same direction."[491] Combined with the aforementioned words and omissions, Williams claimed it "spoke convincingly against the similarity of the two texts."[492] Thus, Williams concluded that though the case against authenticity "has been somewhat suspect, the underlying reality behind the position remains strong."[493]

In due course, Maurice A. Robinson—whose study was mentioned and criticized by Williams—wrote a two-part response that answered some key points in Williams's article.[494] Robinson began, "I suggest that this study, like most others claiming to deal definitively with matters of style and syntax, remains flawed, and serves only to further muddle the discussion."[495] After mentioning that Williams's study had "many fallacies," Robinson said he would "select five that occur in close sequence in the middle of the article, in the order they occur."[496]

The first was the mention of ἕτερος being out of step with the Markan use of ἄλλος. After quoting Williams's footnote, Robinson pointed out that Williams used an example from Luke to buttress his claim. To this, Robinson replied: "But such a line of reasoning simply is incorrect on two major

489. Ibid., 408–9.
490. Ibid., 417.
491. Ibid.
492. Ibid.
493. Ibid.
494. Robinson, "Maurice Robinson Responds."
495. Ibid.
496. Ibid.

grounds: first, one cannot make Lukan word preference a touchstone for Markan style and usage (this particularly if one holds to Markan priority!); second, the seeds in the Markan version of the parable in fact are not different—rather, the same type of seed is merely sown in different soils. Within a proper Markan context, ἄλλος then remains the only appropriate term for the Sower, whereas in 16:12, ἕτερος is clearly required. This then becomes a non-issue."[497] The second fallacy mentioned by Robinson was Williams's point on the absence of the word εὐθύς. Robinson wrote, "Yet there are many long stretches of Mark in which εὐθύς does not occur that extend far beyond the twelve verses of the LE."[498] Specifically, Robinson listed "2:13–3:5 (20vv); 3:7–4:4 (33vv); 6:55–7:34 (37vv); 8:11–9:14 (43vv); 9:25–10:51 (78vv); 11:4–14:42 (154vv), etc."[499] To this Robinson added, "In fact, even in the portion up to 16:8, the last appearance of εὐθύς was in 15:1—some 55 verses earlier!"[500] The third fallacy was Williams' mention of the absence of the word πάλιν. Robinson responded: "Leaving aside the fact that πάλιν is far more characteristic of John, indeed Mark does hold second place among the four gospels in the use of this word. However, the same facts apply as in the case of εὐθύς: numerous long stretches exist in Mark in which πάλιν simply does not appear."[501] The list of passages illustrating this point was lengthy: "Examples include 1:1–2:1 (45vv); 4:1–5:20 (60vv); 5:22–7:31 (109vv), etc. And once more, even in the portion up to 16:8, the last occurrence of πάλιν was at 15:13—some 42 verses earlier. Once more, Williams' claim is flawed."[502] Robinson's fourth point from Williams's article addressed the "unexpected shift" between verses eight and nine. "Williams notes that 'the nominative singular participle in v. 9 seems to have no referent,' and that this 'participial function in Mark 16:9 is different from what is found in the rest of the Gospel.' He further notes that 'one could hardly argue that Jesus has been the subject up to this point,' even though that 'while he has been mentioned [16:6–7], the events have primarily surrounded the women who have come to the tomb. Therefore, this sudden and uninformed shift weighs against authenticity.'"[503] However, Robinson

497. Ibid.
498. Ibid.
499. Ibid.
500. Ibid.
501. Ibid.
502. Ibid.
503. Ibid.

pointed out a similar shift in Mark 15:44–46. After listing the passage in both Greek and English, Robinson asserted:

> The point in parallel here is that, even though "while [Joseph] has been mentioned, the events have primarily surrounded [Pilate]." In fact, the shift from an obliquely mentioned Joseph of v.45 to him suddenly becoming the subject in v.46 is awkward in the same manner as Jesus becoming subject in 16:9 after having been mentioned obliquely in 16:6–7. The situation is further compounded in view of the fact that the aorist participles ἀγοράσας and καθελών otherwise match the γνούς of v.45, where Pilate is the clear subject. Such an awkward shift of referent forces the reader to do the same sorting out of the intended subject in 15:46 as occurs in 16:9. Thus, in view of this near neighbor parallel instance, the issue in 16:9 should not be considered "different from what is found in the rest of the Gospel," contra Williams' claim to that effect.[504]

The fifth fallacy named by Robinson addressed the combination of ἐκβάλλω and παρά in 16:9, which Williams cited as an "oddity."[505] Williams went on to say: "In fact, the combination . . . is not found anywhere else in the NT. Thus, its presence in 16:9 is not only awkward for Mark but it would be unusual for any NT author . . . The conjunction would have to carry a sense that is unknown in the NT—that of separation."[506] To Williams's claim that ἐκ or ἀπό would be more appropriate, Robinson replied:

> Yet this entire claim is seriously flawed, since Williams focuses on the weakly supported minority reading of several aberrant MSS (C* D L W 0112 33 579 892 pc) while totally failing to mention the overwhelming majority reading of this passage found in all other witnesses, which is ἀφ' ἧς ἐκβεβλήκει and not παρ' ἧς ἐκβεβλήκει. This variant is clearly noted in the Nestle apparatus, even though the editors (peculiarly) chose to follow the aberrancy of παρά rather than the more correct consensus involving the fully appropriate ἀπό. At best, failure to take note of the variant that would obviate this difficulty is an unconscious oversight on Williams' part; at worst, it is a matter of unfairly stacking the deck by ignoring and not mentioning the known legitimate alternatives even when such are immediately available.[507]

---

504. Ibid.
505. Williams, "Bringing Method," 410–11.
506. Ibid.
507. Robinson, "Maurice Robinson Responds."

Robinson concluded his reply to Williams by reiterating "these five examples represent only a portion of what I see as serious methodological flaws in Williams' "Method or Madness" article."[508] He further stated that such flaws "seriously call into question both the method and its conclusions."[509]

Roger Pearse edited a volume in 2010 which offered a new translation of the writings of Eusebius of Caesarea.[510] It included not only the Greek version, but also both Greek and Latin fragments—as well as Syriac, Coptic, and Arabic fragments. According to Miller, "The fragments . . . have never been crtically edited, since their first publication nearly two centuries ago. Nor will such an edition appear soon."[511] The reason given was the cost involved in such an enterprise. Nonetheless, Pearse's volume offered a fresh translation of Eusebius that particularly shed new light on what was said concerning Mark 16:9–20. Not only that, the additional writings—which Kelhoffer apparently did not have access to when he wrote his article on Eusebius—provided context for all that Eusebius said in response to certain questions from Stephanus and Marinus. The translation of *Gospel Problems and Solutions, To Marinus* offered by Miller differed in crucial ways from that given by Kelhoffer, and raised new questions concerning whether Eusebius really believed that 16:9–20 was spurious.[512]

Addendum: Critical Introductions, 1968–2011

Besides the work done in commentaries and articles, critical introductions addressed the issue of the ending of Mark. Willi Marxsen dealt with the subject in his work, published in 1968.[513] He rejected 16:9–20, saying, "Scholars are agreed that both the shorter and the longer ending are secondary additions which seek to bring Mark into line with traditions from other Gospels."[514] Marxsen acknowledged problems with verse 8 being the ending, particularly the command in verse 7 for the women to tell the disciples about the resurrection. Rejecting the idea that the actual ending was

508. Ibid.
509. Ibid.
510. Pearse, *Eusebius of Caesarea*.
511. Ibid., ix.
512. Those issues will be addressed in detail in chap. 3.
513. Marxsen, *Introduction to the New Testament*, 139–42.
514. Ibid., 139.

Does Mark 16:9–20 Belong In The New Testament?

either lost or damaged, Marxsen posited a different approach: he proposed that verse 7 "was inserted into this context as a result of the evangelist's editorial work."[515] He further stated that this would be in line with his aim, "obviously to point his readers to Galilee—and to draw their attention to a 'vision' there."[516] The close parallel in 14:28, according to Marxsen, was also an "obviously editorial" verse.[517] To Marxsen, "It is possible that Mark's references are meant to point to the parousia which he evidently expects will take place in Galilee and—as we can gather from various statements—in the near future."[518]

Donald Guthrie laid out a concise yet thoughtful treatment of Mark 16:9–20 in his introduction, published in 1970.[519] Guthrie acknowledged, "The overwhelming majority of manuscripts contain the full twenty verses, and the earliest Christian writings which show acquaintance with Mark assume their genuineness."[520] After then listing the external evidence against inclusion of the passage, Guthrie listed three deductions:

> (1) The longer ending must have been attached to the Gospel at a very early period in its history; (2) the shorter ending is not well attested and must have been added in an attempt to fill a gap, a testimony to the circulation of Gospels ending at 16:8; (3) indeed, the most satisfactory explanation of all the textual evidence is that the original ended at 16:8 and that the three endings were different editorial attempts to deal with verse 8. If these deductions are correct the mass of mss containing the longer ending must have been due to the acceptance of this ending as the most preferable.[521]

Guthrie briefly listed the internal evidence against the passage and concluded, "This ending wears the appearance of compilation distinct from the rest of the Gospel."[522] After rejecting the idea that verse 8 was the intended conclusion, Guthrie listed proposals as to what happened: the ending was lost or damaged, or something happened to Mark to keep him from finishing. While acknowledging that such was feasible, he was hesi-

---

515. Ibid., 141.
516. Ibid.
517. Ibid.
518. Ibid., 142.
519. Guthrie, *New Testament Introduction*, 76–79.
520. Ibid., 76.
521. Ibid., 76–77.
522. Ibid., 77.

tant to advocate them. Guthrie then raised an intriguing possibility: "Mark intended a continuation volume similar to Acts and would not therefore have regarded 16:8 as the virtual end of his story."[523] If true, this would go a long way towards explaining the apparent problems. Yet according to Guthrie, "It would seem that the only course open is to admit that we do not know the original ending."[524] He was not willing to go beyond what the evidence apparently called for—a scholarly trait which served Guthrie well in his introduction.

Donald J. Selby offered a very brief treatment of 16:9–20 in his introduction, published in 1971.[525] He concluded that verse 8 was the end of the Gospel, but said, "Almost certainly the grammar calls for something else."[526] Selby further hypothesized, "It is not unlikely that only a few words have been lost."[527] Just four years later, Werner Georg Kümmel devoted a section of his Introduction to 16:9–20.[528] He said, "Today it is generally accepted that the account of the resurrection and the ascension which is found in most manuscripts and versions was not part of the original Mark."[529] Some of what Kümmel wrote was a response to Linnemann's hypothesis that 16:15–20 was the original ending of Mark, which he rejected based on linguistic considerations. Yet, Kümmel said that 16:9–20 "must have originated as early as the second century since it is known to Tatian and Irenaeus (who knows it as the end of Mark)."[530] Kümmel concluded, "It is clearly evident from these various attempts to discover an ending of Mark beyond 16:8 that early on there was an uneasy feeling that Mark could not end at 16:8. Matthew and Luke must have had that same uneasiness as well, since their divergence beyond Mark 16:8 shows that, though they expanded Mark, it already ended at 16:8."[531] Kümmel did not accept the idea that the ending was either lost or damaged, and proposed that ending the Gospel on

---

523. Ibid., 78. In a footnote, Guthrie said "many scholars have maintained that such a continuation was actually written and was used by Luke for the first part of Acts."

524. Ibid.

525. Selby, *Introduction to the New Testament*, 109.

526. Ibid.

527. Ibid.

528. Kümmel, *Introduction to the New Testament*, 98–101.

529. Ibid., 98–99.

530. Ibid., 100.

531. Ibid.

Does Mark 16:9–20 Belong In The New Testament?

a note of fear "is a wholly appropriate conclusion" when emphasizing the message of the angels in the text.[532]

In 1988, Hans Conzelmann and Andreas Lindemann briefly mentioned Mark 16:9–20.[533] They rejected the passage as original and said it was a later addition and an "artificial construction."[534] David L. Barr addressed the passage in his introduction, published in 1995.[535] He rejected inclusion of 16:9–20, and said "many manuscripts indicate by some sign that they were not part of the original Gospel."[536] He further argued that verse 8 was the intended ending, saying "the fear of the women is not simply their failure, but also as evidence of their finally grasping the meaning of the second half of Mark's story."[537] Two years later, Raymond E. Brown briefly mentioned 16:9–20 in his introduction.[538] Brown did not take a definitive position, but seemed to agree that the original ending was lost and that 16:9–20 was added later. Yet, Brown did say that he believed the passage was canonical.[539]

Lee Martin McDonald and Stanley E. Porter discussed the ending of Mark in their introduction, published in 2000.[540] They began, "Although most NT scholars today recognize that Mark 16:9–20 is a late addition to the Gospel, not all agree that 16:8 was the original ending of Mark."[541] Rejecting the possibility that the Gospel could have ended at that point, they wrote "It is more likely that the original ending—and possibly the original introduction of the Gospel—has been lost, either because of extended use of the manuscripts or damage to the manuscripts during a time of persecution."[542] The authors also did not accept the idea that the Gospel could have ended with the women staying silent, because "this does not fit in with Mark's purpose of presenting Jesus as the Son of God."[543] Concern-

532. Ibid., 101.
533. Conzelmann and Lindemann, *Interpreting the New Testament*, 52.
534. Ibid.
535. Barr, *New Testament Story*, 236–38.
536. Ibid., 237.
537. Ibid., 237–38.
538. Brown, *Introduction to the New Testament*, 148–49.
539. Ibid., 148.
540. McDonald and Porter, *Early Christianity*, 290–91.
541. Ibid., 290.
542. Ibid.
543. Ibid.

ing 16:9–20, they affirmed it "is not original to Mark but was added later by Christians who were concerned with the abrupt ending of the Gospel."[544] The external evidence was alluded to but not presented. A table was included which presented possible parallels between verses in 16:9–20 and contents of the other Gospels.[545] The authors speculated that the reason for the loss of the original ending was "the form in which the Gospel was first circulated," the codex.[546] They further concluded that "the church supplied what was missing by offering a brief digest of the conclusions of the other canonical Gospels and portions of Acts."[547] Paul J. Achtemeier, Joel B. Green, and Marianne Meye Thompson devoted a brief section to Mark 16:9–20 in their introduction, published in 2001.[548] The authors rejected the authenticity of all the possible endings to Mark. Yet, they wrote that the "evidence cannot prove decisively that the Gospel ended with verse 8."[549]

David A. deSilva discussed 16:9–20 in his introduction, published in 2004.[550] After briefly mentioning the possible endings of Mark, deSilva gave reasons why he believed the longer ending was not original: the fact that it was omitted from early manuscripts, Matthew departing from Mark's narrative at Mark 16:8, and the combination of external evidence and internal evidence.[551] However, deSilva said concerning 16:9–20 that its "status as canonical Scripture is beyond question."[552] After discussing the possibility that the Gospel could have ended at verse 8 (which he rejected), deSilva affirmed his belief that the original ending was lost.[553] Yet he also devoted almost a whole page to the lessons that could be learned from an abrupt ending, saying it could motivate people to speak out about the resurrection and live for Christ "much better in this postmodern age than any commissioning speech, for the story of Jesus itself cannot be completed until the church in every age proclaims the resurrection."[554]

544. Ibid.
545. Ibid.
546. Ibid.
547. Ibid., 291.
548. Achtemeier et al., *Introducing the New Testament*, 143.
549. Ibid.
550. DeSilva, *Introduction to the New Testament*, 224–26.
551. Ibid., 224–25.
552. Ibid., 224.
553. Ibid., 224–25.
554. Ibid., 226.

Does Mark 16:9–20 Belong In The New Testament?

D. A. Carson and Douglas J. Moo dealt with 16:9–20 in their introduction, published in 2005.[555] They began, "Since it is found in the bulk of the manuscripts and can be traced to the first half of the second century, this long ending can lay some claim to be considered as the original ending of Mark's Gospel."[556] However, they then presented five arguments against the originality of 16:9–20 which they said "are very strong":[557] the two oldest manuscripts do not contain the verses; Jerome and Eusebius seem to call them into question; the existence of two other endings suggests uncertainty; 16:9–20 contains "several non-Markan words and expressions"; and the longer ending does not flow naturally after verse 8. The authors then gave three possibilities as to the original ending: Mark may have intended to write more but was prevented from it; Mark may have written a longer ending, yet it may have been lost in the course of transmission—possibly due to the loss of the last page of a codex; and, Mark may well have intended to end at verse 8. It is this last possibility that Carson and Moo seemed to advocate: "But the confusion and astonishment of the women (v.8) leaves us wondering about just what it all means. And that is just the question Mark wants us to ask—and find answers to."[558] In a similar vein, John Drane addressed 16:9–20 in his introduction, published in 2011.[559] In his brief treatment, Drane affirmed that verse 8 is the end of Mark. He said there is "no evidence that Mark was originally longer."[560] He added that he believed 16:9–20 was a later addition. Drane added (similar to Carson and Moo) that Mark may have deliberately intended to provoke his readers to further reflection.

Considering all that had been written, the discussion concerning Mark 16:9–20 had thus advanced from the mid-1960s. Then, the question of inclusion of the passage seemed to be closed. Yet several factors contributed to a more open discussion. Fresh discoveries concerning the external evidence, new theories concerning composition and ending of ancient texts, and a new generation of scholars on both sides not satisfied with traditional answers opened the door for full participation. Most still objected to the idea of Mark 16:9–20 as being an original part of the Gospel. But the

---

555. Carson and Moo, *Introduction to the New Testament*, 187–90.
556. Ibid., 188.
557. Ibid., 189.
558. Ibid., 189–90.
559. Drane, *Introducing the New Testament*, 191.
560. Ibid.

climate was more favorable to contemplate whether the passage could be included, and whether it was canonical.

CHAPTER 2

External Evidence

As has been indicated, the number of manuscripts containing 16:9–20 is large. Kelhoffer said, "Roughly 99 percent of the surviving copies of the Second Gospel agree with the Textus Receptus and include Mark 16:9–20 at some point after Mark 16:8."[1] In this, he echoed the finding of Kurt and Barbara Aland, who wrote: "It is true that the longer ending of Mark 16:9–20 is found in 99 percent of the Greek manuscripts as well as the rest of the tradition."[2]

Elliott stated: "Only two early Greek MSS . . . end Mark at 16:8."[3] The evidence against Mark 16:9–20 also cuts across all Greek text types. The two manuscripts Elliott references which omit the passage are the two earliest manuscripts of Mark 16 in existence. When one considers the work that has been done in this area, one name keeps reoccurring: Bruce Metzger. Metzger continued to revisit the passage over a forty-year span. His work played a crucial role in clarifying the external evidence.

---

1. Kelhoffer, "Witness of Eusebius' *ad Marinum*," 79.

2. Aland, and Aland, *Text of the New Testament*, 292. This is significant, considering they are against the authenticity of the passage, and say it's a later addition—though incorrectly listing some witnesses against the passage, as will be seen below.

3. Elliott, "Last Twelve Verses," 82.

External Evidence

Bruce Metzger and the Changing Perspective concerning Mark 16:9–20

In 1964, Metzger's position concerning the passage was not significantly different from the near-universal scholarly view. While acknowledging all options, Metzger seemed to reject 16:9–20 as belonging in the Gospel.[4] It was during this time—while Metzger was on sabbatical from Princeton Theological Seminary—that he began preparation on what would become *A Textual Commentary of the Greek New Testament*.[5]

In the midst of his work on the project, he encountered "every so often . . . some question—whether great or small,"[6] which had to be resolved before the final product was produced. As it happened, 16:9–20 was one of those problems. Metzger's comments concerning some of the research done up to that point of time in the Ethiopic manuscripts are revealing: "Previously published statements by generally careful and reliable scholars were inadequate, confused, and contradictory. The same manuscripts were cited as containing or as not containing these verses, with or without a shorter ending standing between verses 8 and 9."[7]

In due course, Metzger was able to resolve the problem (as shown earlier). It was perhaps with a bit of sarcasm that he wrote: "Fortunately, not all of the problems that confronted me in writing the textual commentary entailed such extensive research."[8] This work perhaps piqued his interest in the passage itself—especially in view of his discoveries (discussed above) that manuscript 2386 was not a witness against the passage and that no Ethiopic manuscripts of Mark omitted the passage, thus seeming to contradict what had previously been affirmed by scholars.

In 1977, discussing the Armenian version, Metzger affirmed the absence of the passage in the majority of the earlier Armenian copies—yet particularly focused upon one, written AD 989 and introduced by a rubric "of the presbyter Ariston." Metzger commented, "Some scholars, following Conybeare's suggestion, have thought that the words are intended to identify the long ending of Mark as the work of the Ariston who is mentioned by Papias as one of the disciples of the Lord. On the other hand, the

---

4. Metzger, *Text of the New Testament*, 322–26.
5. Metzger, *Reminiscences of an Octogenarian*, 166.
6. Ibid., 167.
7. Ibid.
8. Ibid., 168.

Does Mark 16:9–20 Belong In The New Testament?

identification has been contested by, for example, B. W. Bacon and Clarence R. Williams, who took the Ariston to be Aristo(n) of Pella, who, according to one interpretation of a statement of Moses of Chorene, was the secretary of the Evangelist Mark."[9] Metzger quickly pointed out that others thought the rubric was added in the fourteenth or fifteenth century by an unknown scribe, but was silent concerning his view on the question. In 1987 Metzger's position concerning the passage seemed to modify, at least in print. While still affirming that it was not a product of the same hand that penned the rest of the Gospel, he affirmed its canonicity—with "good reason"—based upon its antiquity and incorporation into such second-century writers as Justin Martyr and Tatian.[10] While investigating the external evidence—and taking away pieces of evidence against its authenticity—Metzger in turn went where it led. Scholars took note of his work and in many cases adjusted their view of the passage.

An Examination of the Manuscript Evidence Against the Passage

Greek Manuscript Evidence Against 16:9–20

The UBS 4th revised edition listed fifteen pieces of evidence against 16:9–20.[11] One of these, manuscript 304, is questionable. Maurice Robinson made these comments after examining a microfilm of the document:

> The primary matter in 304 is the commentary. The Gospel text is merely interspersed between the blocks of commentary material, and should not be considered the same as a "normal" continuous-text MS. Also, it is often very difficult to discern the text in contrast to the comments. Following γάρ at the close of 16:8, the MS has a mark like a filled-in "o," followed by many pages of commentary, all of which *summarize* the endings of the other gospels and even quote portions of them. Following this, the commentary then begins to summarize the ἕτερον δέ the ερά άhe enρκοῦ, presumably to cover the non-duplicated portions germane to that Gospel in contrast to the others. There remain quotes and references to the

---

9. Metzger, *Early Versions of the New Testament*, 163.
10. Metzger, *Canon of the New Testament*, 269–70.
11. Aland et al., *Greek New Testament*, 189. Those listed were ℵ, B, 304, syr[s], cop-sa[ms], arm[mss], geo[1, A], Eusebius, mss[acc. to Eusebius], Epiphanius[1/2], Hesychius, mss.[acc. to Severus], Jerome, and mss[acc. to Jerome]. Of these, only the first three were extant Greek manuscripts.

External Evidence

other Gospels in regard to Mary Magdalene, Peter, Galilee, the fear of the women, etc. But at this point the commentary abruptly ends, without completing the remainder of the narrative or the parallels. I suspect that the commentary (which contains only Mt. and Mk.) originally continued the discussion and that a final page or pages at the end of this volume likely were lost . . . I would suggest that MS 304 should *not* be claimed as a witness to the shortest ending.[12]

Other manuscripts that have been cited in the past as omitting the passage—p45, 16, and 1420—are all damaged. In the case of p45, which dates to AD 225, it omits all of Mark 16, as well as seven other chapters.[13] Manuscript 16 is missing verses 6–20 and manuscript 1420 is also in a state of disrepair—1420 is similar to 2386 in that a page is missing after 16:8.[14] This gives an indication that something happened in the process of transmission of the text. More evidence of similar disruption is not difficult to find.

Vaticanus and Sinaiticus

The two manuscripts which clearly omit 16:9–20 are Vaticanus (B) and Sinaiticus (א), both dating ca. fourth century AD and representing the Alexandrian text. Vaticanus lacks five New Testament books and part of a sixth in addition to Mark 16:9–20.[15] Sinaiticus, discovered in the mid-nineteenth century by Tischendorf at the monastery of St. Catherine on Mount Sinai, was penned by at least three different scribes.[16] It is also the only uncial containing all twenty-seven books of the New Testament. Elliott suggested that both א and B represent one witness against the passage, and not two independent witnesses. He also stated, "The Greek external evidence is not crystal clear."[17] While Elliott was not suggesting acceptance of 16:9–20 and likely was referring to the disruption in the textual stream, his comments are helpful in clarifying matters.

---

12. Elliott, "Nt Manuscripts 1–500."
13. Parker, *Introduction to the New Testament Manuscripts*, 287–88.
14. Kelhoffer, "Witness of Eusebius," 98n80.
15. Metzger, *Manuscripts of the Greek Bible*, 74.
16. Collins, *Codex Sinaiticus and Codex Alexandrinus*, 5–8.
17. Elliott, "Last Twelve Verses," 86.

Does Mark 16:9–20 Belong In The New Testament?

The End of Mark in Vaticanus

Below is an image of Vaticanus at Mark 16:8:[18]

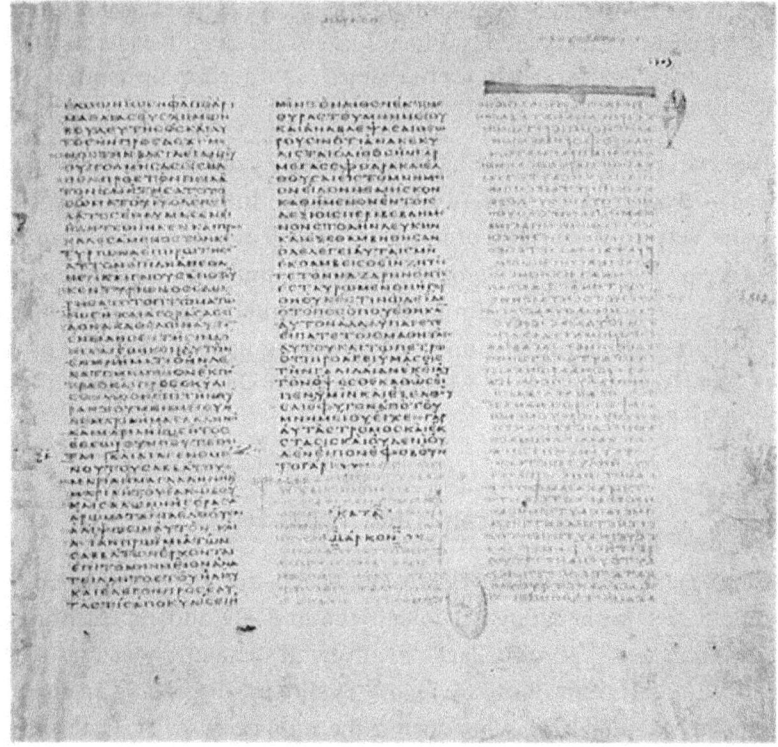

18. Manuscript GA 03, Center for the Study of New Testament Manuscripts, http://www.csntm.org/Manuscript/View/GA_03. Image used by permission from the Center for the Study of New Testament Manuscripts (www.csntm.org).

External Evidence

The End of Mark in Sinaiticus

Below is an image of Sinaiticus at Mark 16:8:[19]

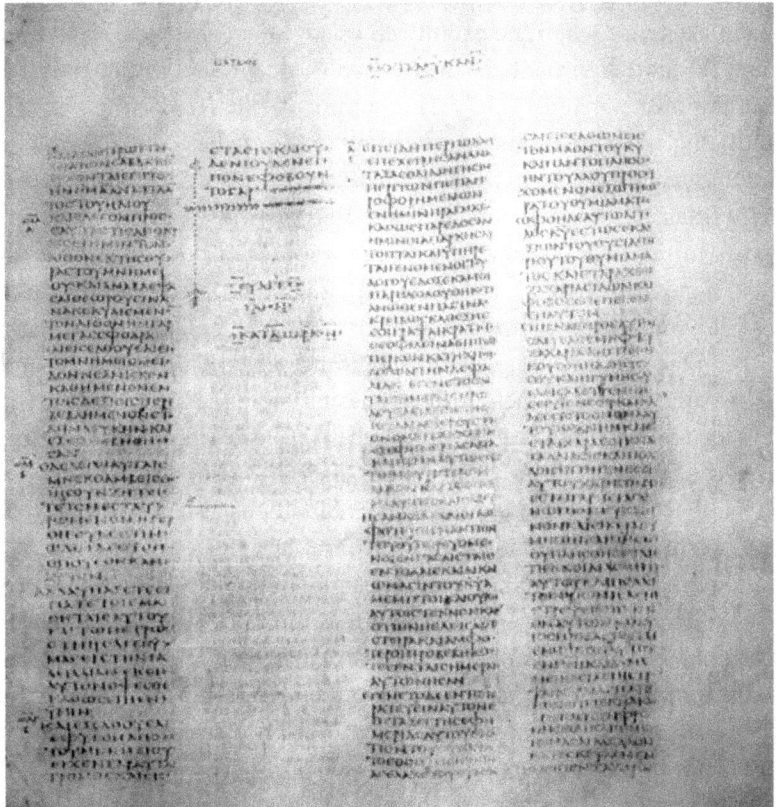

A Closer Look at the Endings of Vaticanus and Sinaiticus

If the endings of both manuscripts were intentional, several problems are apparent. Croy articulates these difficulties well: "We are forced to believe that Mark has committed grammatical and/or stylistic gaffes at the conclusion of his Gospel. We are forced to believe that Mark was either inept, perverse, or astonishingly modernistic as a narrator."[20] Westcott and Hort posed a feasible reason why the scribe of Vaticanus—after 16:8—left the

---

19. Manuscript GA 01, Center for the Study of New Testament Manuscripts, http://www.csntm.org/Manuscript/View/GA_01. Image used by permission from the Center for the Study of New Testament Manuscripts (www.csntm.org).

20. Croy, *Mutilation of Mark's Gospel*, 171.

blank space that exists at that point: "In B, the scribe, after ending the Gospel with v. 8 in the second column of a page, has contrary to his custom left the third or remaining column blank; evidently because one or other of the two subsequent endings was known to him personally. The omitted words were in existence when the extant MS was written, and were known to its scribe."[21] Elliott commented: "Such a gap is exceptional in the New Testament half of this manuscript."[22] This comment, plus Wallace's, opens some potentially fertile areas. The handwriting of the scribes could be examined using modern technology to ascertain exactly how many scribes had possibly written the manuscripts. Is it possible that this phenomenon, where it exists in the Old Testament sections, is found in portions written by a scribal handwriting that is the same as that which copied Mark?

Elliott continued: "It is almost as if the scribe hesitated here. Perhaps his exemplar had the so-called longer ending of Mark, i.e., vv. 9–20, and he had instructions not to include it. His hesitation made him leave the gap to allow for second thoughts, even though, as we are often told, the missing verses could not in practice have been inserted in such a gap if the same size handwriting was to be employed."[23] Sinaiticus also has a cancel-sheet replacement which contains the text from Mark 14:54 to Luke 1:56.[24] The blank space is similar to that of Vaticanus, though it is unclear whether verses 9–20 could fit.[25] Also, 15:47–16:1 is omitted, "and that amounts to about five lines of text."[26] According to Elliott's calculations, 16:9–20 could have fit columns 5 to 10, "although it would have been *very* tight."[27] Elliott's assessment seems reasonable: "these MSS are not straightforward in this matter." Yet verses 9–20 are excluded from two of the oldest manuscripts of the New Testament. It speaks to the weight given B and ℵ that the majority of critical editions of the Greek New Testament, as well as many modern

---

21. Westcott and Hort, *Introduction to the New Testament*, 29–30.

22. Elliott, "Last Twelve Verses," 83. This is in contrast to the assertion by Wallace, "This is *not* a 'wholly singular phenomenon.' Although it is certainly Vaticanus' normal custom to begin a new book at the top of the column following the conclusion of the previous book, this MS breaks that rule on *four* occasions." Wallace, "Mark 16:8," 17. The "four occasions" to which he refers are OT references, not NT.

23. Elliott, "Last Twelve Verses," 84. As noted earlier, Elliott stated that it had been demonstrated by several that it was feasible to insert the passage in the text.

24. Robinson, "Long Ending," 51.

25. Milne and Skeat, *Scribes and Correctors of the Codex Sinaiticus*, 9–11.

26. Elliott, "Last Twelve Verses," 85.

27. Ibid.

External Evidence

English translations, end at verse 8. France said that this "is the virtually unanimous verdict" of modern scholarship.[28] "Until the great Alexandrian codices were known, few paid attention to the scattered references to a Gospel of Mark that lacked a proper conclusion."[29]

Versional Evidence Against 16:9–20

Metzger listed the Old Latin Codex Bobbiensis (it^k), dating to the fourth century and representing the Western text; the Sinaitic Syriac, dating to the third century, also Western; about 100 Armenian manuscripts, representing the Caesarean text; and the two oldest Georgian manuscripts, dating to 897 and 913, also Caesarean.[30] Bobbiensis adds the shorter (or, "Intermediate") ending, which is universally rejected as being authentic: "But they reported briefly to Peter and those with him all that they had been told. And after this Jesus himself sent out by means of them, from east to west, the sacred and imperishable proclamation of eternal salvation." The text of Bobbiensis contains "only about half of Matthew and Mark."[31] It also is "almost identical with that of Cyprian,"[32] which would connect it with the beginning of the third century. Based on the reason that it is a "colorless" ending, Wallace asked, "Why would it have been added to the Gospel? The obvious answer is that the Gospel MS that the scribe had in front of him ended at v. 8."[33] If so, then this is another indication of a problem in the transmission of the text. The Sinaitic Syriac is one of two Old Syriac Gospel-manuscripts, representing the Western text and preserving a form of text that dates to the second or third century.[34] The divided state of the Armenian version concerning 16:9–20 may suggest that it did not originally contain the passage.

To this may be added several manuscripts along with Bobbiensis that precede 16:9–20 with the shorter ending. Majuscule manuscripts L, Ψ, 099, and 0112, dating ca. seventh-ninth centuries, do this. The margin of the Harclean Syriac, dating AD 616, represents the Western text. Several Sahidic and Bohairic manuscripts, from the third-fourth centuries, represent the

28. France, *Gospel of Mark*, 685.
29. Juel, "Disquieting Silence," 1.
30. Metzger, "Textual Commentary," 122–23.
31. Metzger and Ehrman, *Text of the New Testament*, 102.
32. Kenyon, *Text of the Greek Bible*, 146.
33. Wallace, "Mark 16:8," 25.
34. Metzger and Ehrman, *Text of the New Testament*, 96.

Does Mark 16:9–20 Belong In The New Testament?

Alexandrian text. Several Ethiopic manuscripts from the sixth century and representing the Byzantine text also insert the short ending at this point.³⁵

Metzger wrote, "Finally it should be observed that the external evidence for the shorter ending resolves itself into additional testimony supporting omission of verses 9–20. No one who had available as the conclusion of the Second Gospel the twelve verses 9–20, so rich in interesting material, would have deliberately replaced them with four lines of a colorless and generalized summary."³⁶ Thus Metzger stated that the documentary evidence supporting the shorter ending should be added to that supporting ending the Gospel at verse 8.³⁷

An Examination of Evidence For the Passage

Greek Manuscript Evidence For 16:9–20

Below is an image of Codex Alexandrinus (A), which dates to the fifth century:³⁸

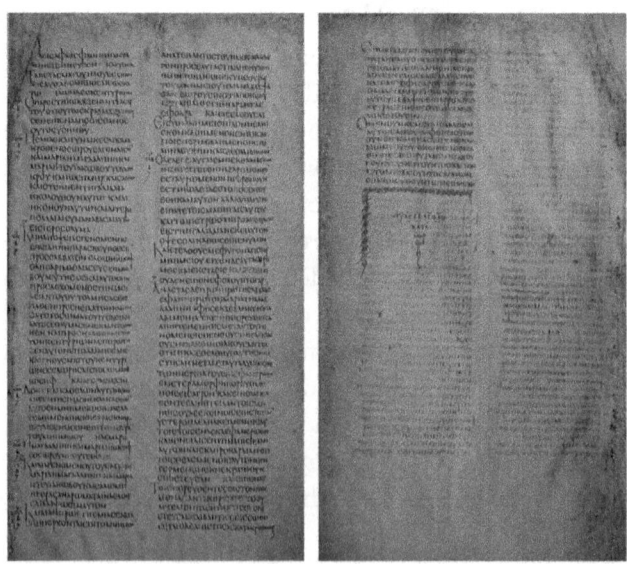

35. Aland et al., *Greek New Testament*, 11*, 27*, 28*, 189.
36. Metzger, *Textual Commentary*, 126.
37. Ibid.
38. Manuscript GA 02, Center for the Study of New Testament Manuscripts, http://www.csntm.org/Manuscript/View/GA_02. Image used by permission from the Center for the Study of New Testament Manuscripts (www.csntm.org).

External Evidence

An accepted tenet of textual criticism is to "weigh" instead of "count" manuscripts. Yet the reading of two of the "Big Three" manuscripts takes precedence over the third. Granted, the age of ℵ and B—as has been shown—is part of the reason for such precedence (along with the fact that A is Byzantine). Since A dates within fifty years of ℵ and B, and also includes all of the New Testament (except for Matt 1–25, which has been lost due to damage), its importance is clear. The UBS Committee heavily relied upon ℵ and B—so much so, that even Elliott felt compelled to critique the practice; after quoting from the Committee concerning selected passages, he wrote: "Such comments betray the reluctance of the editors to deviate too far from those hypnotic MSS. ℵ B. We should not be surprised by this . . . The cult of MSS. rather than the cult of readings is a questionable principle, especially in a text which purports to be eclectic."[39] While one may take issue with his wording, it should encourage prudence in the approach taken to the text.

Along with Alexandrinus, the fifth-century MS *Ephaemi Rescriptus* (C), of the Alexandrian text, also contains the passage. To this may be added Bezae Cantabrigiensis (D), from the Western text, also from the fifth century, along with Codex Sangallensis (Dentury, alonCoridethianus (Qoridethianus (with Cod century and from the Caesarean text. The "Family 13" (f¹³) collection (Caesarean text) includes it, as well as 28 33 157 180 565 597 700 892 1006 1010 1071 1241 1243 1292 1342 1424 1505.[40]

Metzger stated: "Not a few manuscripts which contain the passage have scribal notes stating that older Greek copies lack it, and in other witnesses the passage is marked with asterisks or obeli, the conventional signs used by copyists to indicate a spurious addition to a document."[41]

---

39. Elliott, "Second Look," 328.

40. Aland et al, *Greek New Testament*, 189. The committee did not list the manuscripts in question.

41. Metzger, *Textual Commentary*, 123.

Does Mark 16:9-20 Belong In The New Testament?

Minuscule 1

Minuscule 1 has 16:8 ending at the bottom of a page:[42]

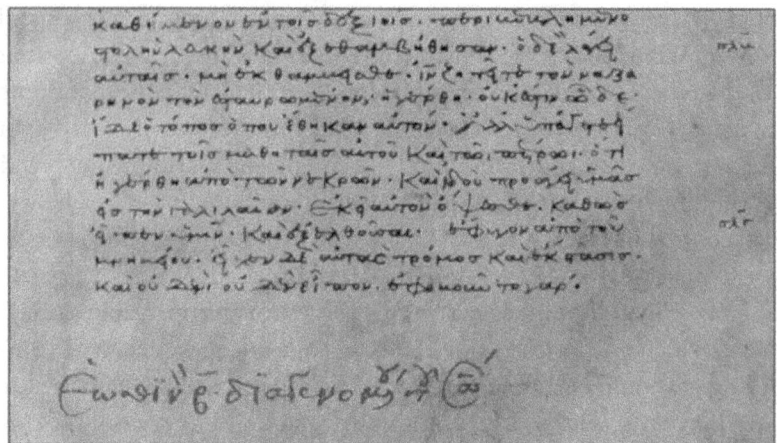

On the top of the next page, there is an annotation:[43]

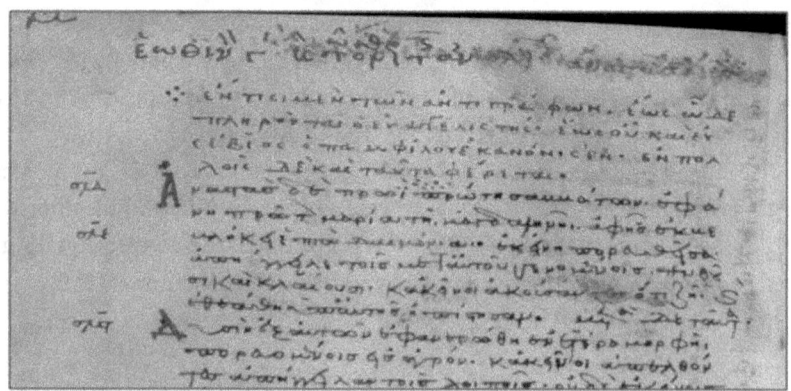

Even though the annotation says that the Eusebian Canons stop at 16:8, someone added an expanded form of the section numbers in the margin. Someone also added (in bright red) rubrics to identify the beginnings of the second and third readings (which begin at 16:1 and 16:9).

---

42. Institut für die neutestamentliche Textforschung, Westfälische Wilhelms-Universität Münster, http://ntvmr.uni-muenster.de/manuscript-workspace. Permission granted via e-mail by Ulrich Schmid, July 3, 2012.

43. Ibid.

External Evidence

Minuscule 22

Minuscule 22 has τέλος (in red) written after 16:8, followed by an annotation between 16:8 and 16:9: "In some of the copies, the Gospel comes to a close here, but in many, this also appears." The annotation is accompanied by an asterisk in the form of a "+" with four dots arranged NE/SE/SW/NW, and the note is indented on both sides:[44]

Minuscule 118

Minuscule 118 has an ordinary ἀρχή symbol between 16:8 and 16:9 (on fol. 105v), showing the lector where to begin the third reading:[45]

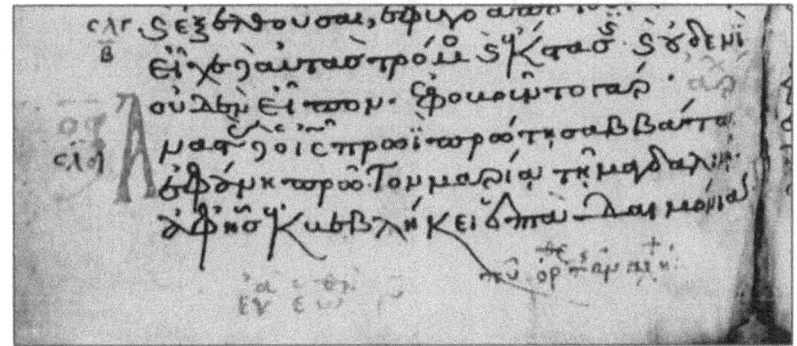

44. Ibid.
45. Ibid.

Does Mark 16:9–20 Belong In The New Testament?

In the lower margin on the left is the abbreviated rubric that means "third Heothina-Gospel." The word "Heothina" refers to a special set of eleven early morning readings.

The same ἀρχή symbol continually appears in 118. On fol. 75v, between Mark 1:11 and 1:12, there is an ἀρχή symbol in the outer margin, and a τέλος symbol in the third line:[46]

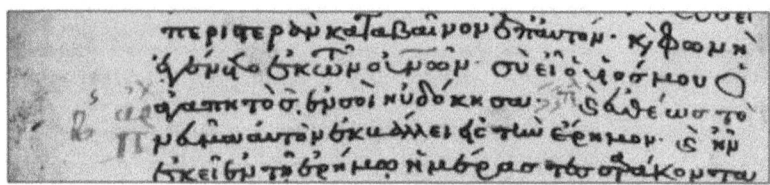

On fol. 92v, between Mark 10:16 and 10:17, there is an ἀρχή symbol in the outer margin, and a τέλος symbol in the third line:[47]

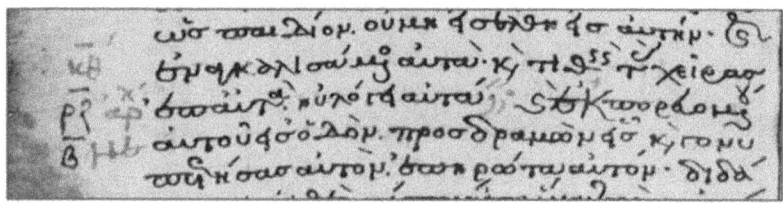

On fol. 112v, between Luke 2:52 and 3:1, there is an ἀρχή symbol in the outer margin, and a τέλος symbol in the third line:[48]

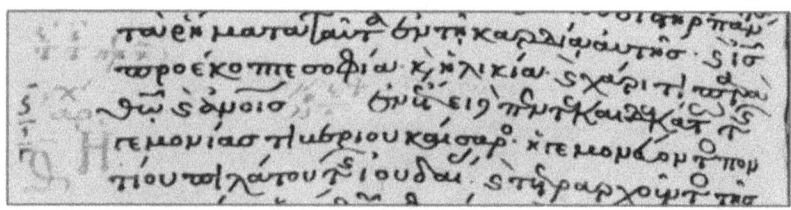

46. Ibid.
47. Ibid.
48. Ibid.

External Evidence

Minuscule 131[49]

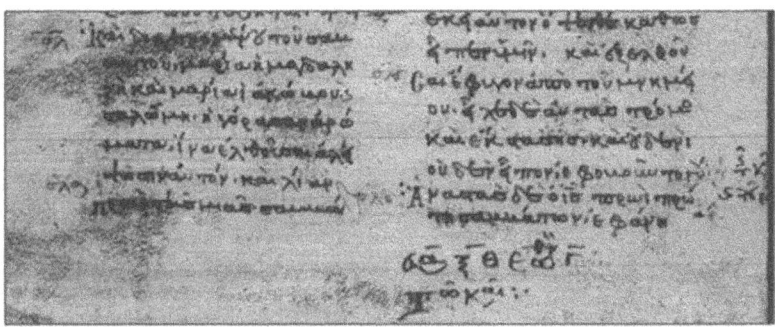

In 131, in image #1600, tightly written in the right margin, are abbreviations indicating a lection break. Notice the abbreviated note in the lower margin identifying the third Heothinon; the three-dot symbol accompanies this note. Compare the format here to the next picture, in which Mark 16:1 begins the second Heothinon-lection in the last line. An abbreviated note meaning "Heothinon #2" is in the left margin. Again, the three-dot symbol accompanied both the note, and the beginning of the lection to which it refers:[50]

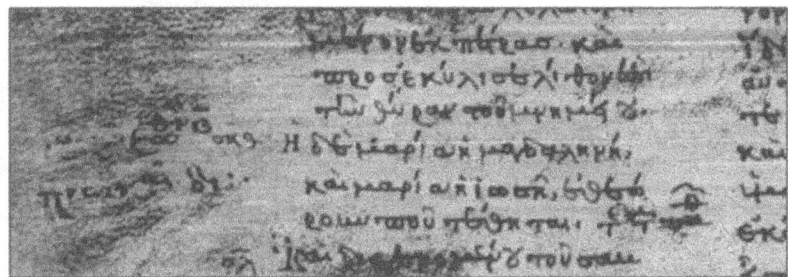

In image #1490, one can see a use of lection-related symbols in each column: in the left column, after Mark 13:13, a τέλος mark is accompanied by an overlined β, signifying "End of #2." A three-dot symbol is in the far left margin. In the right column, after Mark 13:23, a τέλος mark is accompanied by an overlined γ, signifying "End of #3." A three-dot symbol appears two lines later, to the left of the column. These are the ends of the second and third lections for the seventeenth week of the year:[51]

49. Ibid.
50. Ibid.
51. Ibid.

Does Mark 16:9–20 Belong In The New Testament?

Minuscule 157

Minuscule 157 has marks to indicate lection breaks throughout the Gospels. On image #3250, an arch symbol is between Mark 16:8 and 16:9, with thick dots on each side. In the right margin is an abbreviated note identifying this lection as the fourth Heothinon (although it is actually the third). Section numbers can also be seen in the right margin in this picture: 234, at the beginning of 16:9, and 235 at the beginning of 16:11:[52]

Codex 187[53]

Codex 187 does not have any asterisk or obelus accompanying Mark 16:9–20; it has an illustration (one of many throughout the manuscript) between verse 8 and verse 9. The illustration has two parts, depicting Mary

---

52. Ibid.
53. Ibid.

External Evidence

Magdalene encountering Jesus, and Mary Magdalene reporting to the eleven disciples. Section numbers appear in the margin.

Minuscule 199[54]

At the top of the page, a rubric in minuscule 199 identifies Mark 16:9–20 as the third resurrection-gospel (i.e., the third Heothinon). The incipit for this lection is also provided. And, it is identified as the reading for the morning of Ascension Day. When Mark 16:8 ends, a paragraph ends. An ἀρχή symbol is in the left margin; the word τέλος—spelled out horizontally—sits in the otherwise empty space left on the line after the end of 16:9. Mark 16:9 begins on the next line. The A in Ἀναστάς is red, in the margin. Section number 234 is given in the left margin.

In the right margin is a short abbreviated note, written in red; it means, "In some copies this does not occur, but it [that is, the text] stops here." Here is a close-up of the annotation:[55]

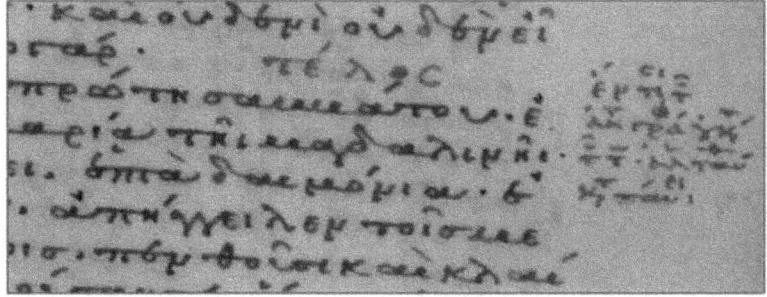

54. Ibid.
55. Ibid.

Does Mark 16:9–20 Belong In The New Testament?

Minuscule 205[56]

A note in the margin of 205 is the same as that found in Minuscule 1: "In some of the copies, the Gospel comes to a close here, and so do Eusebius Pamphili's Canons. But in many, this also appears."

Minuscule 209

In minuscule 209, Mark 16:9–20 is identified in the left margin as the third Heothinon. Mark 16:8 stops about halfway through the line; 16:9 begins the next line (Jesus' name is in the text in the opening phrase of verse 9). In the left margin is the same annotation that is found in codices 1 and 1582:

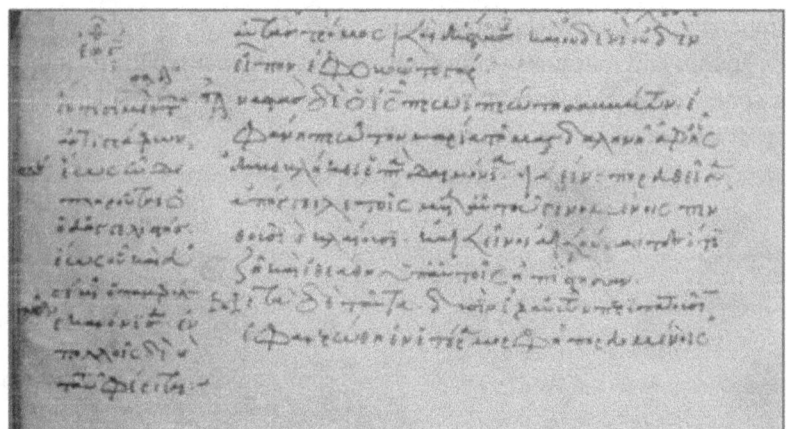

Minuscule 1221

Minuscule 1221 has marks to indicate a lection break; the same marks occur at other lection breaks. In the upper margin is a rubric identifying the

56. Ibid.

third Heothinon (which consists of Mark 16:9–20) and supplying its introductory phrase to be used when the passage is read aloud:[57]

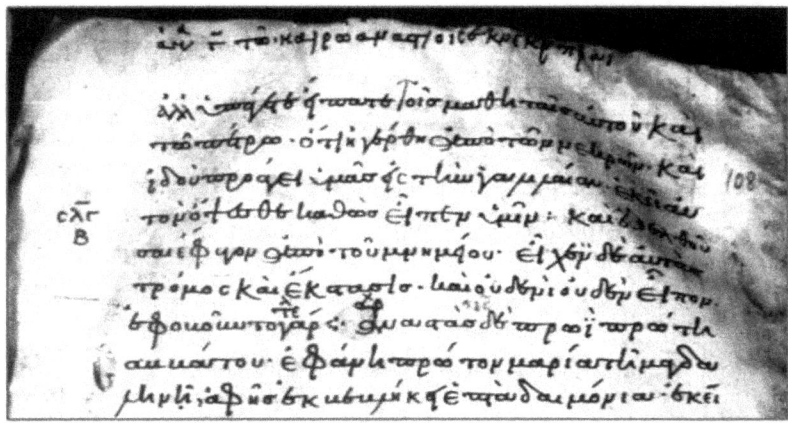

Just in case one looks at this and still imagines that the marks between 16:8 and 16:9 are some strange form of asterisks or obeli, instead of marks which signify ordinary lection breaks, here are a few more examples of those marks from manuscript 1221:

Between Mark 2:12 and 2:13 (fol. 73r)—a chapter break (at the far right of the fourth line):[58]

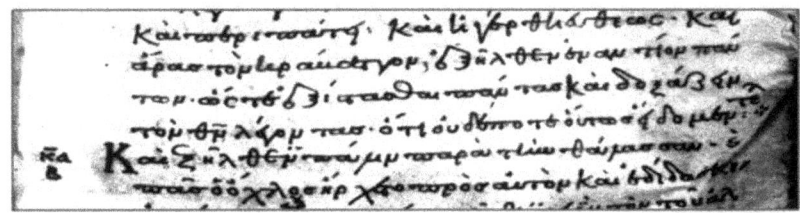

Halfway through Mark 5:24 (fol. 79v)—a chapter break and a lection break (at about the middle of the third line):[59]

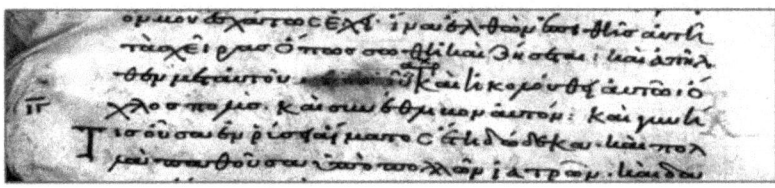

57. Ibid.
58. Ibid.
59. Ibid.

Does Mark 16:9–20 Belong In The New Testament?

Between 6:6 and 6:7 (fol 81r)—a chapter break (at the far right of the third line):[60]

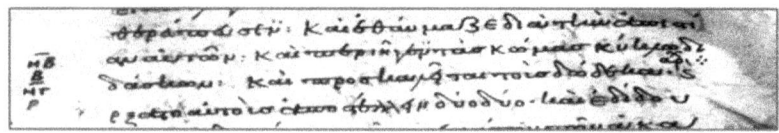

Notice the four-dot symbol. It appears again in the lower margin of the same page. Its purpose is to notify the lector to introduce the lection with the introductory phrase which is written in the margin:[61]

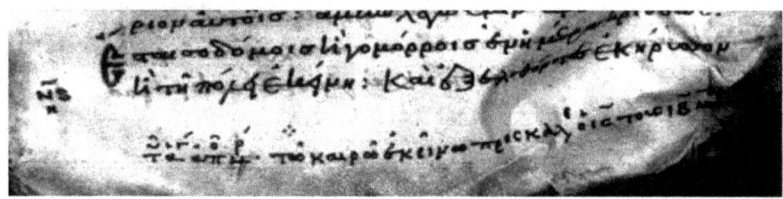

Between Luke 1:25 and 1:26 (fol. 113v):[62]

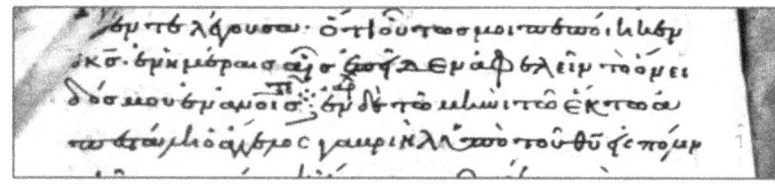

Again the four-dot symbol accompanies a note in the margin for the lector:[63]

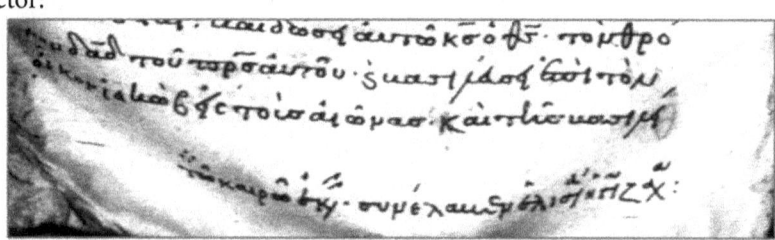

Between Luke 1:56 and 1:57 (fol. 115r):[64]

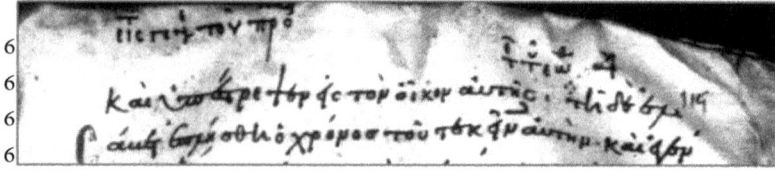

64. Ibid.

External Evidence

A τέλος symbol with the four-dot symbol at the end of Luke 2:20, and an ἀρχή symbol with the four-dot symbol about halfway through Luke 2:22 (fol. 117r):[65]

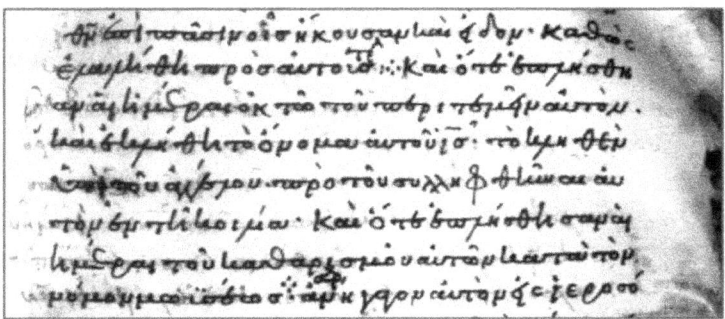

Between Luke 2:40 and 2:41 (fol. 118r)—the four-point symbol appears twice, with a τέλος mark and an ἀρχή mark. The four-dot symbol also accompanies the note in the lower margin:[66]

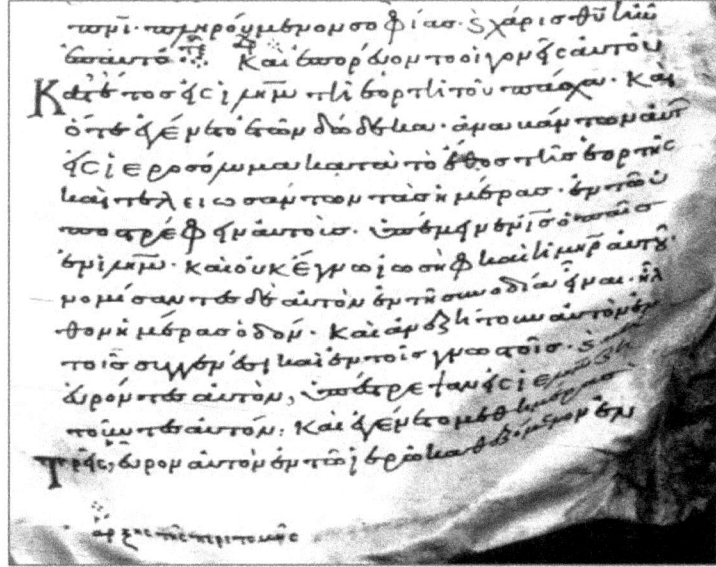

65. Ibid.
66. Ibid.

Does Mark 16:9-20 Belong In The New Testament?

Minuscule 1582

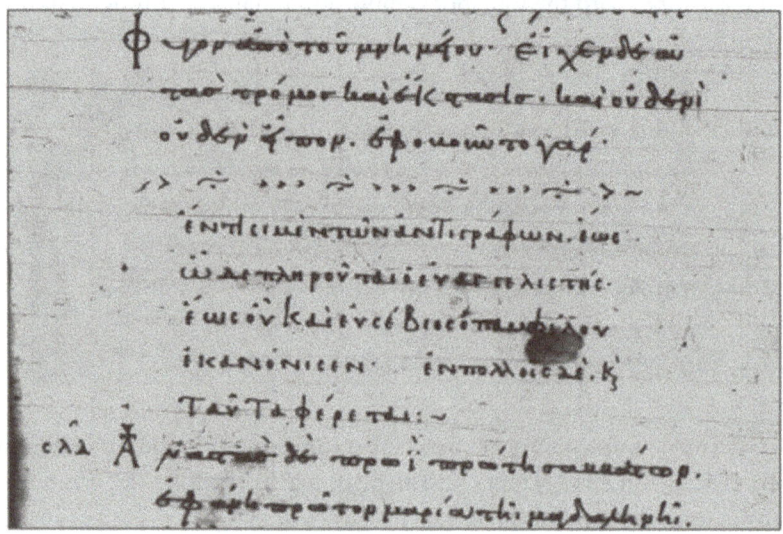

On fol. 133r, between verse 8 and verse 9, the same annotation that appears in Codex 1 is present; here, too, it is in the same column in which the text is written, not in the margin) that says, "In some of the copies the Gospel is finished here, and so do the Eusebian Canons. But in many this also appears," followed by verse 9 (to which is assigned, in the margin, section #234).

Also notable in 1582 is the following note on fol. 134r, in the margin alongside Mark 16:19: "Irenaeus, who lived near the [time of] the apostles, in the third book of his work Against Heresies, wrote about this as Mark's." (This annotation also appears in manuscript 72):[68]

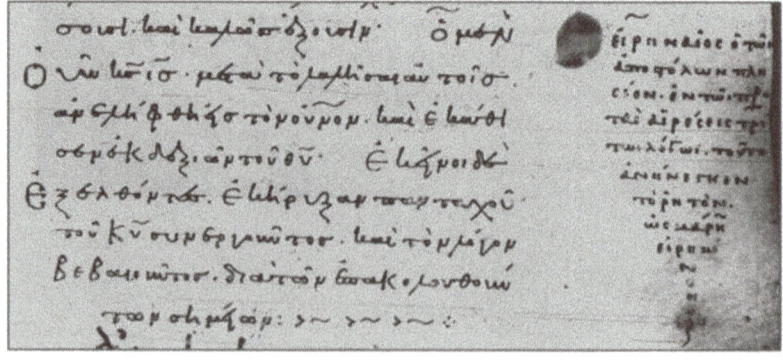

67. Ibid.
68. Ibid.

External Evidence

Minuscule 2346

The following picture features text from Mark 16, framed by commentary on the outer edges of the page. In 2346, the end of Mark 16:8 and the beginning of Mark 16:9 are both on the ninth line. A four-dot symbol is between them, indicating a lection break; the τέλος and ἀρχή symbols are alongside the end of verse 8, and the beginning of verse 9, in the left margin. At the top of the page is the rubric identifying the lection that begins on this page: the third Gospel reading (i.e., the third Heothinon—Mark 16:9–20), followed by the introductory phrase for the lector to use when reading the lection aloud in the church services:[69]

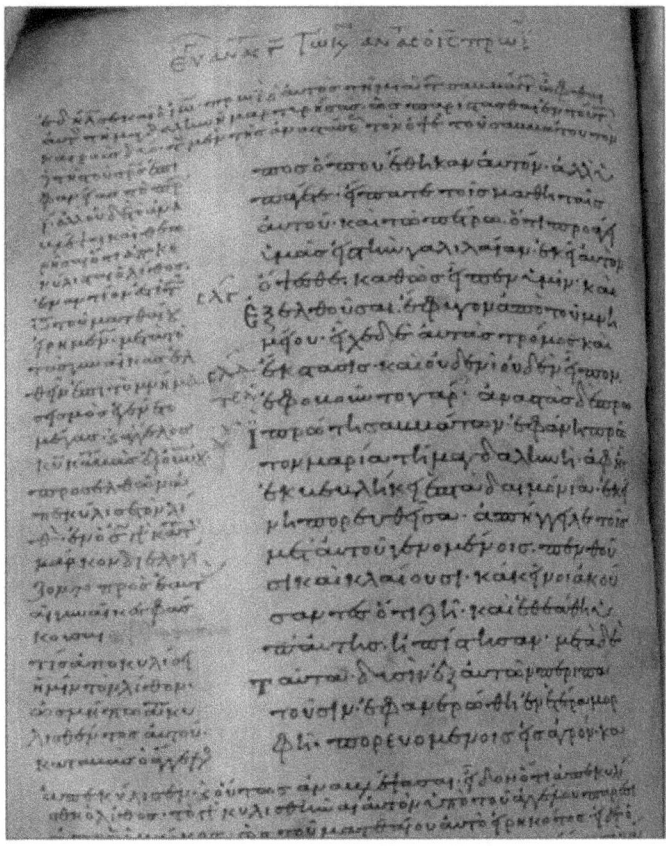

69. Ibid.

Does Mark 16:9–20 Belong In The New Testament?

Manuscript 1241

In 1241, sometimes the copyist made it easier for the lector to finish a sentence or phrase, by placing a final word below the last complete line of text:[70]

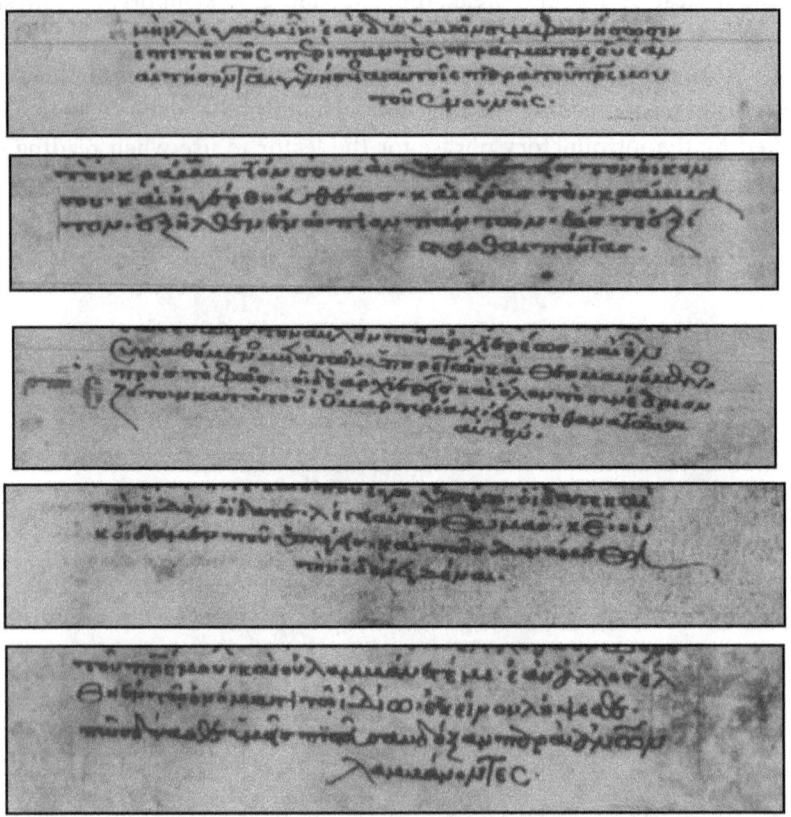

Below is most of the page of 1241 on which Mark 16:8 ends. Notice the marginal note on the right that identifies 16:1 as the beginning of the second Heothinon. Also notice the "+" in the text at the end of chapter 15, and at the end of 16:8:[71]

---

70. Ibid.
71. Ibid.

External Evidence

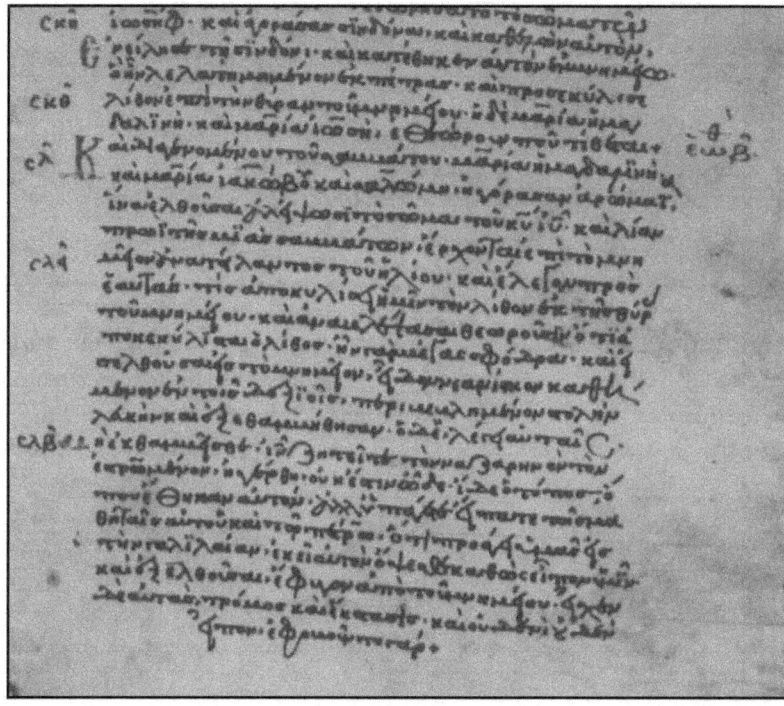

Below is the top of the next page, where 16:9 begins. Notice the margin note identifying the passage as the third Heothinon:[72]

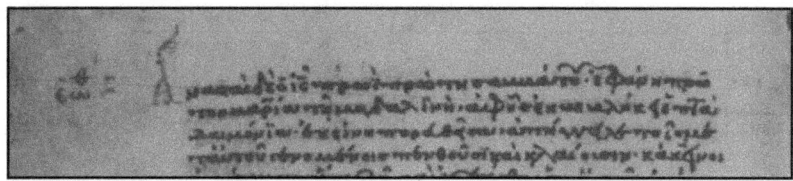

Below is the end of Luke (which is also the end of one of the Heothina):[73]

72. Ibid.
73. Ibid.

Does Mark 16:9–20 Belong In The New Testament?

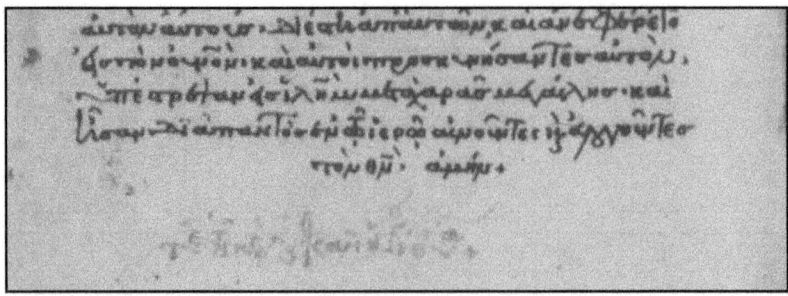

The last line is centered, and there is a "+" at the end, the same as the end of Mark 16:8. Before drawing conclusions, notice the treatment of Heothina #8. At the bottom of the page, John 20:18 is given the same treatment as Mark 16:8:[74]

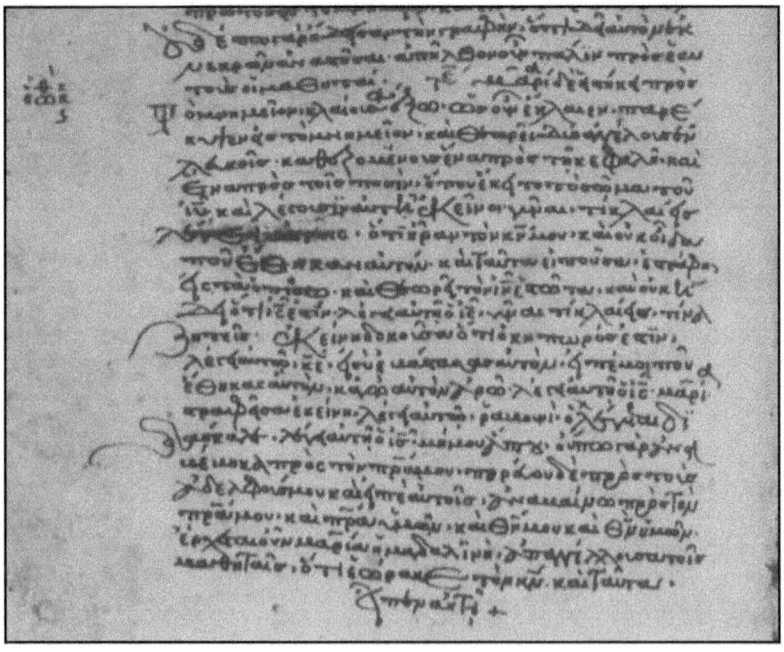

The copyist was making it easier for the lector to identify the end of these Heothina sections when they happened to conclude at the end of a page. Unless one proposes that the copyist thought that John 20:18 was somehow the end of John, it does not seem reasonable to assume that the evidence can be construed that the copyist thought Mark 16:8 was

74. Ibid.

External Evidence

somehow the end of Mark. The significance of this is that the "critical marks or obeli" that supposedly indicate a problem with the text in the non-annotated manuscripts do not. The marks were to help lectors locate the ends of lections.

What of the manuscripts which Metzger described containing scribal notes seeming to indicate that older Greek copies do not have them? There is a group of fourteen manuscripts, falling into two groups. One set of manuscripts with an annotation about Mark 16:9–20 consists of 20, 215, 300, and 199. Manuscripts 20, 215, and 300 contain the Jerusalem Colophon, an annotation stating that the manuscript has been checked using ancient and approved copies at Jerusalem.[75] In 20 and 300 the colophon states after the end of Mark, "The Gospel according to Mark, similarly written and checked from the best copies—1,700 lines, 237 chapters [or, sections]." In 300, the colophon at the end of the Gospel of Matthew says, "The Gospel according to Matthew, written and checked from the old copies at Jerusalem, in 2,514 lines":[76]

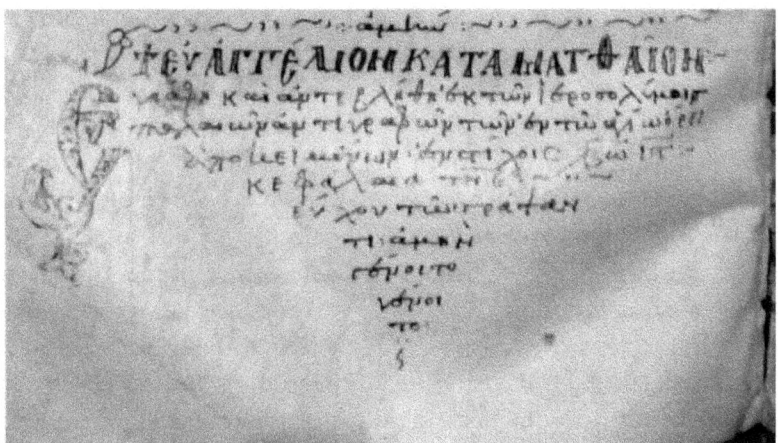

Manuscripts 20, 215, and 300 have the following note at, or near, Mark 16:9 (with some words abbreviated): ἐντεῦθεν ἕως τοῦ τέλους ἐν τίσι τῶν ἀντιγράφων οὐ κεῖται· ἐν δέ τοῖς ἀρχαίοις πάντα ἀπαράλειπτα κεῖται—"From here to the end forms no part of the text in some of the copies. But in the ancient ones, it all appears intact."[77] Those who have gotten the impression that the notes that accompany Mark 16:9–20 state that older copies lack

---

75. Wasserman, "Greek Manuscripts in Sweden," 85–86.
76. Ibid., 106.
77. Burgon, *Last Twelve Verses*, 118–19.

Does Mark 16:9–20 Belong In The New Testament?

the passage may be surprised to learn that the note in 20, 215, and 300 says instead that the ancient copies contain the passage.

The next group of annotated manuscripts is in f1, of the Caesarean text. A subset of this group consists of 1, 205, 205abs, 209, and 1582. They contain the following note, with slight variations: Ἐν τίσι μέν τῶν ἀντιγράφων ἕως ὧδε πληροῦται ὁ Εὐαγγελιστής, ἕως οὗ καί Ἐυσέβιος ὁ Παμφίλου ἐκανόνισεν· ἐν πολλοῖς δέ ταῦτα φέρεται·—"Now in some of the copies, the evangelist's work is finished here, as is also Eusebius Pamphili's Canon-list. But in many, this also appears."[78] As seen above, in Codices 1 and 1582, this note is situated directly above 16:9. Even though this note explicitly says that the Eusebian Canons do not include Mark 16:9–20, the section numbers in 1 and 1582 include the passage: Section 234 begins at 16:9, 235 begins at 16:10, and 236 begins at 16:12.

Five secondary members of this group are also secondary members of f1: 15, 22, 1110, 1192, and 1210. In these manuscripts, a note prefaces 16:9: Ἐν τίσι τῶν ἀντιγράφων ἕως ὧδε πληροῦται ὁ εὐαγγελιστής. Ἐν πολλοῖς δέ καί ταῦτα φέρεται.—"In some of the copies, the Gospel is completed here, but in many, this also appears."[79] This is essentially the same note that is displayed in 1 and 1582, minus the phrase about the Eusebian Canons. Considering that textually 1 and 1582 are closer to the archetype of f1, it seems reasonable to deduce that the note was originally framed as in 1 and 1582, and the phrase about the Eusebian Canons was removed at a time and place where the Eusebian Canons had been expanded so as to include the passage. Like the previous note, this note defends rather than accuses Mark 16:9–20, contrasting "some" copies that lack the passage with "many" copies that include it.

The text of 199 in Luke is aligned with the text of the uncial/minuscule Λ /566 (a codex from the 800's in which Matthew and Mark are written in minuscule lettering and Luke and John are written in uncial lettering), which has the Jerusalem Colophon at the end of each Gospel. Minuscule 199's margin note states, Ἐν τίσι τῶν ἀντιγράφων οὗ κεῖται τοῦτο ἀλλ' ἐνταῦθα καταπαῦει—"In some of the copies this does not occur, but it stops here" (that is, at the end of 16:8).[80]

The statement that "Not a few manuscripts which contain the passage have scribal notes stating that older Greek copies lack it" may be

---

78. Ibid., 120.
79. Ibid., 119.
80. Kelhoffer, "Witness of Eusebius' *ad Marinum*," 107.

External Evidence

brought into focus by observing what some do say. One manuscript (199) says that some copies do not contain 16:9–20. Ten manuscripts (1, 15, 22, 205, 205abs, 209, 1110, 1192, 1582, and 1210) say that some copies do not contain 16:9–20 but many copies do contain it. Three manuscripts (20, 215, and 300) say that some copies do not contain 16:9–20 but the ancient copies do contain it. None of these manuscripts say that the ancient copies do not contain 16:9–20. The notes in the fourteen manuscripts do not state that 16:9–20 is spurious. Except for the short note in MS 199, they state either that the ancient copies contain the passage, or that while it is not found in some copies, many copies contain it. And, rather than constituting fourteen independent lines of evidence, the manuscripts containing these annotations consist of two clusters of related manuscripts: one group shares the Jerusalem Colophon, and the other represents the Caesarean Text. The UBS text did not (at least in print) list all of the manuscripts that were in question.[81] The manuscripts listed above simply indicate that there was an awareness of an issue within the textual stream.

Versional Evidence For 16:9–20

The UBS textual apparatus, in listing the evidence in favor of inclusion, put *Lect* at the beginning of the list of versions. This indicates "the reading of the majority of the lectionaries selected, together with the text of the edition published by Apostoliki Diakonia, Athens."[82] Several Old Latin versions are on the list, some dating to the fifth century: it$^{\text{aur, c, dsupp, ff2, l, n, o, q}}$. The Vulgate, from the fourth century and of the Western text, includes the verses (more will be said about this below). The Curetonian Syriac, (syr^c) from the late 300s of the Western text, is extremely mutilated, but contains 16:17–20. To this may be added the Peshitta (syr^p), the Gospels text of which was translated into Syriac no later than the late 300s, the Palestinian (syr^{pal}) from the sixth century and the Harklensis (syr^h) from the seventh century—all from the Byzantine text.[83] The passage is also found in the Bohairic (cop^{bo}) and Fayyumic (cop^{fay}) manuscripts of the Coptic version.[84] There is a form of the Armenian version (arm), from the Caesarean text,

---

81. Perhaps later editions of the UBS text will name them.
82. Metzger, *Textual Commentary*, 22*.
83. Ibid., 25*–28*.
84. Ibid., 28*.

Does Mark 16:9–20 Belong In The New Testament?

which includes the passage from the fifth century.[85] Farmer asserted: "It is clear that the acceptance of the last twelve verses of Mark was widespread. Throughout the ancient church . . . the evidence for knowledge and acceptance of the authenticity of the last twelve verses of Mark in the ancient church is impressive."[86] The passage is also represented by all Greek text types. Thus, the manuscript evidence indicates that there were two editions of the ending in circulation.

Patristic Evidence Witnesses Against Inclusion

Clement of Alexandria, Eusebius of Caesarea, and Origen

At first glance, the patristic evidence seems decisive. Clement of Alexandria, ca. AD 215,[87] is silent about the long ending. Origen, ca. AD 253/254,[88] also shows "no knowledge of the existence of these verses."[89] According to Kelhoffer, Eusebius of Caesarea, ca. AD 339,[90] is explicit in his comments: "The solution to this might be twofold. For, on the one hand, the one who rejects the passage itself, [namely] the pericope which says this, might say that it does not appear in all the copies of the Gospel according to Mark. At any rate, the accurate ones of the copies define the end of Mark with the words of the young man who appeared to the women and said to them, 'Do not fear. You are seeking Jesus the Nazarene.'"[91]

To this Metzger added: "The original form of the Eusebian sections (drawn up by Ammonius) makes no provision for numbering sections of the text after 16.8."[92] Kelhoffer raised the question of Eusebian authorship

---

85. Ibid.
86. Farmer, *Last Twelve Verses*, 34.
87. Aland et al, 33*.
88. Ibid.
89. Metzger, *Textual Commentary*, 123.
90. Aland et al., *Greek New Testament*, 3rd ed., 33*.
91. Eusebius, *Gospel Problems and Solutions, To Marinus*, 1, trans. Kelhoffer, "Witness," 84.
92. Metzger, *Textual Commentary*, 123. This seems to go against what is listed later in the UBS apparatus: "mss$^{acc.\ to\ Eusebius}$" in favor of inclusion, as well as the same reference in favor of omission. Metzger did not explain in his *Textual Commentary*, though it likely referred to Eusebius knowing of the LE but contending that it was not in most of the manuscripts that he had examined (which will be examined below).

of the writing and said that it needs to be tested.[93] Jerome, ca. AD 419/420, notes that the long ending is found in "scarcely any copies of the Gospel—almost all the Greek codices being without this passage."[94] Yet it is curious to interpret a writer's non-use of twelve verses as if this shows that they were absent from his copies of Mark, when it can be shown that the same writer did not use eleven chapters of Mark. Parker stated: "Those who wish to argue for the originality of the Long Ending point to the weakness of this argument, and not unreasonably. It cannot be argued that the Long Ending was unknown to or rejected by Clement and Origen."[95] There are two statements of Origen that possibly indicate an awareness of the passage. In *Against Celsus*, Origen writes:

> And there is nothing absurd in a man having died, and in His death being not only an example of death endured for the sake of piety, but also the first blow in the conflict which is to overthrow the power of that evil spirit the devil, who had obtained dominion over the whole world. For we have signs and pledges of the destruction of his empire, in those who through the coming of Christ are everywhere escaping from the power of demons.[96] . . . Moreover, the Holy Spirit gave signs of His presence at the beginning of Christ's ministry, and after His ascension He gave still more; but since that time these signs have diminished.[97]

Arguing from silence concerning Origen and Clement is limited, at best. While one cannot say they were aware of the passage, neither can one say they rejected it.

The fourth revised edition of the UBS Greek New Testament changed the list of witnesses against the passage. Whereas previous editions had named Clement and Origen as witnesses against it, the fourth revised edition removed them from the list.[98] As for Eusebius, Kelhoffer attempted to show how the two answers to the first question of Marinus were logically incompatible; he lamented that "many scholars who cite 'Eusebius' as a witness either for or against the authenticity of the Longer Ending highlight the answer that is more congenial to their argument without explaining the

---

93. Kelhoffer, "Witness of Eusebius," 81.
94. Jerome, *Epistle* 120.
95. David Parker, *Living Text of the Gospels*, 136–37.
96. Origen, *Against Celsus* 7.17.
97. Origen, *Against Celsus* 7.8.
98. Aland et al., *Greek New Testament*, 189.

origin of the other conflicting testimony."⁹⁹ A recent translation of Eusebius by David J. D. Miller is as follows:

> The answer to this would be twofold. The actual nub of the matter is the pericope which says this. One who athetises that pericope would say that it is not found in all copies of the Gospel according to Mark: accurate copies end their text of the Markan account with the words of the young man whom the women saw, and who said to them: "Do not be afraid; it is Jesus the Nazarene that you are looking for, etc. . . .," after which it adds: "And when they heard this, they ran away, and said nothing to anyone, because they were frightened." That is where the text does end, in almost all copies of the Gospel according to Mark. What occasionally follows in some copies, not all, would be extraneous, most particularly if it contained something contradictory to the evidence of the other evangelists. That, then, would be one person's answer: to reject it, entirely obviating the question as superfluous. Another view, from someone diffident about athetising anything at all in the text of the Gospels, however transmitted, is that there is a twofold reading, as in many other places, and that both are to be accepted; it is not for the faithful and devout to judge either as acceptable in preference to the other. Supposing the latter point of view to be granted as true, the proper thing to do with the reading is to interpret its meaning.¹⁰⁰

Later in the same paragraph, discussing Mary Magdalene, Eusebius says: "In this way, therefore, he appeared to her 'early in the morning' in Mark also." That this is a reference to Mark 16:9 is acknowledged by the translator.¹⁰¹ Eusebius thus seemed to attribute the statement to Mark.

Eusebius referred to the passage again, in *Gospel Problems and Solutions* 2, in response to another query: "There is then no difficulty in saying that one of them was the Magdalene who, in Matthew, came to the tomb late on the Sabbath; and then again that other, also a Magdalene, came there early in the morning, in John, and that she is the one of whom it is stated in Mark (according to some copies) that 'he had cast seven devils' out of her."¹⁰²

---

99. Kelhoffer, "Witness of Eusebius," 92n63.
100. Pearse, *Eusebius of Caesarea*, 97, 99.
101. Ibid., 98.
102. Ibid., 113.

External Evidence

While it seems here that Eusebius doubted the reference to Mark 16:9 as Markan, there is yet a third reference made to the passage. *Gospel Problems and Solutions* 3 contains this assertion: "Then the Mary in John would be a different person, who gets there later than the others, early in the morning; this would be the same one from whom, according to Mark, he had cast out seven devils."[103] This statement, along with the translation of *Gospel Problems and Solutions* 1 above, seems to contradict the idea that Eusebius believed Mark 16:9–20 was spurious. He was indeed aware of textual problems, as indicated by the answer to Marinus's first question. Eusebius states "one person's answer: to reject it, entirely obviating the question as superfluous."[104] The first approach only made sense because the manuscripts of his day were in the condition that was described by him. His solution would not have made any sense if Marinus and others had not known about how some manuscripts of Mark ended. Some of them known to Eusebius had 16:9–20 and others did not. He acknowledged what some would say in answering the questions posed by Marinus. The textual transmission stream had indeed been interrupted at some point. Yet, Eusebius also attributed verses from the passage to Mark later in his response to Marinus.

Jerome

As to Jerome, the quotation cited earlier is his translation of Eusebius's statement from Greek into Latin. Though Wallace argued that it reflects Jerome's own opinion,[105] this must be discounted—since Jerome included verses 9–20 in the Vulgate, while excluding other verses that did not have sufficient manuscript verification. Two years prior to this, Jerome wrote to Augustine: "Let me therefore frankly say that I have read all these; and storing up in my mind very many things which they contain, I have dictated to my amanuensis sometimes what was borrowed from other writers, sometimes what was my own, without distinctly remembering the method, or the words, or the opinions which belonged to each."[106] This indicates that Jerome was already using other sources; further, he was not heavily engaged in the editing process. In several other works, Jerome stated that he relied

---

103. Ibid., 119.
104. Ibid., 97.
105. Wallace, "Mark 16:8," 22.
106. Jerome, *Epistle* 75, 3.4.

upon secretaries to do much of the work he could have done.[107] While there is no direct indication that he did the same in the matter of the citation from 16: 9–20, it does raise the question if the same practice was used. In another work, Jerome referred approvingly to the Long Ending (verse 14): "Even the Apostles showed unbelief and hardness of heart."[108] Wallace—in arguing for the validity of using Jerome against verses 9–20—attempted to explain why Jerome included the verses in the Vulgate.[109] Regardless of the reason, Jerome did include it in the Vulgate. It seems he believed that the passage belonged in the Gospel.

Witnesses For Inclusion

There are several patristic witnesses in favor of the genuineness of verses 9–20. In some cases they predate not only the manuscript evidence but also the testimony of Eusebius and Jerome.

Papias

Papias, whose *Five Books on the Sayings of the Lord* was completed by AD 110, had only bits and pieces of his work later cited by various writers. Though no evidence is available that Papias quoted directly from 16:9–20, he may have been familiar with the passage. Eusebius indicated this: "But as regards them let it be noted that Papias, their contemporary, mentions a wondrous account that he received from the daughters of Philip. For he recounts a resurrection from the dead in his time, and yet another paradox about Justus who was surnamed Barsabbas, as having drunk a deadly poison and yet, through the grace of the Lord, suffered no harm."[110] An allusion to Mark 16:18 as personified by Justus is thus possible, but not certain.

---

107. This is seen in his works *Against Vigilantius*, *Epistle* 84, and *Epistle* 117—all dating prior to *Epistle* 120.
108. Jerome, *Against the Pelagians*, 2.15.
109. Wallace, "Mark 16:8," 23.
110. Eusebius, *Ecc. History*, 3.39.

External Evidence

Epistle of the Apostles

The *Epistula Apostolorum*, or *Epistle of the Apostles*, is an anonymous composition.[111] First discovered in 1895 in Cairo, the first publication of its text was in 1913. It was translated from Greek into Coptic and Ethiopic (the Ethiopic alone being complete), as well as a small Latin fragment. Hannah proposed that the *Epistle of the Apostles* evidenced a collection of all four Gospels, thus placing them as early as the 140s.[112] While not explicitly quoting from 16:9–20, the author seems to have been familiar with the passage—as indicated by several instances in his writing. It speaks of Jesus' position in heaven where he "sits at the right hand of the throne of the Father,"[113] a reference to Mark 16:19. It also describes the women at the tomb "weeping and mourning."[114] This phrase is identical to that used in Mark 16:10. There is also this statement: "Come, our Master has risen from the dead. And Mary came and told us. And we said unto her: What have we to do with you, O woman? He that is dead and buried, can he then live? And we did not believe her, that our Savior had risen from the dead."[115] This seems to indicate that the author was at least familiar with the passage; he describes the apostles collectively rejecting the testimony of the women who had seen Jesus (as in Mark 16:11–14). Further, the text states: "Then she went back to our Lord and said unto him, 'None of them believed me concerning your resurrection.'"[116] Again, this seems to parallel 16:11. Consider also these citations: "Then the Lord said to Mary and to her sisters, 'Let us go to them.' And he came and found us inside, veiled . . . And he said to us, 'Why do you doubt and are not believing?'"[117] This seems to be another allusion to the collective disbelief of the apostles, only found in 16:11–14—especially verse 14, where Jesus rebukes the apostles for rejecting the testimony of those who had come to tell them of his resurrection. Later, it has Jesus saying, "Go and preach to the twelve tribes of Israel and to the Gentiles and Israel and to the land of Israel towards East and West,

---

111. Muller, "Epistula Apostolorum," 1:251.
112. Hannah, "Four-Gospel 'Canon,'" 632.
113. *Epistle of the Apostles* 3.
114. Ibid., 10.
115. Ibid.
116. Ibid.
117. Ibid., 11.

Does Mark 16:9–20 Belong In The New Testament?

North and South."[118] This could be from Mark 16:15.[119] Taken as a whole, the author of *Epistle of the Apostles* seems to demonstrate a familiarity with 16:9–20.[120] In his commentary on Mark, Robert H. Stein rejected 16:9–20 as authentic. He yet acknowledged that *Epistle of the Apostles* used the passage,[121] as did Hengel—who declared "the connections . . . are particularly striking."[122] Hengel also concluded that the account of the resurrection found in *Epistle of the Apostles* matches best with 16:9–20, dating *Epistle* "at the latest in the middle of the second century, and very probably earlier," and 16:9–20 "to the first decades of the second century."[123]

Justin Martyr

Justin Martyr, who dates ca. AD 153,[124] shows a familiarity with the passage. The phrase ἐξελθόντες πανταχοῦ ἐκήρυξαν[125] ("having gone forth, preached everywhere") is the same as found in Mark 16:20, with one difference. The order of the last two words is reversed.[126] While it is feasible that Justin knew the passage, there are those who take issue. In the most recent critical text published of Justin's *Apology*, the editors do not list 16:20 as a Scripture cited.[127] Yet, the very words chosen by Justin seem to be more than just coincidental. The phrase from both works is virtually the same. It is probable that Justin was at least alluding to Mark 16:20. Kelhoffer used Justin as a witness to the antiquity of the passage, and also referenced words

---

118. Ibid., 30.

119. But see Hannah, "Four Gospel 'Canon,'" 625, who *contra* Hornschuh and Hill, believes it fits better with the Intermediate Ending.

120. Hannah says it is "possible, but far from certain" that the author reflected knowledge of 16:9–20. He regarded that as "unfortunate," because of the date assigned to 16:9–20 by Kelhoffer. "Thus, if it could be shown that the author of the *Epistula* in fact knew the long ending it could potentially provide crucial evidence for the origin of the *Epistula*" (ibid).

121. Stein, *Mark*, 728.

122. Hengel, *Studies in the Gospel of Mark*, 168.

123. Ibid. Hengel also rejected Markan authorship of the passage, and stated that he believed the "harmonizer and epitomator" drew freely from the Gospels and Acts, along with other sources.

124. Minns and Parvis, *Justin, Philosopher and Martyr*, 33.

125. *Justin Martyr, First Apology* 45.5 (Minns and Parvis, 198).

126. In the UBS text the phrase is ἐξελθόντες ἐκήρυξαν πανταχοῦ.

127. In fact, at the phrase in 1.45.5, Minns and Parvis have no notation.

and phrases used by Justin that possibly reflect knowledge and use of the passage.[128] Assuming Justin cited it, it would indicate that the long ending existed prior to AD 150.[129]

Irenaeus

Irenaeus also dates toward the middle of the second century. In *Against Heresies*, there seem to be two citations from 16:9–20. In book 1, there is this statement concerning Jesus, which is a reference to verse 19: "Then he was assumed into heaven, where Jesus sits at the right hand of his Father."[130] In book 3 there is a quotation from Mark 16:19: "Also, towards the conclusion of his Gospel, Mark says: 'So then, after the Lord Jesus had spoken to them, He was received up into heaven, and sitteth on the right hand of God.'"[131] This statement about Mark 16:19 is specifically mentioned in a Greek margin note in Codex 1582 and in Codex 72 (which implies that the note was present in the archetype of Family 1, in the late 400's). Westcott and Hort accepted this quotation by Irenaeus as genuine.[132] One might dispute this by pointing to the uncertainty of the text. The writings of Irenaeus are known in a Latin translation of a later date, and how much it was emended is unknown. However, Kelhoffer had no problem citing Irenaeus as using the passage. Kelhoffer refers to it as an "unambiguous citation of Mark 16:19 as a part of the end of Mark's Gospel."[133] Because of the patristic evidence, Kelhoffer stated that 16:9–20 dates at least to the early decades of the second century.[134] In light of the support of Markan authorship of 16:9–20 by mid-second-century authors—whether one accepts or rejects 16:9–20—the passage is ancient, well-attested, and accepted by the early church. This is borne out by the number of third-century patristic writers who quoted from 16:9–20 and attributed it to Mark.

---

128. Kelhoffer, "Miracle and Mission," 170–75.
129. Farmer, *Last Twelve Verses*, 31.
130. Irénée de Lyon, *Contre les hérésies*.
131. Irenaeus, *Against Heresies*, 3:10:5.
132. Westcott and Hort, *Introduction to the New Testament*, 39.
133. Kelhoffer, *Miracle and Mission*, 170.
134. Ibid., 175.

Does Mark 16:9–20 Belong In The New Testament?

Tertullian

Tertullian was listed in the third edition (corrected) UBS text as supporting inclusion of the passage.[135] However, the reference to Tertullian was noticeably absent in the fourth edition. In at least four of Tertullian's writings (*Against Praxeas, Scorpiace, Apology, Persecution*) he at the least alludes to the passage, although not directly quoting from it. Two of the citations seem to point directly to 16:9–20. From Tertullian's *Apology*: "Thereafter, having given them commission to preach the gospel through the world, He was encompassed with a cloud and taken up to heaven."[136] From *On Running Away From Persecution*: "So we preach throughout all the world; nay, no special care even for Israel has been laid upon us, save as also we are bound to preach to all nations."[137] These two quotations utilize phraseology similar to what is said by Jesus in 16:15: "Go into all the world, and preach the Gospel to every creature." Aland affirmed that Tertullian used 16:9–20.[138] Tertullian wrote in the early third century, passing away sometime after AD 220.

Vincentius of Thibaris

In AD 257, Vincentius of Thibaris seemed to refer to verses 17–18 of the passage: "We know that heretics are worse than Gentiles. If, therefore, being converted, they should wish to come to the Lord, we have assuredly the rule of truth which the Lord by His divine precept commanded to His apostles, saying, 'Go ye, lay on hands in my name, expel demons.' And in another place: 'Go ye and teach the nations, baptizing them in the name of the Father, of the Son, and of the Holy Ghost.' Therefore first of all by imposition of hands in exorcism, secondly by the regeneration of baptism, they may then come to the promise of Christ. Otherwise I think it ought not to be done."[139] This appears to be a reference to the promise made by Jesus concerning miraculous gifts, though the wording is not identical. The

---

135. Aland et al., *Greek New Testament*, 3rd ed., 196f.

136. Tertullian, *Apology* 21.

137. Tertullian, *On Running Away from Persecution*, 6.

138. Aland and Aland, "Bemerkungen Zum Schluss Des Markusevangliums," 157–80; ss cited in Snapp, "External Footprints."

139. Vincentius of Thibaris, as quoted in Cyprian, "Seventh Council of Carthage," trans. Ernest Wallis, in Roberts and Donaldson, eds., *Ante-Nicene Fathers*, 5:569.

laying on of hands is not linked to the expelling of demons in 16:9–20. Yet, the context of the citation by Vincentius has a similarity to the long ending, especially since the latter quote is from the end of Matthew.

The Gospel of Nicodemus

The *Gospel of Nicodemus* also includes citations from verses 15–19. Two places utilize it—the first being from *Part I: The Acts of Pilate*: "We have seen Jesus and his disciples sitting on the mountain called Mamilch; and he was telling his disciples, Go into all the world, and preach to all creation. The one who believes and is baptized will be saved, but the one who disbelieves will be condemned. These signs will accompany those who believe: they will cast out demons in my name; they will speak in new tongues; they will pick up snakes; and if they drink anything poisonous, it will not harm them; they will lay their hands on the sick and they will become well."[140] The second citation is found in *Part II: The Descent of Christ into Hell*. It places Jesus on the Mount of Olives saying: "Go into all the world and preach the Gospel. Whoever will believe and be baptized will be saved; but whoever will not believe will be condemned."[141] The date for the *Gospel of Nicodemus* is disputed. Ehrman and Plese state the difficulties:

> There is no certainty that Justin actually knew a Gospel comparable to the one that lies before us, although he may have heard of the existence of one. If Epiphanius knew our text (what little he says about it corresponds to what we have here), then it must have been written by the middle of the fourth century. But given the extensive variation in the textual tradition of the text, it is also possible that there were multiple forms of the tradition circulating in different times and places. And so some scholars date the composition of this work not until the fifth or sixth centuries (Elliott), others put it in the middle of the fourth century (Klauck), and yet others, somewhat optimistically, place it all the way back in the second century (Scheidweiler). Possibly Zbigniew Izydorczyk (1997) is the most judicious in suggesting that the composition lying at the foundation of our surviving manuscripts was created

---

140. Ehrman and Plese, *Apocryphal Gospels*, *Acts of Pilate* 14.1. The authors commented that the most recent scholar to attempt a critical edition of the Greek text was Tischendorf, in 1853. They did indicate that one was under way for the Corpus Christianorum Series Apocryphorum: 419, 422.

141. Ibid., *Descent of Christ into Hell* 14.1.

in the fourth century, based on traditions in circulation already some two hundred years earlier.[142]

Kelhoffer tentatively placed the date of the document prior to Justin, though he acknowledged the connection with Justin was uncertain.[143]

On Rebaptism

One other third-century witness to 16:9–20 is *On Rebaptism*, which was anonymously composed ca. AD 258:[144] "And some of themselves, when they had seen Him, believed not, but doubted; and they who were not then present believed not at all until they had been subsequently by the Lord Himself in all ways rebuked and reproached."[145] The date of composition of the second- and third-century witnesses to 16:9–20 for the most part predates the earliest Greek manuscripts and provides attestation as to the existence, acceptance, and circulation of the passage.

What Does the External Evidence Indicate?

When all the data are considered, several things are clear. First, there was an issue with the Greek text at the ending of Mark, possibly as early as the second century. This is borne out by the number of references to manuscripts ending at verse 8, the existence of the shorter ending, the two oldest manuscripts not containing 16:9–20, and the patristic witnesses who call attention to copies of Mark ending at verse 8. Second, Mark 16:9–20 was in circulation, accepted by some patristic witnesses as part of Mark and written by Mark, and accepted by the early church, in the second century (likely in the early part of the century). Third, the evidence both for and against inclusion of the passage is represented by all Greek text types. Whether one accepts or rejects Mark 16:9–20, one thing is clear: the external evidence for inclusion is stronger than has been presented by some scholars in the past.

---

142. Ibid., 420.

143. Kelhoffer, "Miracle and Mission," 177.

144. Aland, et al., *Greek New Testament*, 3rd ed., 37*.

145. *On Rebaptism* 9.7. It is listed as favorable to the passage in the UBS 4th ed. text, 189.

CHAPTER 3

Internal Evidence

Could the Gospel Have Ended with ἐφοβοῦντο γάρ?

Concerning whether the Gospel of Mark could have ended with ἐφοβοῦντο γάρ ("for they were afraid"), Bruce Metzger expressed the misgivings of many scholars: "ἐφοβοῦντο γάρ of Mark xvi.8 does not represent what Mark intended to stand at the end of his Gospel."[1] This echoed the judgment of Westcott and Hort: "It is incredible that the evangelist deliberately concluded either a paragraph with ἐφοβοῦντο γάρ, or the Gospel with a petty detail of a secondary event, leaving his narrative hanging in the air."[2] Nevertheless, it is a popular trend among modern scholars to advance the notion that Mark intended to end at verse 8: "If Mark wrote first, he created a new literary genre that would be later called *Gospel*. I suspect that because of the magnitude and uniqueness of Jesus, Mark also wanted to point to him in such a way that got the readers involved in the story. Of *all* the Gospels, Mark tends to leave it to the *reader* to form an opinion about Jesus rather than telling the reader what he must believe . . . Mark wants them to work things out for themselves—not in an academic, detached way, but by coming to grips with Jesus of Nazareth."[3]

---

1. Metzger, *Text of the New Testament*, 228.
2. Westcott and Hort, *Introduction to the New Testament*, 46.
3. Wallace, "Mark 16:8," 37.

Does Mark 16:9–20 Belong In The New Testament?

Building upon the work of van der Horst,[4] several scholars proposed that the author of Mark utilized what are now considered modern literary styles. Petersen suggested that the modern literary technique of "reader-response" came from the Gospel.[5] Boomershine's view was that the idea of narrative criticism was inspired by Mark.[6] Hester posited "ironic conclusion" as the key to understanding the abrupt ending.[7] Danove even went so far as to assert that "a conclusion in γάρ is at least acceptable according to the canons of contemporary literary practice."[8] Could a book end with γάρ? Van der Horst argued for the thirty-second treatise of Plotinus's *Ennead* as an example. This chapter division is the only example in all of Greek literature of a "book" ending in γάρ. This is not the end of the *Ennead*, only one treatise. Also, it is clear that Plotinus here is not being abrupt, only making an obvious conclusion. Croy stated: "As van der Horst himself acknowledges, the writings of Plotinus have been cut up and rearranged by his pupil, Porphyry. This 'final γάρ' example actually did have a continuation prior to being edited. The 32nd treatise of Plotinus, therefore, is a dubious example of γάρ ending a book."[9] Cox embarked on an extensive search of ancient works for a similar ending to Mark 16:8. He "found that one thousand and five sentences end with γάρ followed by a period and roughly 500 sentences end with γάρ followed by a question mark."[10] As has been seen, Cox found that although sentences and paragraphs could (and did) end with γάρ, the situation was different when it applied to an ancient book: "The ISC did not list any ancient works that end with γάρ except Mark 16:8 followed by 16:9–20 in the textual marks."[11] Even this does not emphasize the more important point: of all extant ancient works, none have the kind of ending found at Mark 16:8. That is to say, none end with any kind of suspense or unresolved questions. Some of those who advocate verse 8 being the end say that this is exactly the point—that the author of Mark was a literary genius. Yet, this seems to make the author of the Gospel too clever by half. While listing the reasons in favor of verse 8 being the end, Stein

---

4. Van der Horst, "Can a Book End," 121–24.
5. Petersen, "When Is the End," 151–66.
6. Boomershine, "Mark 16:8," 225–39.
7. Hester, "Dramatic Inconclusion," 61–86.
8. Danove, *End of Mark's Story*, 130.
9. Croy, *Mutilation of Mark's Gospel*, 49.
10. Cox, *History and Critique of Scholarship*, 152.
11. Ibid., 157.

Internal Evidence

registered this objection: "The various explanations given would not have convinced first-century readers of Mark. These explanations seem to arise from a twentieth-century existentialism that revels in paradox. It is based less on understanding Mark's own purpose in writing his Gospel than on modern literary theory."[12] France was even more emphatic in his rejection.

> For me the "abruptness" of the ending consists not primarily in the stylistic form of its final sentence, but in the "unfinished" nature of its contents . . . And my own inclination is to side with the increasingly unfashionable minority who find an intentional ending at 16:8 an unacceptably "modern" option . . . I do not find any of them persuasive, because they all seem to presuppose an inappropriately "modern" understanding of literary technique both in terms of how writers wrote and of how readers might be expected to respond. The natural response to v. 8 is surely to assume that this apologetically damaging anticlimax *cannot* be the end.[13]

Basic rules of hermeneutics point away from a primarily modern "grid" being placed over the ancient text. The situation is akin to some modern interpretations of the book of Revelation—paying scant attention to first-century readers, while focusing all too much on twenty-first-century circumstances. The comments by France are to the point: "Ancient authors were more in the habit of saying as clearly as possible what they meant and what conclusions they intended their readers to draw than of teasing the reader with unfulfilled promises and undelivered messages."[14] Far from being straightforward and clear, an ending which leaves the women afraid and the disciples cowering does not inspire much confidence.

Conversely, E. J. Pryke—while advocating the view that the Gospel ended at verse 8—said that Mark did so in spite of his lack of ability:

> An analysis of the twelve sentences with φοβεῖσθαι reveals that half of them simply state the fear of the parties concerned, which are the people, the disciples, or the women at the tomb. The other six are more precise, referring to Herod's fear of John, the disciples' inability to answer, the scribes' and the chief priests' fear of Jesus, the scribes, the chief priests' and the elders' fear of the people. *With so many grammatical and stylistic errors* in a Gospel which also abounds in parenthesis, asyndeton, and anacolouthon, and in the case of *an author who was no literary genius*, arguments based

---

12. Stein, *Gospel of Mark*, 735.
13. France, *Gospel of Mark*, 672–73, 683.
14. Ibid., 671–72.

on style can be very precarious. Considering, however, that in 9:6, 11:18, 12:12 γάρ is found, the usage seems well in keeping with the redactional style and theology of the author. The positioning of the explanatory γάρ clause after the main statements does not support Taylor's plea that "the natural sequel to ἐφοβοῦντο γάρ would be a μή clause." It might be so if *the author were a better writer, or other than Mark*. Such a sequence is well supported by the redactional syntax, and theology, elsewhere in the Gospel. Coupled with this, we should recall the ambiguity and difficulty of interpretation in the opening of the Gospel. Marcan usage then would support 16:8 as the genuine ending of the Gospel, and in keeping with style and literary ability.[15]

There are several arguments in favor of the ending of Mark continuing beyond verse 8, as presented by Gundry. Among them are these:

> Sometimes Mark closes pericopes on the note of fear (4:41; 9:32; 11:18; 12:12), but more usually he strikes this note earlier (5:33, 36; 6:20, 50; 9:6; 10:32; 11:32) . . . Γάρ-clauses end pericopes in 1:38; 3:35; 6:52; 10:45; 11:18c; 12:44 (cf. 4:25), but these instances represent only a small fraction of the sixty-six γάρ-clauses scattered throughout the book . . . Since the fact of Resurrection appearances was clearly an element of the primitive preaching (cf. I Cor xv.5ff., and also Acts i.22, ii.32, iii.15, x.41, xiii.31), it is highly improbable that Mark intended to conclude his Gospel without at least one account of a Resurrection appearance.[16]

In Mark 14:28 Jesus told his disciples, "But after I have risen, I will go ahead of you into Galilee." At the empty tomb in Mark 16:7, an angel reaffirmed, "He will go ahead of you into Galilee." This presupposes a meeting—which took place in Mark 16:14–18. The Great Commission was given by Jesus on a mountain in Galilee (Matt 28:16). Without 16:9–20, the promise to meet in "Galilee" in Mark is never realized—it is a loose end. Some suggest that Mark was never able to write the ending, or that there existed an ending that was subsequently lost.[17] Joel Marcus tried to rebut this argument by comparing Mark's story of Jesus to a film about the life of John F. Kennedy:

> Imagine a film about the life of John F. Kennedy that concludes with footage of the fateful visit to Dallas on November 22, 1963.

15. Pryke, *Redactional Style*, 45; emphasis added.
16. Gundry, *Mark*, 1011–12.
17. Stein, *Mark*, 737.

Internal Evidence

> The motorcade threads its way through the streets of downtown Dallas; President and Mrs. Kennedy sit in an open convertible, waving happily to the crowds in the bright sunshine—and there the movie ends. There is no depiction of the gunshots ringing out, of the President slumping forward, of the limousine suddenly picking up speed, of the First Lady cradling the President's head in her lap. But these events are all the more powerfully evoked by not being portrayed, because *everyone knows what will happen next*. It may be that Mark's ending is meant to function in a similar way. Everyone in the Markan audience knew that the reunion in Galilee prophesied in 14:28 and 16:7 had actually taken place.[18]

While clever, the reasoning employed by Marcus does not hold up. If Mark's first audience did know about the resurrection of Jesus, would they have also then known about the crucifixion? The question rises, why not leave it off as well? Mark's Gospel was also intended for those who knew nothing of Jesus' life. Ultimately, Marcus's attempt at downplaying the internal argument for a continuation falls short. As has been shown, no ancient book ends with γάρ; and, no paragraph in the Gospel of Mark ends with γάρ. Since the arguments in favor of such an ending have a distinctly twentieth- or twenty-first-century flavor, one is compelled to reject them. How would first-century readers of the Gospel have reacted to an account of the life of Jesus—written by a close companion of Peter—without an account of the resurrection from the tomb? Such an approach to the book virtually ignores not only the evidence from the text, but also the first-century setting of the Gospel. There must have been more to the text of Mark 16.

Could Mark Have Used Certain Words That Are Found in Mark 16:9–20?

Metzger summarized two of the main internal arguments against inclusion:

> The longer ending, though current in a variety of witnesses, some of them ancient, must also be judged by internal evidence to be secondary. (a) The vocabulary and style of verses 9–20 are non-Markan (e. g. ἀπιστέω, βλάπτω, βεβαιόω, ἐπακολουθέω, θεάομαι, μετά ταῦτα, πορεύομαι, συνεργέω, ὕστερον are found nowhere else in Mark; and θανάσιμον and τοῖσ μετ᾽ αὐτοῦ γενομένοις, as designations of the disciples, occur only here in the New Testament). (b) The connection between ver. 8 and verses 9–20 is so awkward that

---

18. Marcus, *Mark*, 2:1095.

it is difficult to believe that the evangelist intended the section to be a continuation of the Gospel.[19]

Sixteen words used in this section are not used elsewhere in the Gospel of Mark. Three of these words are used more than once in this section, and this section does not contain two of Mark's favorite words. The word εὐθύς (meaning "immediately") is used forty-three times by Mark; Pryke states that its function is "as a connecting word, and at the same time as a stylistic device which creates movement and liveliness."[20] The word πάλιν ("again") is used twenty-eight times in Mark; Pryke states that the "main function of πάλιν, therefore, is as a linking word, referring back to the previous incidents of a similar character (teaching, journeys, missions). Its function appears to be twofold: it helps to weave together the disjointed pericopae, making a 'Gospel' which moves on from stage to stage, its ultimate point being the Passion and Resurrection."[21] The additional words to what Metzger listed are πενθέω, ἕτερος, μορφή, ἕνδεκα, παρακολουθέω, ὄφις, and ἀναλαμβάνω. Also to be included are πορεύομαι, θεάομαι and ἀπιστέω. Williams listed the same sixteen words.[22] Terry replied by making two points:[23]

> In all fairness, however, it should be pointed out that eight of these sixteen do have their word root used elsewhere in Mark. Πορεύομαι may not be used before this section, but its compounds are used 25 times elsewhere (εἰσπορεύομαι—8 times; ἐκπορεύομαι—11 times; παραπορεύομαι—4 times; προσπορεύομαι—once; συμπορεύομαι—once); in fact πορεύομαι itself is a variant reading in Mark 9:30. It is certainly no surprise to find this word used three times in this section. Ἀπιστέω is not found elsewhere in Mark, but its noun form ἀπιστία ("unbelief") is found not only in this section (v. 14), but twice elsewhere (6:6; 9:24). Μορφή is not found elsewhere in the four Gospels, but μεταμορφόομαι ("transfigure, transform") is found in Mark 9:2. Παρακολουθέω and ἐπακολουθέω are found only here in Mark, but ἀκολουθέω is used 19 times in Mark and συνακολουθέω twice. Θανάσιμος occurs only here in the New

---

19. Metzger, *Textual Commentary*, 125.
20. Pryke, *Redactional Style*, 87.
21. Ibid., 97.
22. Williams, "Bringing Method to the Madness," 405.
23. Wallace, in his chapter "Mark 16:8 as the Conclusion to the Second Gospel," referenced Terry in two footnotes (30). Wallace stated: "In particular, Terry's treatment of the cumulative argument is weak, even though he is able to show quite successfully that many of the anomalies in 16:9–20 can be found scattered throughout the rest of Mark."

Internal Evidence

Testament, but θάνατος ("death") is found six times in Mark and θανατόω ("put to death") twice. Ἀναλαμβάνω is found only here in the Gospels, but λαμβάνω is used 21 times in Mark. And although συνεργέω occurs only here in the Gospels, ἐργάζομαι is found once and ἔργον twice in Mark. In addition, it should be pointed out that three of these sixteen words are found only in the post-resurrection accounts in the story of Jesus' life (i.e., in the Gospels plus Acts 1). They are ἀπιστέω ("disbelieve"), ἕνδεκα ("eleven"), and ἀναλαμβάνω ("take up"). It is therefore not unusual to find these words only here in Mark because of the subject matter.[24]

Yet, the indisputable fact that Mark knew the word πορεύομαι does not mitigate the simple fact that he never uses it up to 16:8. Also, Mark established a pattern of communicating "depart" with ὕπαγε and never the imperative or participle of πορεύομαι.

Kelhoffer, in his analysis of Farmer's review of the internal evidence, said: "It is not sufficient only to assert *that* Mark had used a certain word in 1:1–16:8 or that he *could* have done so at a certain point in the LE."[25] While quick to say he was not "making light" of such an approach and that they were "important initial observations," Kelhoffer added that they "are not conclusive in themselves," and that he wished to "redefine their significance."[26] He asserted: "When there are sufficient data, it is more useful to consider the Gospel of Mark more broadly to observe Mark's own *patterns of writing*: when Mark wanted to express 'x,' 'y,' and 'z' how did he usually do this?"[27]

Williams, though acknowledging that Kelhoffer came closest to enunciating a clear method of analysis, stressed that past attempts to disprove Markan authorship based on internal evidence "have yielded a somewhat less-than-convincing result."[28] He continued, "Thus, the strength of their conclusions often greatly exceeds the evidence from which the deductions are extracted."[29]

To be sure, "Nothing can be inferred about the genuineness of this section of Mark from the presence of any one of these words; rather, it is the

---

24. Terry, "Style of the Long Ending," 3.
25. Kelhoffer, *Miracle and Mission*, 66.
26. Ibid.
27. Ibid; emphasis original.
28. Williams, "Bringing Method to the Madness," 398.
29. Ibid.

Does Mark 16:9–20 Belong In The New Testament?

large number of them which calls the style of the passage into question."[30] Mark 15:40–16:4, a passage of similar size, is also similar in the number of new words found. There are not just sixteen such words, but twenty to twenty-two, depending on textual variants. An analysis of the Gospel shows that there are 555 words that are used only once, and that "the distribution of words used only once is not uniform in Mark."[31] Mark 1:1–12 contains sixteen words used only once, and 14:1–12 contains twenty.[32] Below is a chart of words in Mark used only once, based upon the statistics for infrequently used words found in Kubo's *Reader's Lexicon*:

Chapter	Number of Words Used Only Once	Number of Verses	Hapax Legomena	Ratio WUOO/Verses
1	39	45	6	.86
2	16	28	3	.57
3	13	35	1	.37
4	42	41	2	1.02
5	25	43	4	.58
6	46	56	3	.82
7	41	36 *	6	1.14
8	23	38	2	.61
9	43	48 *	10	.90
10	40	52	5	.77
11	14	32 *	2	.44
12	46	44	5	1.05
13	40	37	3	1.08
14	70	72	5	.97
15	53	46 *	5	1.15
16:1-8	4	8	0	.50
Subtotals	555	661	62	.84
16:9-20	13	12	1	1.08
Totals	568	673	63	.84

*Verses are missing from chapters 7, 9, 11, and 15 due to textual variants.[33]

The chart below illustrates the comparison of 16:9–20 with the sections in Mark from the UBS text:[34]

---

30. Terry, "Style of the Long Ending," 4.
31. Ibid.
32. Ibid.
33. Ibid., 4–5.
34. Ibid., 5.

Internal Evidence

Number of Sections	Number of Words Used Only Once per Section	Number of Verses per Section	Total Hapax Legomena	Ratio WUOO/Verses
Long Ending				
4	Range: 1-6; Ave. 3.25	2-5	1	.33-2.00 Ave. 1.08
Rest of Mark				
37	Range: 0-12; Ave. 3.32 (chapters 1-16) (chapters 12-16)	2-5	16	.00-2.40 Ave. .88 Ave. 1.10
29	Range: 1-16; Ave. 6.38	6-9	15	.13-2.29 Ave. .90
17	Range: 1-15; Ave. 8.24	10-13	15	.09-1.30 Ave. .74
7	Range: 8-30; Ave. 15.29	15-23	16	.53-1.36 Ave. .84

By either measurement, 16:9–20 compares favorably. For twelve verses composed of sections this size in the last five chapters of Mark (around the climax), the number of words to be expected that are used only once would be thirteen, which is exactly what is found. Of the sixteen words not found elsewhere in Mark, three—πορεύομαι, θεάομαι and ἀπιστέω—are used more than once in 16:9–20, which is cited as evidence against inclusion. An analysis of words that are used more than once within a twelve-verse span of text and only within that span in Mark reveals that there are seventy-seven such words in the undisputed verses of Mark plus five proper nouns. If the selection is limited to a six-verse span (the largest span actually used in 16:9–20), the number of words drops to fifty-eight plus three names. The chart below illustrates the point:[35]

Times Used	Twelve Verse Spread words	names	Six Verse Spread words	names
2 times	53	2	42	1
3 times	14	2	11	1
4 times	4	1	4	1
5 times	5	–	–	–
6 times	1	–	1	–

Terry compared the ratio of "unique-words-used-more-than-once-to-verse" in 16:9–20 (.25) with 2:18–22 (1). Concerning 2:18–22 he said it "contains at least seven words that are used only once in Mark, including two hapax legomena."[36] Williams's assessment of attempts to defend the

35. Ibid.
36. Ibid.

authenticity of 16:9–20 did not take such data into account: "For the most part, the major defenses have gone about "proving" their case by simply establishing *possibility*. That is, attempts at defending the authenticity of the pericope have often been made by simply offering comparable discrepancies from other works and thereby opening the door for the possibility of the same in Mark 16. In essence, the strategy is grounded in the notion that, if all things are possible, the longer ending could be authentic."[37]

Williams then appealed to the uniqueness of 16:9–20 as a reason to reject the passage: "A key difference between the longer ending and other portions of Mark's Gospel is the external questionability of the former. Whereas peculiar grammatical features are found throughout the narrative, in this case stylistic variation is located in the midst of a passage that is textually questionable. Thus, it is the combination of textual uncertainty and stylistic peculiarity that negates any *equivalent* comparisons with other portions in Mark."[38]

As mentioned earlier, the passage does not contain two of Mark's favorite words: εὐθύς and πάλιν. The text reveals that the last fifty-three verses do not use them. Terry asserted: "Looking at Mark as a whole, there are 650 sets of twelve consecutive verses, not considering the last twelve verses. Out of these, 373 sets do not contain εὐθύς or εὐθέως; that is, more than 57 percent do not have them. Also, 399 sets do not contain πάλιν; that is, more than 61 percent do not have this word. And finally, it may be noted that 229 sets do not contain εὐθύς, εὐθέως, or πάλιν; that is, more than 35 percent do not contain any of these words. It is hardly an objection to say that the last twelve verses are in the same category with more than one-third of the sets of twelve consecutive verses in the rest of the book."[39] While this analysis may seem peculiar, it seems to be a valid approach. The formula for consecutive verses is Number of Consecutive Verses = Total Number of Verses—Size of Verse Set + 1.[40] If all possible twelve-verse units of Mark are considered, beginning with Mark 1:1–12, and then considering Mark 1:2–13, and then considering Mark 1:3–14, and so forth until one reaches 16:9–20, only 373 such units contain εὐθύς (or εὐθέως). Nevertheless, this difficulty is not so easily dismissed.

---

37. Williams "Bringing Method to the Madness," 398–99; emphasis original.
38. Ibid., 399f.
39. Terry, "Style of the Long Ending," 7.
40. Terry, phone conversation with the author, July 6, 2012.

Internal Evidence

The word πορεύομαι occurs only in Mark 16:9–20 but nowhere else in Mark, even though compound verbs with this root plus a prefixed preposition do occur. The word θνήσκω occurs only in Mark 15:44 in the Gospel. The singular occurrence of ὕστερον in Mark 16:14 seems to be evidence against Markan authorship. Yet there is a single occurrence of the adverb πάλαι (Mark 15:44) and the subordinating conjunction ἐπέι (Mark 15:42). Given that New Testament authors had the intellect and ability to write in different styles, it is not difficult to consider 16:9–20 utilizing different words and phrases from the rest of the Gospel—especially if the passage was not the intended finished product, but a preliminary draft.

Is the Passage a Summary of the Other Gospel Accounts?

Mark 16:9–20 is a collection of two- and three-verse summaries of action. This seems to be in contrast to Mark generally giving the greatest narrative detail and lingering over the action with historical presents and imperfect tense verbs to bring out its significance in Jesus' ministry and road to the cross.[41] Yet, the ending of Mark contains information not found in the other Gospels, such as Jesus appearing in a different form to the two on the road to Emmaus, and the information on drinking poison. Also, Mark was capable of writing in a frugal style: a comparison of episodes shared by Matthew, Mark, and Luke generally shows that Mark's presentation of events is fuller. However, there are exceptions—such as Mark's presentation of Christ's temptations and the transfiguration, and his treatment at the beginning of the Gospel where he does summary treatment of John's preaching and Jesus' baptism.

Two times the disciples were told to go to Galilee where Jesus would appear to them (Mark 14:28; 16:7), clearly indicating that Mark's ending would include the appearance in Galilee. But at first glance it appears only Matthew and John actually record obedience to that command (Matt 28:16; John 21). This seems to be evidence that something is missing, as the current ending appears at first glance to not record the twice-commanded journey to Galilee. This objection is problematic. On the one hand, it is objected that the long ending is a summary of the other Gospels. This is evidence that the intended ending of the Gospel could not have been at 16:8. Yet, it is also objected that it does not include the same material as the other Gospels. Mark's summary notes need not indicate the obvious

---

41. Written correspondence from Jim Smeal, October 22, 2012.

Does Mark 16:9–20 Belong In The New Testament?

location, although one should expect Mark to indicate the Galilee location in the finished product.

France objected that the passage has "something of a 'secondhand' flavor," and looks "like a pastiche of elements drawn from the other Gospels and Acts."[42] Apparently, he believed that whoever put the passage together knew all four Gospels. Some questions must therefore be asked.[43] Why did this individual decide not to continue and conclude the scene that is underway in 16:8, so as to correspond to the events in Matthew 28:8-10? Why did this individual restate the day and time, after seeing them stated at the beginning of Mark 16? Why did he focus solely on Mary Magdalene, with no mention of her companions who were in the narrative spotlight in verse 8? It is claimed that the supposed author made no attempt to deceive readers that Mark wrote this ending. But why, although he had seen in Mark 16:7 that Mark's narrative called for a scene in Galilee, did he describe some appearances which anyone familiar with the Gospel of Luke would place in, or near, Jerusalem? What is being echoed in Mark 16:11, in which the disciples reject Mary Magdalene's report that Jesus was alive and had been seen by her? John 20 does not say that the disciples did not believe her, and Luke 24 does not picture Mary Magdalene reporting that she had seen Jesus; it even depicts a disciple saying that the women did not see Jesus. France's attempt to answer this by supposing that the author depended upon John 20:18 as he wrote Mark 16:10–11a, but upon Luke 24:11 and 41 as he wrote 16:11b, is problematic for two reasons. First, it involves an unlikely use of source materials. Second, it requires that the author overlooked the contents of his other piece of source material—Matthew 28—in which the disciples comply with the women's report by going to Galilee.

What is being echoed in Mark 16:13–14, where the main group of disciples rejects the report of the two travelers, and then later Jesus appears to the eleven and rebukes them? This cannot be based upon the single scene in Luke 24:35ff., where Jesus appears to the main group of disciples as the two travelers are still speaking. And *contra* France, Mark 16:14's report of a rebuke of the eleven disciples does not correspond to the episode about Jesus and Thomas in John 20:24–29. France has proposed a parallel that is not there. What is being echoed in Mark 16:17–18? No other Gospel's conclusion features an account of Jesus prophesying about signs. But France

---

42. France, *Gospel of Mark*, 687.

43. The questions in the next four paragraphs were raised in an email from Snapp, October 15, 2012.

Internal Evidence

proposed this as evidence that the author was also familiar with the book of Acts, and summarized all its contents by inventing this prophecy. France did say that familiarity with the book of Acts would not be likely to induce an author to put into Jesus' mouth a prophecy about believers picking up snakes (which is not exactly what happens in Acts 27) and drinking poison without harmful effects (which happens nowhere in Acts).

Why did the author refrain from using John 21? An ending needed to be supplied for a text in which a post-resurrection appearance by Jesus in Galilee to Peter and the others was very strongly foreshadowed. Yet although the author found exactly such an ending in John 21, he did not use it at all. What is being echoed in several small details throughout Mark 16:9–20? It is not unlikely that Mark knew that Jesus cast out seven demons from Mary Magdalene, and that he would include this detail if he wrote a summary of Jesus' post-resurrection appearances. Would a second-century copyist have attempted to construct an ending for Mark 1:1–16:8 by first restating the day and time, and then by reintroducing Mary Magdalene (without her companions), and then by delving into Luke 8:2 in search of words to describe her, and then, after finding Luke's words Μαρία ἡ καλουμένη Μαγδαληνή, change them to Μαρία τῇ Μαγδαληνῇ, and after finding Luke's words ἀφ' ἧς δαιμόνια ἑπτὰ ἐξεληλύθει, change them to παρ' ἧς ἐκβεβλήκει ἑπτὰ δαιμόνια? The theory proposed by France requires that the author undertook such a task, hunting-and-finding-and-changing source material many times over in the course of writing the twelve verses. It is clear that the author made no attempt to deceive readers into thinking this was Mark's original ending because of the awkward elements mentioned earlier.

Someone attempting to construct an ending for Mark's Gospel would likely consult the other Gospels if he had access to them, if only to ensure that his account did not contradict what was already recorded. This scenario is feasible by considering what one does not see—the triune baptismal formula and any demonstration of Christ's physicality, although these would things that a second-century copyist would almost inevitably take from the other accounts if he had them. There are also certain words used in Mark 16:9–20 that are not found in the parallel accounts in Matthew and Luke. Such words as σωθήσεται in 16:16, πιώσιν in 16:18, and ἐκάθισεν in 16:19 are common words found in the other two Gospels.[44] Yet they are absent from the corresponding passages concerning the post-resurrection appearances. Instead of a copyist in the early second century constructing Mark

---

44. Hoffman et al., *Synoptic Concordance*.

Does Mark 16:9–20 Belong In The New Testament?

16:9–20, an alternative theory is feasible for the similarities between Mark 16:9–20 and the other accounts of Christ's post-resurrection appearances. The author's familiarity with the same events which the other authors independently recorded could account for the parallels. Instead of a summary of other Gospel accounts by a later author with little or no connection to the apostle Peter, the passage could be a summary from hearing a firsthand account of the events described.

What of the Lack of Historical Presents and Imperfect Tense Verbs?

An objection to Markan authorship of 16:9–20 is based on the lack of historical present and imperfect tense verbs. Mark 16:1–8 contains six present indicative verbs (including three historical presents) and four imperfect tense verbs to dwell on the action. Mark 16:9–20, in contrast, have zero historical presents and zero imperfect tense verbs to describe the resurrection appearances. In the rest of Mark, the occurrence of indicative mood verbs in the aorist, present, and imperfect tenses is 541–519–292, respectively. In the last 12 verses of Mark, the occurrence is 14–1–0 for aorist, present, and imperfect indicative mood verbs, respectively—seemingly a radical departure. The only present indicative mood verb is in verse 11, which is necessary in indirect discourse. The narrative style of verses 9–20 thus seems to be dramatically unlike that of Mark 1:1–16:8.[45]

Historical presents and imperfect verbs are definite characteristics of Mark's Gospel, but there is a certain unevenness in his style. Take, for example, the following passages. In Mark 6:21–29, there are nine verses with 172 Greek words, including eleven Greek words found once in Mark. Additionally, there are sixteen aorists and one present (vs. 25, direct discourse) with no imperfects. In Mark 16:9–20, there are twelve verses with 171 Greek words, including eleven Greek words found once in Mark. Additionally, there are fourteen aorists and one present (vs. 11, indirect discourse) with no imperfects.[46]

Much depends on the subject matter of each narrative. In Mark 6:21–29, Mark is telling about King Herod on his birthday and his oath that led to the beheading of John the Baptist. Eleven Greek words are here found nowhere else in the Gospel of Mark, the same number as found in Mark 16:9–20. And some of these words are found nowhere else in the

---

45. Written correspondence from Jim Smeal, October 22, 2012.
46. Written correspondence from David Warren, October 29, 2012.

Internal Evidence

entire Greek NT. Both passages above are equal in length (about 170 Greek words each). Both are loaded with aorists in the indicative, but with no imperfects, and each only has one present indicative, both due to the necessities of discourse.[47] What of the point concerning Mark's ratio of tenses in the indicative—541 aorists, 519 presents, and 292 imperfects? In the entire Gospel of Mark, there is a 541 to 519 to 292 ratio = 1.9 to 1.8 to 1. In Mark 6:21–29, there is a 16 to 1 to 0 ratio = 16 to 1 to 0. In Mark 16:9–20, there is a 14 to 1 to 0 ratio = 14 to 1 to 0. Compare this to the last twelve verses of Mark chapter 15 (Mark 15:36–47): in Mark 15:36–47, there are twelve verses with 202 Greek words, including eighteen Greek words found once in Mark. There are also thirteen aorists and one present (vs. 36, direct discourse, conditional), with ten imperfects.[48] Here in the last twelve verses of chapter 15 is a completely different ratio with nearly as many imperfects as aorists, but still only one present indicative (again due to the necessities of discourse). Observe the number of words found only here in the Gospel of Mark. What do these data imply? There is no significant pattern that can be applied across the board to other passages in the Gospel and then determine their genuineness, or whether 16:9–20 belongs.[49]

But, why the dominance of the aorist in a few passages? Mark does not want to dwell on the action as continuous regarding Jesus' baptism, the verses that narrate John's execution (although lots of presents and imperfects are in the setup to that event), and the actual description of Joseph of Arimathea's burial of Jesus (surrounded itself by imperfects). There are a few events in which Mark did not want to dwell on the progress of the action and employed almost exclusively aorist tense verbs when using the indicative mood. The reason for that is because Mark wanted to narrate those events in summary fashion. Every author does that occasionally. But why would he summarize the appearance events?

Does the Transition between 16:8 and 16:9 Omit 16:9–20?

There are five reasons why the transition between verses eight and nine is referenced by those who oppose inclusion of 16:9–20: The subject of verse 8 is the women, whereas Jesus is the presumed subject of verse 9. The other women of verse 1–8 are forgotten in verses 9–20. In verse 9 Mary

47. Ibid.
48. Ibid.
49. Ibid.

Does Mark 16:9–20 Belong In The New Testament?

Magdalene is identified even though she has been mentioned only a few lines before. While the use of ἀναστας δὲ ("Now rising") and the position of πρώτῃ ("first") are appropriate at the beginning of a comprehensive narrative, they are ill-suited in a continuation of verses 1–8. The use of the conjunction γάρ ("for") at the end of verse 8 is very abrupt.

With regard to the first two reasons, while there is not an exact parallel containing all these features in the rest of the Gospel, they are found in different transitions between sections in Mark. There are five verses in Mark— 2:13; 6:45; 7:31; 8:1; and 14:3—which possess several features bearing upon the first two objections. First, each of the verses starts a new section. Second, Jesus is presumed to be the subject. Third, Jesus is not included in the previous verse. Fourth, the verse prior must have a subject different from Jesus. Fifth, the subject mentioned in the verse prior is not again referred to in the new section. All of this can indicate that these are unpolished notes of one who heard a firsthand account of the events described.

Verse nine does not continue what is discussed in verses 1–8 (the empty tomb); rather, it is the beginning of a new section (the resurrection appearances of Christ). The author does not mix the two proofs. Thus the words in question are appropriate to verse 9, because it starts a new section. Final γάρ is not in Mark. Yet, though Mark does not use γάρ in two word clauses, there are two passages (1:16; 11:18) that use γάρ in three word clauses, and seven passages (1:38; 3:21; 5:42; 9:49; 14:70; 15:14; 16:4) that use γάρ in four word clauses. Nevertheless, it is not as simple as Terry seems to try to make it.[50] When one simply reads Mark 16, it is clear that the transition is not smooth. Hort emphasized this very difficulty as evidence against the genuineness of the passage.[51] At any rate, verses 9–20 seem to comprise a summary.

The Designation of the Apostles in 16:10

Metzger referenced two phrases used to designate the apostles—θανάσιμον and τοῖσ μετ' αὐτοῦ γενομένοις—which are nowhere else used in the New Testament.[52] Yet, θανάσιμον in verse 18 does not refer to the apostles; rather, it refers to a "deadly thing" which is drunk. The latter phrase, τοῖσ μετ'

---

50. And, Terry himself conceded that the abrupt transition is a definite problem. Phone conversation with the author, July 6, 2012.

51. Westcott and Hort, *Introduction to the New Testament*, 48–50.

52. Metzger, *Textual Commentary*, 125.

Internal Evidence

αὐτοῦ γενομένοις, does indeed refer to the apostles. The fact that γενομένοις is an aorist participle makes sense within the context of 16:9-20, where the resurrection appearances of Jesus are discussed. Mark 16:9-20 is the only place in the Gospel where this phrase, as applied to the apostles, would be found. The shorter expression οἱ μετ' αὐτοῦ ("those with him") is found three other times in Mark (1:36; 2:25; and 5:40).

Some Internal Evidences For Inclusion

Mark is well-known for his fondness for presenting things in groups of three, and Mark 16:9-20 exhibits this characteristic. The post-resurrection appearances are arranged in three scenes: the appearance to Mary Magdalene (9-11), to the two travelers (12-13), and to the eleven (14-18). The triple use of ἐφάνη/ἐφανερώθη is striking. Mark employs the terms ἀναστῆναι (8:31, 9:10), ἀναστῇ (9:9), and ἀναστήσεται (9:31, 10:34) to refer to Christ's resurrection, although other terms could have been used. The use of Ἀναστάς in 16:9 is thus a Markan feature. Mark uses the word πρωΐ (1:35, 11:20, 13:35, 15:1, and 16:2) more frequently than the other Gospel writers. Its presence in 16:9 is Markan. Mark uses the word ἀγρόν proportionately more often than the other Gospels. Its presence in 16:12 is consistent. Mark's words in 14:9—κηρυχθῇ τὸ εὐαγγέλιον εἰς ὅλον τόν—have a strong verbal parallel with the wording in 16:15: εἰς τὸν κόσμον ἅπαντα κηρύξατε τὸ εὐαγγέλιον. The term ἐφανερώθη, which occurs in 16:12 and 16:14, is a distinctly Markan term. Mark uses φανερώθη in Mark 4:22. The term σκληροκαρδίαν which occurs in 16:14 is rather uncommon, but it also appears in Mark 10:5. The use of κατακριθήσεται is Markan. He uses κατακρινοῦσιν in 10:33 and κατέκριναν in 14:64. The term ἀρρώστους, which refers to sick people in 16:18, appears in Mark 6:5 and 6:13. The tern πανταχοῦ in 16:20 is also found in the Alexandrian Text in Mark 1:28. A related term (either πάντοθεν, in the Alexandrian Text, or πανταχόθεν in the Byzantine Text) is used in Mark 1:45. This, too, is a characteristic Markan term. Although Mark uses κἀκεῖνον as an absolute twice in Mark 12:4-5, it is notable that in Mark 16:9-20 this phenomenon—rare in Mark 1:1-16:8—is concentrated. The words ἐκείνη (16:10), κἀκεῖνοι (16:11), ἐκείνοις (16:13), and ἐκεῖνοι (16:20) are all used as pronouns. This is a feature that suggests Mark 16:9-20 was written as a summary, unlike most of the rest of the book. The text itself does not suggest a reason why the author would suddenly resume using the summarizing style that he employed at the outset of

Does Mark 16:9–20 Belong In The New Testament?

chapter 1. Another internal feature that suggests Markan authorship of the passage is the theme of the "failure of the apostles." Five times in 16:9–20, this is referenced. This theme is prominent in the last half of the Gospel of Mark, and is thus consistent. Finally, the reference to the ascension (while also mentioned in Luke) is internally consistent with the Gospel of Mark; he quotes from Psalm 110 in two places—Mark 12:36 and Mark 14:62.

Does the Internal Evidence Weigh Against the Passage?

When scholars such as Elliott and Wallace either do not address or else pass over answers to their arguments, it gives one pause. To claim, as did Elliott, that "it is self-deceiving to pretend that the linguistic questions are still 'open,'"[53] or to characterize 16:9–20 as "an inferior piece of writing, plodding and grey,"[54] is not helpful. Thomas's words are just as problematic, describing those "who for theological reasons feel compelled to cling to 16:9–20."[55] To their credit, Kelhoffer and Williams both recognized that those kinds of statements are not needed: "Since Mark did not write the LE, it is either a 'false' (and embarrassing) interpolation or not worthy of serious attention by NT scholars";[56] "To some, even raising the possibility of the passage's authenticity might seem gratuitous."[57] Overlooked in all of this is the fact that there are those who recognize the similarities between 16:9–20 and the rest of Mark. Kelhoffer acknowledged, "Numerous parts of 16:9–20 bear a striking resemblance to Mark 1:1–16:8."[58] Kelhoffer maintained that the author of the passage consciously imitated the Gospel and drew upon the other three.

Hort spoke concerning the internal evidence:

> We do not think it necessary to examine in detail the intrinsic evidence supposed to be furnished by comparison of the vocabulary and style of verses 9–20 with the unquestioned parts of the Gospel. Much of what has been urged on both sides is in our judgement trivial and intangible. There remain a certain number

---

53. Elliott, "Last Twelve Verses," 89.
54. Ibid., 91.
55. Thomas, "Reconsideration," 419.
56. Kelhoffer, *Miracle and Mission*, 32.
57. Williams, "Bringing Method to the Madness," 397. Williams cited Kelhoffer approvingly, and referenced Elliott as an example to make his point.
58. Kelhoffer, *Miracle and Mission*, 49.

Internal Evidence

of differences which, taken cumulatively, produce an impression unfavourable to identity of authorship. Had these verses been found in all good documents, or been open to suspicion on no other internal evidence, the differences would reasonably have been neglected.[59]

Writing a century later, Koester went a step further. He stated that the "vocabulary and style" of the passage "are fully compatible with the Gospel of Mark."[60] This does not mean that either Hort or Koester accepted 16:9–20 as an original part of Mark;[61] Hort even stated that the passage "manifestly cannot claim any apostolic authority."[62] Yet, neither one rejected the passage out of hand as not belonging to the Gospel based upon internal evidence alone. Elliott said, "In many ways the non-Markan character of Mark 1:1–3 is more pronounced than that of Mark 16:9–20."[63] While Williams attempted to show the supposed non-Markan style of 16:9–20 based on his own methodological study,[64] Robinson showed how that study fell short of its goals.[65] When even Elliott—as hostile as he is against the passage—can accept it as canonical, then the internal evidence by itself cannot be a sufficient basis to exclude the passage. This is all the more so because of its evident antiquity. As early as the second century, the church accepted 16:9–20 as part of the Gospel and as being from Mark. Thus, there was oral tradition circulating that the evangelist was connected to the passage. This may explain why the internal differences between 16:9–20 and the rest of Mark were not highlighted by early patristic witnesses.

Another thing to consider is the subjective nature of internal evidence. While important, many times the conclusions drawn are not definitive. This led Petzer to question the whole endeavor: "Contrary to the way in which the criterion is formulated and functions in New Testament textual criticism, it cannot be expected or presupposed that the language employed in the New Testament documents will of necessity be consistent, or, to put it differently, the stylistic patterns identified in those documents cannot be employed as a means of determining what was written in them

---

59. Westcott and Hort, *Introduction to the New Testament*, 48.
60. Koester, *Ancient Christian Gospels*, 295.
61. In the same reference, Koester described 16:9–20 as "certainly secondary."
62. Westcott and Hort, *Introduction to the New Testament*, 51.
63. J. Elliott, "Mark 1.1–3," 586.
64. Williams, "Bringing Method to the Madness."
65. Robinson, "Evangelical Textual Criticism."

originally."[66] While Petzer's view was that the New Testament was as much a product of redactors as the authors,[67] he nevertheless highlighted some of the problems in relying heavily upon internal evidence to determine authorship. "The fact that an author wrote parts of his text in the style of another author means that the influence of other authors is present in the text under observation."[68] Also, "the involvement of different authors, albeit indirectly, presupposes difference in language and style, because no two authors write in the same way." This has application for the Synoptics, if one takes the view that sources were used. "Because such an involvement of sources is not acknowledged in the pattern used as the norm, it can also not be identified as such in the application of that norm, with the result that the differences lead to a conclusion that the disputed passage was not originally part of the text under consideration."[69] Such conclusions are definitely in the minority. Petzer did suggest "the text must, so to speak, define and reconstruct itself,"[70] instead of attempting to use implications from linguistic and stylistic patterns to settle disputed passages.[71] To that, at least, agreement can be reached.

Internal evidence is indeed important in textual criticism, as it is with Mark 16:9–20. If one allows an author the ability to write in different ways (as is the case with John—in his Gospel and epistles, as opposed to Revelation), or in summary fashion, then it is feasible that Mark wrote 16:9–20. Since Mark was a companion of Peter, and his Gospel parallels Peter's sermons in the book of Acts, it is reasonable to assume, as Papias had asserted, that Mark took notes of Peter's own words of his eyewitness accounts—all under the inspiration of the Holy Spirit. Mark would then use those notes to construct his finished Gospel. Mark 16:9–20, seen in this light, is thus a summary of what Peter preached and taught concerning the last days of Jesus on the earth. However, it is evident that there was a problem with the transmission of the text. This is reflected in the various pieces of manuscript and patristic evidence which indicate an issue at the end of Mark—particularly Vaticanus and Sinaiticus, the damaged copies of some

---

66. Petzer, "Author's Style," 186.
67. Ibid., 190.
68. Ibid.
69. Ibid.
70. Ibid., 194.

71. It seemed that Petzer had given up on the whole enterprise, and focused solely on his belief in the supposed role of redactors in the New Testament.

Internal Evidence

manuscripts, and the testimony of Eusebius and Jerome as to some copies ending at verse 8. It is also possibly seen in the abrupt transition between verses eight and nine, as well as the words in the passage used only once in the Gospel. How does one account for the origin of Mark 16:9–20, as well as the two endings in the textual stream? The final chapter will set forth a proposal to answer those questions.

CHAPTER 4

A Proposal Concerning the Origin of Mark 16:9–20

The statement by Clark in 1965 concerning Mark 16:9–20 still appears reasonable today: "we should consider the question still open."[1] The evidence is presented in a more balanced way than before, especially in light of all that has been written on the subject in subsequent years. Advocacy of inclusion of the passage is better received at present, though a decided majority of scholars reject its authenticity. Yet, the fact remains there was a disruption in the transmission of the text concerning the long ending. This is evidenced first from the blank space at the end of Mark in Vaticanus and the cancel-sheet replacement at the end of Sinaiticus. Added to this are p45, manuscript 13, manuscript 16, manuscript 1420, and manuscript 2386, which are all damaged at the end of Mark. This is further seen from some of the statements from some of the versions—"in some places" the text ends at verse 8. However one interprets Eusebius, it is evident he was aware of a textual problem at the end of Mark. Jerome repeated what Eusebius wrote, later included the passage in the Vulgate, yet still acknowledged that some manuscripts ended at verse 8. While the silence of Origen and Clement cannot definitively be used against the passage, it may also suggest their knowledge of a textual problem.

---

1. Clark, "Theological Relevance," 10.

A Proposal Concerning the Origin of Mark 16:9–20

Three Possibilities

Mark Intended to End the Gospel at Verse 8

This option, while still widely held, is unlikely. The reasons given earlier were listed by Stein, who also added this:

> The assumption that 16:8 is the intended ending of the Gospel and the attempted explanations to justify this almost all lose sight of the main character in the story, Jesus Christ, the Son of God, and focus instead on the minor characters, the women. The focus of the story, however, involves the message of the angel, who is God's reliable spokesperson in the account. Since this message tells of the disciples' meeting Jesus, who is awaiting them in Galilee, it is clear that the reader is prepared by Mark to hear something about that meeting, which the readers knew took place. Consequently, I believe that when we take into consideration Mark's intended purpose in 16:1–8, which is to tell about Jesus Christ, the Son of God, we must conclude that Mark did not intend 16:8 to serve as the conclusion of his Gospel.[2]

Stein also listed a number of recent scholars who took the position that 16:8 was not the intended ending for the Gospel. Stein asked, "Does this indicate a trend?"[3] As indicated earlier, those who take the position that the Gospel ended intentionally at verse 8 seem to interpret throughout the lens of modern literary criticism. Stein offered this cogent assessment:

> Mark wrote his Gospel with his intended audience in mind, rather than 20th-and 21st-century commentators who find delight in Mark's abrupt and confusing ending at 16:8. It is interesting to note that Julius Wellhausen, one of the early writers who advocated the appropriateness of 16:8 as Mark's intended ending, concluded that Mark 16:7 was not Markan but a later addition to his Gospel. He could not conceive of Mark having intended to end his Gospel at 16:8 and allowing 16:7 to be in his Gospel. Our knowing that both Mark 14:28 and 16:7 clearly reveal Mark's own editorial hand makes an intended ending at 16:8 even more difficult to accept.[4]

---

2. Stein, "Ending of Mark," 96–97.
3. Ibid., 98.
4. Ibid., 95.

Does Mark 16:9–20 Belong In The New Testament?

The Ending at Verse 8 Is Missing—Whether by Accident or Excision

Given the fact that several manuscripts evidence damage at the end of Mark, there is the possibility that the original ending of Mark was lost. This would explain the various endings. Farmer suggested that the removal of 16:9–20 was because certain scribes excised the passage on account of the references to picking up snakes and drinking poison.[5] Fee pointed out a weakness in this theory: "The whole argument that 'omission' spread out from Alexandria can be turned on its head to show that inclusion spread out from Roman influence (Irenaeus, Tatian, Old Latin, etc.)."[6] Similarly, Wallace suggested that pressure from Rome caused Mark 16:9–20 to be added to the Gospel.[7] However, there is no indication that the church in Rome had developed an overarching ecclesiastical structure that early. It is not clear, for example, that any kind of group was tasked with enforcing orthodoxy. Added to this is the evidence which seems to indicate that the early church was not overly concerned with the state of the text.[8] Elliott, while rejecting Farmer, suggested that a possible reason for exclusion of a "lost" ending was that it contained an appearance of Jesus to Peter: "Because of the later reluctance to credit him with this revelation, that ending needed to be removed."[9] This assumes more than is warranted. The evidence at hand simply suggests that there was a possible disruption at the end of Mark. Streeter suggested that the author of John had Mark's original ending which is now lost. The difficulty is in explaining how Mark's Gospel got from Rome to Ephesus without an available copy existing to repair the loss. If this happened very early (almost immediately), why did not Mark's associates run down a copy already sent and repair the loss? If Mark's Gospel circulated for thirty years with the original ending, surely they could have located some copy to recover the original ending.

Could something have happened to the manuscript during the transmission phase? Croy suggested such, and went so far as to postulate both

---

5. Farmer, *Last Twelve Verses of Mark*, 107–8.
6. Fee, "Last Twelve Verses," 463.
7. Wallace, "Mark 16:8," 29n81.
8. Kelhoffer, "Witness of Eusebius," 94–96. Kelhoffer argues that this was apparently the practice of the patristic witnesses who commented on the text; he agrees with Burgon that "the early church fathers were 'but very children in the Science of Textual Criticism.'"
9. Elliott, "Last Twelve Verses," 95–96.

A Proposal Concerning the Origin of Mark 16:9–20

the beginning and the ending of the Gospel had been mutilated.[10] C. F. D. Moule had written some years before concerning this theory:

> It is tempting to postulate a mutilation of Mark at the beginning as well as the end. If one removes "The beginning of the Gospel of Jesus Christ the Son of God"—which is the sort of heading that any scribe might supply, if presented with only a mutilated exemplar to copy—, then the Gospel starts with a relative adverb, καθώς, "just as," which is no less abrupt and improbable as a beginning than γάρ is as an ending. Schluss demonstrates that the earliest available manuscript evidence is entirely silent beyond γάρ; but is it impossible that mutilation took place even before any copies were made, yet was not mended even if the Evangelist was still living? And if the original autograph was on a codex and not a roll, then it only requires the bottom sheet to be lost for beginning and end to go at one stroke. (Even a roll seems to have been easily damaged at the beginning: Roberts 1939) . . . Despite all efforts to defend the view that the Gospel was meant to end at 16:8 or, conversely, to find Mark's hand in part or all of 16:9 ff., it remains difficult not to believe that something has been lost.[11]

If this approach is correct, it is important to attempt to discover at what particular point and how it happened. Hort hypothesized that such did take place, and that 16:9–20 was added by a later copyist who had found the passage independent of the Gospel and thus inserted it at the end of verse 8.[12] Yet it is also feasible that the passage was part of summary notes composed by Mark. Given that the early patristics considered the passage as being part of the Gospel, and even from Mark's hand, such a theory seems more reasonable.

As evidenced by the manuscripts mentioned, something happened that affected them in an adverse way—each one at the end of Mark. Could someone have removed the passage because of what it taught? Farmer suggested that Alexandrian scribes did so, but one person could have done it as easily as a group. Much discussion along these lines has centered on picking up snakes and drinking poison, but there may have also been a problem with the teaching on baptism. If the verses were deliberately excised, it could explain the textual stream that did not contain them. The last page of Mark is missing in several manuscripts, so it apparently would have been

---

10. Croy, *Mutilation of Mark's Gospel*, 113–64.
11. Moule, *Birth of the New Testament*, 131–32n.
12. Westcott and Hort, *Introduction to the New Testament*, 51.

Does Mark 16:9–20 Belong In The New Testament?

easy to tear off. At the same time, there would have been manuscripts that included the verses—which eventually gained wide circulation. Yet, it is difficult to accept that the ending of a Gospel did not survive the transmission process. Also, why would one omit an entire passage to excise one or two verses? An accident could explain the omission in certain manuscripts, although it is odd that such an event is not indicated in any of the early patristic writings. That said, normal wear and tear seems to best explain the damage to several of the manuscripts.

Verses 9–20 Are Markan, Being His Notes

This option is preferable. Mark 16:9–20 is an early document, and has similarities to the Gospel of Mark (whether or not one accepts its genuineness). It was already being used to some extent by the middle of the second century, if not earlier. Both Irenaeus and Tatian used the verses as Scripture on different sides of the ancient Western world (Gaul and Syria, respectively), and it was also probably used by Justin and certainly the author of the *Epistle of the Apostles*. Its presence from that point (second century) and its eventual overwhelming dominance in the manuscript tradition suggest that it may have been in some form connected to Mark. This proposal is based on several reasons. By the time Mark composed his Gospel he had already written—as preliminary inspired notes about Christ's post-resurrection appearances and based on Peter's sermons—the material that is known as Mark 16:9–20.[13] This is suggested because of the similarities between 16:9–20 and the rest of the Gospel. Mark was then permanently interrupted (whether by his death or persecution) when he wrote 16:8, leaving his account unfinished—thus accounting for the awkward transition between verses eight and nine. Theodor Zahn, while rejecting the passage as authentic, proposed how the Gospel was circulated ending at verse 8:

---

13. Farmer suggested that vv. 9–20 represented "redactional use of older material by the evangelist and belonged to the autograph" (107). Farmer's redactional theory is unnecessary and unprecedented in the rest of Mark, though. My position is quite different in that it does not assume the material was redacted, and because of the proposal (explained below) concerning why the material was a part of the Gospel in the Byzantine textual tradition. It is also different from what Hort replied to, in that Hort was answering those who speculated that the passage was written and added by Mark after the Gospel was completed, while my theory states that Mark had already written these notes and that it was placed after the end of v. 8 by one of his companions.

A Proposal Concerning the Origin of Mark 16:9–20

An accident to the original MS. has been suggested, which must have taken place before any copies were made. But if this happened before the book left his hands, why did not the author correct it before he permitted his book to be copied, i.e., before it was issued? More probably death, or some other compelling circumstance, arrested his pen. If he died before the completion of the work, the friends for whom it was originally intended would have felt it their duty to copy and issue the posthumous work without additions. If, however, as the tradition seems to show, Mark published the book himself, its incompleted form would be incomprehensible only in case that a few lines were wanting which the author and editor could have added at any time. On the other hand, the small compass of the work, in comparison with the other historical books of the NT, leaves room for the conjecture that Mark intended to add several portions to his work . . . If he began to write the Gospel before the death of Peter (64), but did not publish the same until after the death of Paul (67), things enough could be mentioned which must have interrupted the pen of this spiritual son of Peter and younger friend of Paul in the city where both the apostles had died as martyrs, and which also in the time immediately following must have prevented him from at once completing his book as he desired. If, in these circumstances, he yielded to the request for its issue, it would not have been something unheard of or irrational. It is perfectly possible also that during the months and years while he and others were hoping for the completion of the interrupted work he had given the unfinished book to several friends to read, and that they had made several copies without his being able to prevent it. At all events, the incomplete character of the book is proof that it was handed down in the Church in the form in which it came from the author's pen, since the first attempt to recast the work would have been directed toward furnishing it with a conclusion. The varied and slow success of the later attempts in this direction show how difficult it was to change the form of a book after it had once found a circle of readers in the Church. Nor is the result different if we assume that it is not the original work of Mark which has had the misfortune, either by accident or intention, of losing its conclusion, but only a later working over of the same; for how could a new working over of the Gospel, which was never completed, have replaced the original work, which was complete, and which had already come to be highly esteemed by many?[14]

---

14. Zahn, *Introduction to the New Testament*, 2:479–80.

Does Mark 16:9–20 Belong In The New Testament?

If Zahn is correct, then copies of the unfinished Gospel were already circulating by the time Mark died. The notes Mark penned for the ending were subsequently placed at the end of the Gospel by a colleague of Mark. The differences in vocabulary and style between 16:9–20 and the rest of the Gospel would thus be accounted. An example of this is the dominance of the aorist tense in the passage. This would be explained because Mark had written the passage as a summary, intending to come back to it and finish it.

This usage of the aorist is not unknown in Mark. There are two passages in the Gospel where Mark makes exclusive use of the aorist tense as opposed to the historical present tense. Mark 1:9–11 concerns the baptism of Jesus by John. Mark uses the aorist tense in the passage in order to summarize what was taking place. Mark 6:21–29 addresses the death of John. In verses 14–21 of that pericope, and starting again at verse 30, Mark uses the historical present consistently. Yet in verses 21–29, he utilizes the aorist—except verse 25, where there is one present tense verb in a direct quote, where Mark has to use it. In this case, Mark did not want to draw attention to the progress of the action—only that it occurred. In verses 14–20, he was delving into the psychology of Herod's actions. Additionally, Mark wanted to emphasize the death of Jesus over that of John. The use of the aorist tense in 6:21–29 would assist in simply summarizing John's death. In 16:9–20, the aorist tense is used consistently. In this case, it is because the passage is part of the notes Mark wrote of Peter's sermons. Mark had intended to finish the Gospel, using the summary material of 16:9–20 as the basis for it. However, he was prevented from doing so—whether by persecution or death. The usage of the aorist tense for a summary, or for notes, is similar to what is seen in the "Summaries" of the *Histories of Rome* by Livy.[15] The original text by Livy utilizes Latin historical presents and imperfects. In the "Summaries" of those thirty-five books, the Latin perfect tense is used—which is the equivalent of the Greek aorist. If a person is writing notes or summaries in Greek, he would likely use the aorist.

While the possibility of deliberate mutilation is appealing in certain ways, it overlooks the fact that no early patristic writers make any mention of such taking place. As mentioned before, the suggestion of deliberate mutilation is too closely aligned to "conspiracy theories." Something indeed happened to several manuscripts at the end of Mark, but is more likely that it was the result of wear and tear. Plus, an edition of Mark was already in circulation without the passage.

15. Adema, "Discourse Modes and Bases."

A Proposal Concerning the Origin of Mark 16:9–20

A point that must be stressed, to which Zahn alluded, is the reception of changes to a text accepted as apostolic. Most scholars agree that Mark 16:9-20 was very early in origin, and that the abrupt ending was also early. If it was known that the Gospel—ending at verse 8—was in circulation prior to Mark's death, then how could the second-century church have allowed an ending to be added by an anonymous author (or authors) which was not clearly apostolic (as many scholars claim), and how could it have gained such wide acceptance in subsequent years? Those who claim that the ending is independent of Mark and not apostolic in origin (such as France, Kelhoffer, Elliott, and Wallace) have the burden of answering those questions in a scholarly, intellectually satisfying way.

It is inconceivable that such an important event as the alteration of a biblical text—much less a Gospel—would have been kept secret in the early church, especially in light of biblical admonitions not to alter the Scriptures. Such admonitions were well known to the early church. Perhaps the most noteworthy is Deuteronomy 4:2, "You shall not add to the word that I command you, nor take from it, that you may keep the commandments of the Lord your God that I command you." This is echoed in Proverbs 30:5–6, "Every word of God proves true; he is a shield to those who take refuge in him. Do not add to his words, lest he rebuke you and you be found a liar." Josephus repeated this principle in *Against Apion*: "We have given practical proof of our reverence for our own Scriptures. For, although such long ages have now passed, no one has ventured either to add or to remove, or to alter a syllable."[16] In the New Testament, this attitude concerning altering Scripture is emphasized in several places. Paul stressed this in 1 Corinthians 4:6, when he commanded "not to go beyond what is written." In 2 John 9–11, a warning was given concerning accepting someone "who goes on ahead and does not abide in the teaching of Christ." This person who alters the teaching is not to be greeted or supported, and does not have the approval of God or Christ.[17] Revelation 22:18–19 is clear: "I warn everyone who hears the words of the prophecy of this book: if anyone adds to them, God will add to him the plagues described in this book, and if anyone takes away from the words of the book of this prophecy, God will take away his share in the tree of life and in the holy city, which are described in this book."

---

16. Josephus, *Against Apion* 1.42.

17. While many hold that the term "teaching of Christ" in the passage refers to the teaching *about* Christ, it is my conviction that the term refers to all that Christ and the apostles taught. For a fuller discussion, see Hester, "Exegesis of 2 John 9–11," in *Among the Scholars*, 75–86.

Does Mark 16:9–20 Belong In The New Testament?

John applied here the words of Deuteronomy 4:2 to, at the very least, the words of the Apocalypse; yet, it is significant that these are the last words of our Lord recorded in Scripture. He is stating the principle, enunciated by Moses and repeated by Agur, Paul, and John, of not altering the word of God.

Kruger mentioned some of these texts in his discussion about the attitudes of early Christians concerning the text of Scripture; he also particularly focused on second-century Christian writings (the *Didache*, Papias, the *Epistle of Barnabas*, Dionysius of Corinth, Irenaeus, and an Anonymous critic of Montanism).[18] He demonstrated that in each case, these Christian writers refer (either explicitly or implicitly) to Deuteronomy 4:2, and apply it to the New Testament. Kruger showed that the *Didache* applied this to the teachings of Jesus; Papias connected the passage to the Gospel of Mark; the *Epistle of Barnabas* cited it concerning written Jesus tradition; Dionysius of Corinth referred to those who changed "the scriptures of the Lord"; Irenaeus complained of those who changed the number 666 in Revelation; and the Anonymous critic of Montanism applied the principle to "the word of the new covenant of the Gospel."[19] Significantly, Kruger also cited Irenaeus concerning the doctrine of the church; it is "being guarded and preserved without any forging of Scriptures . . . neither receiving addition nor [suffering] curtailment."[20]

If, as some claim, the passage was crafted by an anonymous author who was not connected with the apostles, then how does one reconcile the acceptance of 16:9–20 with the subsequent rejection of pseudonymous second-and third-century documents which had no connection to the apostles? This is further complicated by the fact that second- and third-century writers cited 16:9–20, and attributed it to Mark. If it was known

---

18. Kruger, "Early Christian Attitudes."

19. Ibid., 74–76.

20. Ibid., 76. Kruger later makes it clear that he himself does not see a contradiction between the Scriptural admonitions (along with the quoted views of early Christians), and the apparent reality that some Christians changed the text and altered its wording. He writes, "Early Christianity was more complex . . . it becomes clear that a high view of these texts (and concern over transmission) is not mutually exclusive with the existence of significant textual variation." Ibid., 79. He apparently tries to negotiate a middle ground, allowing for major changes (such as Mark 16: 9–20), while acknowledging the overall attitude towards Scripture by the early church. Such an attempt is not convincing, given the clear Scriptural admonitions against alteration and the evidence presented here that early Christians accepted Mark 16: 9–20 as both canonical and from the hand of Mark.

A Proposal Concerning the Origin of Mark 16:9–20

that this ending had been supplied by another hand (or hands) separate from Mark, such would have been significant. Scholars such as Kelhoffer maintain that the passage is an early attempt to harmonize the Gospels. Yet there is no evidence in the manuscript traditions elsewhere of any type of harmonization of the Gospels in one document.

What is the precedent for an extensive passage, attached later to a Gospel, being accepted as apostolic at an early stage? John 7:53–8:11 would seem to be such a passage, but it is not parallel. Most scholars hold that it is not Johannine, but "obviously a piece of oral tradition."[21] Another important difference is critical. Mark 16:9–20 has attestation from patristic witnesses in the second century, but John 7:53–8:11 does not. Metzger commented, "No Greek Church Father prior to Euthymius Zigabenus (twelfth century) comments on the passage."[22] He continued, "At the same time the account has all the earmarks of historical veracity."[23] Yet, Mark 16:9–20 had early and wide acceptance—with some early witnesses stating that it was written by Mark. The shorter ending, by contrast, was never cited by any early patristic witness, was never widely accepted as was 16:9–20 and is only present in a small number of manuscripts.

It seems reasonable to assume that 16:9–20 was at the very least connected with Mark. While it is feasible that another associate of the apostles wrote the passage, such a conclusion contradicts the evidence. The testimony of early patristic writers lays claim to Mark being the author. In light of clear biblical warnings to not alter Scripture in any way, the affirmations of early Christians against altering New Testament documents, and the consistent rejection of pseudonymous documents, how could the early church have accepted such a lengthy passage—if it had no connection to any of the apostles?

Are Verses 9–20 Canonical?

Kelhoffer wrote: "An awareness of the text-critical problem concerning Mark 16:9–20 does not necessarily lead to a decision to refrain from making use of this passage."[24] Eusebius and Jerome both used the passage, even after acknowledging the omission; thus, the early church included

21. Metzger, *Textual Commentary*, 220.
22. Ibid.
23. Ibid.
24. Kelhoffer, "Witness of Eusebius," 111.

Does Mark 16:9–20 Belong In The New Testament?

Mark 16:9–20. This is seen by the second century authors who cite the verses—such as Irenaeus, the author of *Epistle of the Apostles*, and Justin. Instead of adding text not considered to be Scripture, the inclusion of Mark 16:9–20 was considered part of Scripture. Mark 16:9–20 is an ancient passage used by Christians in answering questions and preaching. Hebrews is an unsigned epistle, and discussion still continues concerning authorship. Yet there is no question whether it was considered canonical. This is also the case with Mark 16:9–20. The difference is that there are patristic witnesses who affirm Markan authorship with no qualification, and even those who question the text—such as Eusebius and Jerome—do not question authorship. When Mark 16:9–20 is cited, canonicity of the passage is not an issue. Kelhoffer made the case that Eusebius considered it to be Scripture.[25]

The early church relied upon four things to determine canonicity: its apostolicity—written by an Apostle or by the companion of an Apostle; its antiquity—written in the time of the Apostles; its orthodoxy—conformity to the "Rule of Faith"; and its catholicity—its widespread and continuous acceptance and use in the churches.[26] Mark 16:9–20 satisfies each of those points. As has been proposed, 16:9–20 was part of the notes Mark had written, intending to finish the Gospel at a later point. If an associate of his placed the passage at the end of the Gospel following Mark's death, this would explain the apostolic connection—it was widely known that Mark was a constant companion of Peter. The notes Mark had taken, through the inspiration of the Holy Spirit, accurately summarized the conclusion of the sermons Mark had heard Peter preach concerning Jesus Christ.

Conclusion

It has been shown that Mark 16:9–20 has Markan characteristics. It was suggested that the twelve verses are notes which Mark wrote as a summary of the post-resurrection appearances of Jesus, which Mark intended to finish. He had already circulated the Gospel which ended at verse 8. For some unknown reason, Mark was prevented from utilizing his notes to complete it. Mark's associates published the Gospel ending at 16:8 after his death or imprisonment. His companions subsequently placed 16:9–20 at the end of Mark, thus publishing a second edition. This, along with the early circulation of the unfinished Gospel, would account for the testimony of Eusebius

---

25. Ibid., 94–95.
26. Bruce, *Canon of Scripture*, 255–62.

A Proposal Concerning the Origin of Mark 16:9–20

and Jerome, the inclusion of the shorter ending in Bobbiensis, as well as other unknown scribes writing in the margins of lectionaries. It would also explain apparent differences in vocabulary and style. The abrupt transition between verses eight and nine in the long ending would be better understood, as would the use of the aorist tense instead of the historical present—since the twelve verses were a summary. The two ancient textual traditions are a result of two editions. The first was published by Mark's associates around the time of his death, imprisonment, or mission trip, while the second edition was published after his passing with Mark's appended notes. The time interval between the two editions was very short. This theory accounts for the two equally attested external traditions as well as the stylistic differences and similarities with Mark 1:1–16:8. Second- to fourth-century attestation of Mark 16:9–20 testifies to its acceptance by the early church as canonical. Thus, modern-day readers of the Gospel of Mark should use the verses as part of Scripture. Apparently the early Christians believed Mark 16:9–20 to contain true statements concerning Jesus, the apostles, and their teaching—and some of them affirmed it being from Mark himself. If those in the present-day approach Mark 16:9–20 as a part of Scripture, they will be including rich material that is valuable to study.

Bibliography

Achtemeier, Paul J., et al. *Introducing the New Testament: Its Literature and Theology.* Grand Rapids: Eerdmans, 2001.
Adema, Suzanne M. "Discourse Modes and Bases: The Use of Tenses in Vergil's *Aeneid* and Livy's *Ab Urbe Condita.*" *Belgian Journal of Linguistics* 23 (2009) 133–46.
Aland, Kurt, and Barbara Aland. "Bemerkungen Zum Schluss Des Markusevangliums." In *Neotestamentica Et Semitica-Studies in Honour of Matthew Black.* Edited by E. Earle Ellis and Max Wilcox. Edinburgh: T. & T. Clark, 1969.
———. "Die widedergefundene Markusschlub? Eine methodologische Bemerkung zur textkritischen Arbeit." *Zeitschrift fur Theologie und Kirche* 67 (1970) 3–13.
———. *The Text of the New Testament.* 2nd ed. Grand Rapids: Eerdmans, 1995.
Aland, Barbara, Kurt Aland, Johannes Karavidopoulos, Carlo R. Martini, and Bruce M. Metzger, eds. *The Greek New Testament.* 4th ed. Stuttgart: Deutsche Bibelgesellschaft, 2001.
Aland, Kurt, Matthew Black, Carlo M. Martini, Bruce M. Metzger, and Allen Wikgren, eds. *The Greek New Testament.* 3rd (corrected) ed. Stuttgart: United Bible Societies, 1983.Anderson, Hugh. *The Gospel of Mark.* Grand Rapids: Eerdmans, 1976.
Barr, David L. *New Testament Story: An Introduction.* Belmont, CA: Wadsworth, 1995.
Black, David Alan, ed. *Perspectives on the Ending of Mark: 4 Views.* Nashville: B & H Academic, 2008.
Bock, Darrell L. "The Ending of Mark: A Response to the Essays." Chapter 5 of Black, *Perspectives on the Ending of Mark: 4 Views.*
Boomershine, Thomas E. "Mark 16:8 and the Apostolic Commission." *Journal of Biblical Literature* 100 (1981) 225–39.
Boomershine, Thomas E., and Gilbert L. Bartholomew. "The Narrative Technique of Mark 16:8." *Journal of Biblical Literature* 100 (1981) 213–23.
Bridges, Carl B. "The Canonical Status of the Longer Ending of Mark." *Stone-Campbell Journal* 9 (2006) 231–42.
Brown, Raymond E. *An Introduction to the New Testament.* New York: Doubleday, 1997.
Bruce, F. F. *The Canon of Scripture.* Downers Grove: InterVarsity, 1988.
Burgon, John W. *The Last Twelve Verses of the Gospel according to St. Mark: Vindicated against Recent Critical Objections and Established.* Repr. Collingswood, NJ: Dean Burgon Society, 2002.
Burkett, Delbert. *Rethinking the Gospel Sources.* New York: T. & T. Clark International, 2004.
Carson, D. A. *The Gospel according to John.* Grand Rapids: Eerdmans, 1991.

Bibliography

Carson, D. A., and Douglas J. Moo. *An Introduction to the New Testament*. 2nd ed. Grand Rapids: Zondervan, 2005.

Childs, Brevard S. *The New Testament as Canon: An Introduction*. Philadelphia: Fortress, 1985.

Clark, Kenneth W. "The Theological Relevance of Textual Variation in Current Criticism of the Greek New Testament." *Journal of Biblical Literature* 85 (1966) 1–16.

Collins, A. Jeffries, ed. *The Codex Sinaiticus and the Codex Alexandrinus*. London: Trustees of the British Museum, 1963.

Conzelmann, Hans, and Andreas Lindemann. *Interpreting the New Testament*. Translated by Siegfried S. Schatzmann. Peabody, MA: Hendrickson, 1988.

Cox, Steven Lynn. *A History and Critique of Scholarship Concerning the Markan Endings*. Lewiston, NY: Mellen, 1993.

Croy, N. Clayton. *The Mutilation of Mark's Gospel*. Nashville: Abingdon, 2003.

Danove, Paul L. *The End of Mark's Story: A Methodological Study*. Leiden: Brill, 1993.

DeSilva, David A. *An Introduction to the New Testament*. Downers Grove: InterVarsity, 2004.

Drane, John. *Introducing the New Testament*. Minneapolis: Fortress, 2011.

Ehrman, Bart D, and Zlatko Plese. *The Apocryphal Gospels: Texts and Translations*. New York: Oxford, 2011.

Elliott, J. K. "The Last Twelve Verses of Mark: Original or Not?" Chapter 3 of Black, *Perspectives on the Ending of Mark: 4 Views*.

———. "Mark 1.1–3—A Later Addition to the Gospel?" *New Testament Studies* 46 (2000) 584–88.

———. "A Second Look at the United Bible Societies' Greek New Testament." *Bible Translator* 26 (1975) 325–32.

———. "The Text and Language of the Endings to Mark's Gospel." *Theologische Zeitschrift* 27 (1971) 255–62.

Elliott, Rich. "Nt Manuscripts 1–500." *Encyclopedia of New Testament Textual Criticism*. http://www.skypoint.com/members/waltzmn//Manuscripts1-500.html#m304.

Farmer, William R. *The Last Twelve Verses of Mark*. Cambridge: Cambridge University Press, 1974.

Fee, Gordon D. Review of *The Last Twelve Verses of Mark*, by William R. Farmer. *Journal of Biblical Literature* 94 (1975) 461–64.

France, R. T. *The Gospel of Mark*. Grand Rapids: Eerdmans, 2002.

Funk, Robert W., et al. *The Five Gospels*. San Francisco: HarperSanFrancisco, 1993.

Geisler, Norman, and Thomas Howe. *The Big Book of Bible Difficulties*. Grand Rapids: Baker, 2008.

Gideon, Virtus E. "The Longer Ending of Mark in Recent Study." In *New Testament Studies: Essays in Honor of Ray Summers in His Sixty-Fifth Year*, edited by Huber L. Drumwright and Curtis Vaughan, 3–12. Waco, TX: Baylor University Press, 1975.

Green-Armytage, A. H. N. *John Who Saw: A Layman's Essay on the Authorship of the Fourth Gospel*. London: Faber & Faber, 1952.

Gundry, Robert H. *Mark: A Commentary on His Apology for the Cross*. Grand Rapids: Eerdmans, 1992.

Guthrie, Donald. *New Testament Introduction*. Downers Grove: InterVarsity, 1970.

Hannah, Darrell D. "The Four-Gospel 'Canon' in the *Epistula Apostolorum*." *Journal of Theological Studies* 59 (2008) 598–633.

Bibliography

Helton, Stanley N. "Churches of Christ and Mark 16:9-20." *Restoration Quarterly* 36 (1994) 33-52.

Hengel, Martin. *The Four Gospels and the One Gospel of Jesus Christ: An Investigation of the Collection and Origin of the Canonical Gospels.* Harrisburg: Trinity, 2000.

———. *Studies in the Gospel of Mark.* Translated by John Bowden. Philadelphia: Fortress, 1985.

Hester, David W. *Among the Scholars.* Morris, AL: Hester, 2000.

Hester, J. David. "Dramatic Inconclusion: Irony and the Narrative Rhetoric of the Ending of Mark." *Journal for the Study of the New Testament* 57 (1995) 61-86.

Hoffman, Paul, et al. *Synoptic Concordance.* 4 vols. Berlin: de Gruyter, 1999.

Hooker, Morna D. *The Gospel according to St. Mark.* London: Black, 1991.

Hug, Joseph. *La finale de l'évangelie de Marc: Mc 16, 9-20.* Études Bibliques. Paris: Gabalda, 1978.

Iverson, Kelly R. "A Further Word on Final Γαρ." *Catholic Biblical Quarterly* 68 (2006) 79-94.

———. "Irony in the End: A Textual and Literary Analysis of Mark 16:8." Paper read at the southwestern regional conference of the Evangelical Theological Society, April 2001. http://bible.org/article/irony-end-textual-and-literary-analysis-mark-168.

Jong, Matthijs J. de. "Mark 16:8 as a Satisfying Ending to the Gospel." In *Jesus, Paul, and Early Christianity*, edited by Rieuwerd Buitenwerf et al., 123-49. Leiden: Brill, 2008.

Juel, Donald Harrisville. "A Disquieting Silence: The Matter of the Ending." In *The Ending of Mark and the Ends of God*, edited by Beverly Roberts Gavena and Patrick D. Miller, 1. Louisville: Westminster John Knox, 2005.

Kaiser, Walter C., ed. *Archaeological Study Bible.* Grand Rapids: Zondervan, 2005.

Kelhoffer, James A. "'How Soon a Book' Revisited: EUAGGELION as a Reference to 'Gospel' Materials in the First Half of the Second Century." *Zeitschrift fur die neutestamentliche Wissenschaft und die Kunde der alteren Kirche* 95 (2004) 1-34.

———. *Miracle and Mission: The Authentication of Missionaries and Their Message in the Longer Ending of Mark.* Tubingen: Mohr Siebeck, 2000.

———. "The Witness of Eusebius' *ad Marinum* and Other Christian Writings to Text-Critical Debates concerning the Original Conclusion to Mark's Gospel." *Zeitschrift fur die neutestamentliche Wissenschaft und die Kunde der alteren Kirche* 92 (2001) 78-112.

Kenyon, F G. *The Text of the Greek Bible.* London: Duckworth, 1975.

Koester, Helmut. *Ancient Christian Gospels.* London: SCM, 1990.

Krauss, Veronika. "'Verkundet das Evangelium der ganzen Schopfung!' Eine exegetischbibeltheologische Untersuchung von Mk 16,9-20." PhD diss., Catholic Theological University of Vienna, 1980.

Kruger, Michael J. "Early Christian Attitudes toward the Reproduction of Texts." In *The Early Text of the New Testament*, edited by Charles E. Hill and Michael J. Kruger, 63-80. London: Oxford, 2012.

Kuhn, Thomas S. *The Structure of Scientific Revolutions.* 2nd ed. Chicago: University Of Chicago Press, 1970.

Kümmel, Werner Georg. *Introduction to the New Testament.* Translated by Howard Clark Kee. Nashville: Abingdon, 1975.

Lincoln, Andrew T. "The Promise and the Failure: Mark 16:7, 8." *Journal of Biblical Literature* 108 (1989) 283-300.

Bibliography

Linnemann, Eta. "Der (wiedergefundene) Markusschluss." *Zeitschrift fur Theologie und Kirche* 66 (1969) 255-87.

Magness, J. Lee. *Sense and Absence: Structure and Suspension in the Ending of Mark's Gospel*. Atlanta: Scholars, 1986.

Mann, C. S. *Mark*. Garden City: Doubleday, 1986.

Marcus, Joel. *Mark: A New Translation with Introduction and Commentary*. Vol. 2. New Haven: Yale University Press, 2000.

Marxsen, Willi. *Introduction to the New Testament*. Translated by G. Buswell. Philadelphia: Fortress, 1968.

McDill, Matthew. "A Textual and Structural Analysis of Mark 16:9-20." *Filologia Neotestamentaria* 17 (2004) 27-44.

McDonald, Lee Martin, and Stanley E. Porter. *Early Christianity and Its Sacred Literature*. Peabody, MA: Hendrickson, 2000.

Metzger, Bruce M. *The Canon of the New Testament: Its Origin, Development, and Significance*. Oxford: Clarendon, 1987.

———. *The Early Versions of the New Testament*. Oxford: Clarendon, 1977.

———. "The Ending of the Gospel according to Mark in Ethiopic Manuscripts." In *Understanding the Sacred Text: Essays in Honor of Morton S. Enslin on the Hebrew Bible and Christian Beginnings*, ed. John Reumann, 165-80. Valley Forge, PA: Judson, 1972.

———. *Manuscripts of the Greek Bible*. Corrected. New York: Oxford, 1991.

———. *Reminiscences of an Octogenarian*. Peabody, MA: Hendrickson, 1997.

———. *Text of the New Testament: Its Transmission, Corruption, and Restoration*. New York: Oxford University Press, 1964.

———. *A Textual Commentary on the Greek New Testament*. London: United Bible Societies, 1971.

Metzger, Bruce M., and Bart D. Ehrman. *The Text of the New Testament: Its Transmission, Corruption, and Restoration*. New York: Oxford, 2005.

Meye, Robert P. "Mark 16:8—The Ending of Mark's Gospel." *Biblical Research* 14 (1969) 33-43.

Milne, H. J., and T. C. Skeat. *Scribes and Correctors of the Codex Sinaiticus*. London: British Museum, 1938.

Minns, Denis, and Paul Parvis, eds. *Justin, Philosopher and Martyr*. New York: Oxford, 2009.

Mirecki, Paul Allan. "Mark 16:9-20: Composition, Tradition and Redaction." ThD diss., Harvard University, Cambridge, MA, 1986.

Moule, C. F. D. *The Birth of the New Testament*. 3rd ed. San Francisco: Harper & Row, 1982.

Muller, C. Detlef G. "Epistula Apostolorum." In *New Testament Apocrypha*, edited by Wilhelm Schneemelcher, 1:251. Rev. ed. English translation by A. J. B. Higgins et al., edited by R. McL. Wilson. Louisville: Westminster John Knox, 1991.

Myers, Ched. *Binding the Strong Man: A Political Reading of Mark's Story of Jesus*. Maryknoll: Orbis, 1988.

Parker, David C. *An Introduction to the New Testament Manuscripts and Their Texts*. London: Cambridge, 2008.

———. *The Living Text of the Gospels*. Cambridge: Cambridge University Press, 1997.

Bibliography

Pearse, Roger, ed. *Eusebius of Caesarea: Gospel Problems and Solutions*. Translated by David J. D. Miller et al. Ancient Texts in Translation 1. Ipswitch, MA: Chieftain, 2010.

Pesch, Rudolf. *Das Markusevangelium*. 2 vols. Herders theologischer Kommentar zum Neuen Testament 2. Frieburg: Herder, 1976–77.

———. Review of *La finale de l'évangile de Marc: Mc 16,9–20*, by Joseph Hug. *Theologische Revue* 75 (1984) 368.

Petersen, Norman R. "When Is the End Not the End? Literary Reflections on the Ending of Mark's Narrative." *Interpretation* 34 (1980) 151–66.

Petzer, J. H. "Author's Style and the Textual Criticism of the New Testament." *Neotestamentica* 24 (1990) 185–97.

Phillips, Robert Lloyd. "Mark 16 in Recent New Testament Studies." MTh thesis, Midwestern Baptist Theological Seminary, 1975.

Pryke, E. J. *Redactional Style in the Marcan Gospel*. London: Cambridge, 1978.

Roberts, Alexander, and James Donaldson, eds. *The Ante-Nicene Fathers*. Translated by Ernest Wallis. 1869. Repr., Peabody, MA: Hendrickson, 1994.

Robinson, Maurice A. "The Long Ending of Mark as Canonical Verity." Chapter 2 of Black, *Perspectives on the Ending of Mark: 4 Views*.

———. "Maurice Robinson Responds to T. B. Williams." *Evangelical Textual Criticism* (blog). Posted October 18, 2010. http://evangelicaltextualcriticism.blogspot.com/2010/10/maurice-robinson-responds-to-tb.html.

Rousseau, Adelin, et al., eds. *Irénée de Lyon, Contre les hérésies*. Translated by Adelin Rousseau et al. Sources chrétiennes 100, 151, 152, 210, 211, 263, 264, 293, 294. Paris: Cerf, 1965–1982.

Schmithals, Walter. "Der Markusschlub, die Verklärungsgeschichte und die Aussendung der Zwolf." *Zeitschrift fur Theologie und Kirche* 69 (1972) 379–411.

Schweizer, Eduard. *The Good News according to Mark*. Translated by Donald Madrig. Richmond, VA: John Knox, 1970.

Selby, Donald J. *Introduction to the New Testament*. New York: Macmillan, 1971.

Shedinger, Robert F. "Kuhnian Paradigms and Biblical Scholarship: Is Biblical Studies a Science?" *Journal of Biblical Literature* 119 (2000) 453–71.

Snapp, James, Jr. "External Footprints and Internal Fingerprints: Consider All the Evidence about Mark 16:9–20." Elwood, IN: Curtisville Christian Church, 2007.

Spencer, Aida Besançon. "The Denial of the Good News and the Ending of Mark." *Bulletin for Biblical Research* 17 (2007) 269–83.

Stanton, Graham N. "The Fourfold Gospel." *New Testament Studies* 43 (1997) 347–66.

Stein, Robert H. "The Ending Of Mark." *Bulletin for Biblical Research* 18 (2008) 79–98.

———. *Mark*. Edited by Robert W. Yarbrough and Robert H. Stein. Grand Rapids: Baker Academic, 2008.

Stock, Augustine. *The Method and Message of Mark*. Wilmington, DE: Glazier, 1989.

Terry, Bruce. "The Style of the Long Ending of Mark." 1996. http://matthew.ovc.edu/terry/articles/mkendsty.htm. Originally published in abbreviated form as: "Another Look at the Ending of Mark." *Firm Foundation* 93 (September 14, 1976).

Thomas, John Christopher. "A Reconsideration of the Ending of Mark." *Journal of the Evangelical Theological Society* 26 (1983) 407–19.

Thomas, John Christopher, and Kimberly Ervin Alexander. "'And the Signs Are Following': Mark 16:9–20—A Journey into Pentecostal Hermeneutics." *Journal of Pentecostal Theology* 11 (2003) 147–70.

Bibliography

Trompf, Gary. "The First Resurrection Appearance and the Ending of Mark's Gospel." *New Testament Studies* 18 (1971–72) 308–30.

Turner, Rex A. *Systematic Theology*. Montgomery, AL: Amridge University, 1990.

Van der Horst, P. W. "Can a Book End with a ΓΑΡ? A Note on Mark XVI.8." *Journal of Theological Studies* 23 (1972) 121–24.

Wallace, Daniel B. "Mark 16:8 as the Conclusion to the Second Gospel." Chapter 1 of Black, *Perspectives on the Ending of Mark: 4 Views*.

Wasserman, Tommy. "The Greek Manuscripts in Sweden with an Excursus on the Jerusalem Colophon." *Svensk Exegetisk Arsbok* 75 (2010) 77–107.

Westcott, Brooke F., and Fenton John Anthony Hort. *Introduction to the New Testament in the Original Greek: With Notes on Selected Readings*. Reprint. Peabody, MA: Hendrickson, 1988.

Williams, Joel F. "Literary Approaches to the End of Mark's Gospel." *Journal of the Evangelical Theological Society* 42 (1999) 21–35.

Williams, Travis B. "Bringing Method to the Madness: Examining the Style of the Longer Ending of Mark." *Bulletin for Biblical Research* 20 (2010) 397–418.

Witherington, Ben. *The Gospel of Mark: A Socio-Rhetorical Commentary*. Grand Rapids: Eerdmans, 2001.

Zahn, Theodor. *Introduction to the New Testament*. 3 vols. Edinburgh: T. & T. Clark, 1909.

www.ingramcontent.com/pod-product-compliance
Lightning Source LLC
Chambersburg PA
CBHW050815160426
43192CB00010B/1767